CW00672518

Revisiting Gendered States

Oxford Studies in Gender and International Relations

Series editors: J. Ann Tickner, University of Southern California, and
Laura Sjoberg, University of Florida

REVISITING GENDERED STATES

Feminist Imaginings of the State in International Relations

Edited by Swati Parashar

J. Ann Tickner

and

Jacqui True

OXFORD
UNIVERSITY PRESS

Oxford University Press is a department of the University of Oxford. It furthers
the University's objective of excellence in research, scholarship, and education
by publishing worldwide. Oxford is a registered trade mark of Oxford University
Press in the UK and certain other countries.

Published in the United States of America by Oxford University Press
198 Madison Avenue, New York, NY 10016, United States of America.

© Oxford University Press 2018

All rights reserved. No part of this publication may be reproduced, stored in
a retrieval system, or transmitted, in any form or by any means, without the
prior permission in writing of Oxford University Press, or as expressly permitted
by law, by license, or under terms agreed with the appropriate reproduction
rights organization. Inquiries concerning reproduction outside the scope of the
above should be sent to the Rights Department, Oxford University Press, at the
address above.

You must not circulate this work in any other form
and you must impose this same condition on any acquirer.

Library of Congress Cataloging-in-Publication Data
Names: Parashar, Swati, editor. | Tickner, J. Ann, editor. | True, Jacqui, editor.
Title: Revisiting gendered states : feminist imaginings of the state in international relations /
edited by Swati Parashar, J. Ann Tickner, and Jacqui True.
Description: New York, NY, United States of America : Oxford University Press, [2018] |
Series: Oxford studies in gender and international relations |
Includes bibliographical references and index.
Identifiers: LCCN 2017030421 (print) | LCCN 2017054883 (ebook) |
ISBN 9780190644055 (Updf) | ISBN 9780190644062 (Epub) |
ISBN 9780190644048 (pbk. : acid-free paper) | ISBN 9780190644031 (hardcover : acid-free paper)
Subjects: LCSH: International relations—Social aspects. | State, The. | Feminist theory. |
Feminism—Political aspects.
Classification: LCC JZ1253.2 (ebook) | LCC JZ1253.2 .R49 2018 (print) | DDC 327.1082—dc23
LC record available at https://lccn.loc.gov/2017030421

9 8 7 6 5 4 3 2 1

Paperback printed by Webcom, Inc., Canada
Hardback printed by Bridgeport National Bindery, Inc., United States of America

CONTENTS

FOREWORD

V. SPIKE PETERSON

You never know where choosing a discipline and writing a dissertation may take you. Having spent almost a decade solo backpacking and occasionally working in the global South, I returned to the United States in 1980 with a lot of questions about power, poverty, and inequalities. Looking for answers (as well as a career path), I entered a doctoral program in international relations (IR)—presumably the most appropriate discipline for studying the array of power relations operating worldwide. I soon realized, however, that mainstream IR scholars had less interest in critical analyses of power than in reproducing disciplinary givens. I had little interest in the latter and, hence, dwindling interest in disciplinary IR.

But there was unexpected good news. In the time I had been away from academic studies in the United States, feminists in various disciplines had generated astute critiques of how "truth claims" were produced, how cultural and material power were coconstituted, and how inequalities of sex/gender, race, class, and national status were inextricably, though complexly, connected. My commitment to disciplinary IR was soon eclipsed by my enthusiasm for studying feminist and other critical interventions in social theory/practice. There were no formal gender courses or programs at the time, and certainly no evidence of attention to gender, sexuality, or race issues in disciplinary IR. Burgeoning critiques of epistemology did penetrate the margins of IR, and exploring these kept me engaged enough to complete the doctoral coursework. But now I had to write a dissertation.

This posed a dilemma: How to conjure a project that would meld my interest and ongoing research in critical and historical studies with the expectations of disciplinary IR scholars indifferent to and uninformed about those studies? In short, my answer was to produce a genealogy of *early* (archaic) state formation and its institutionalization of interactive hierarchies (male-female, propertied/free-slave, insider-outsider) and argue that *modern* state-making and its naturalization of similar hierarchies were profoundly shaped by this history. In other words, IR theory needed to take seriously how early centralizations of political power normalized ways of identifying, thinking, and acting, with implications for understanding the power relations of modern knowledge production, capitalist exploitation, and imperialist—heteropatriarchal and racist—institutions.

I managed to write and defend the dissertation, but this was hardly a strategic route to disciplinary recognition or academic employment! Unexpected good news again: in 1988 a postdoc position at the University of Southern California (USC) enabled me to continue work on critical theories and "gendering the state." Earlier that year, a conference featuring "Women and International Relations" was convened at the London School of Economics, and with the publication of conference papers in a special issue of *Millennium*, "feminist IR" was effectively launched. Ann Tickner participated in that conference and has been a pioneering contributor to and advocate for feminist IR ever since. At USC I was able to organize, with Jane Jaquette, the first US-based feminist IR conference: "Woman, the State and War: What Difference Does Gender Make?" This gathering enabled a range of scholars to become aware of each other's work, and circulation of the conference report, "Clarification and Contestation: Exploring the Integration of Feminist and International Relations Theory," generated even wider awareness of feminist IR as an emerging field of inquiry. The following year Ann Tickner and Peggy McIntosh organized a third conference at Wellesley College. I was fortunate to be the editor of and a contributor to the collection of papers from that conference, which became *Gendered States: Feminist (Re)Visions of International Relations Theory*, published by Lynne Rienner in 1992.

That is the surprising place where choosing a discipline and writing a dissertation took me. And twenty-five years after the Wellesley conference and *Gendered States*, out of a collaborative workshop at Monash University, Ann Tickner and a new generation of scholars have produced the present volume: *Revisiting Gendered States: Feminist Imaginings of the State in International Relations*. The editors and contributors advocate bringing back the "gendered state" as one among various approaches to advancing our understanding of perennial questions—not only for disciplinary IR but well beyond its narrow constructions of power, violence, sovereignty, protection, and security.

As the editors note in their introduction, despite its centrality to the field, the state has been inadequately theorized within mainstream scholarship. Thematic foci of disciplines continually shift, and "bringing the state back in" enjoyed significant attention in the 1980s. Feminist scholars—in anthropology, history, political science, and IR—generated some of the most discerning and fruitful work among those engaged in rethinking the state. As the editors also note, mainstream attention to the state—though not the state's centrality or power—faded as global restructuring, and especially global financial arrangements, altered the playing field of IR. By eroding the decision-making autonomy of states, neoliberal policies rendered *all* states vulnerable to market dynamics and the instability of their fluctuations. Those dynamics generated financial crises that spurred some IR scholars to refocus on theorizing states, though rarely with any consideration of the gendered and racialized aspects of states and the "world order," or growing economic inequalities within and between nations. The outstanding contribution of this volume is to advance the work of filling that enormous gap.

As feminist studies in IR flourished, an ever-wider array of topics was critically examined. Feminists probed more deeply into security issues and political economy, and by adopting intersectional lenses collectively enriched—and complicated—IR accounts of sovereignty, nationalism, citizenship, development, global political economy, human rights, peace studies, and many additional areas of inquiry. Work on the state continued throughout these decades, but the present collection is the first to revisit the "gendered state" as its point of departure. The volume is timely indeed, given the perennially undertheorized status of the concept and the ambiguous and precarious conditions in which the state currently exists.

Most of the contributors assembled here represent a new generation of scholars trained in and pursuing critical, gender-sensitive investigations of world politics. They undertake research decades after *Gendered States* and in a global context marked by dramatic changes *and* entrenched continuities. Readers will be familiar with major socioeconomic shifts and the geopolitical events accorded IR attention; some of the latter feature here in cogently presented case studies. Engaging and building on twenty-five years of theoretical growth, contributors to this volume significantly advance how we understand states, sovereignty, and security as gendered phenomena. Underpinning this stimulating research are analytical shifts variously adopted by the authors: developments and complications of gender, sexualities, and feminist theorizing; the "taking up" of insights from masculinity studies, cultural studies, and constructivist/poststructuralist epistemologies; deeper engagement with antiracist and postcolonial analyses; and pluralistic appreciation of diverse methods and the value of working across disciplinary divides.

The collection is also enriched by contributors adopting feminist and other critical practices favoring wider geopolitical inclusion in field research and case studies. Their important turning away from Anglo-Eurocentrism is evident in which states are the focus of chapter studies: India, Indonesia, Liberia, and Sri Lanka, as well as Australia, Russia, and Sweden. And contributors ably demonstrate the value of less top-down, more bottom-up orientations and taking seriously the everyday and lived experiences of people that produce, and are produced by, the interaction of local-global dynamics.

The innovative approaches and empirical studies richly portrayed in these chapters present a wealth of insights. Of the many contributions, I note especially those "taking up" the politics of affect, emotion, and subjective experience so relentlessly "neglected" or simply trivialized in mainstream IR. As these chapters document, we gain invaluable understanding of how the world actually *"works"* when we acknowledge and attend to the power of emotions. The latter shape subjectivities, priorities, and practices constituting the collectivities we call states, in turn affecting domestic as well as foreign policy and, not least, expressions of and resistances to violence and warfare.

Protectionism is a productive lens for exposing the pervasiveness and potency of affect in the micro and macro dimensions constituting the many worlds of IR. As Judith Stiehm argued many decades ago, the logic of protection is deeply gendered, and in operation invokes masculinist qualities and activities typically at the expense of those who are deemed feminine (read: needing protection): whether they be females, children, dependents, "natives," weak citizens, or "less developed" nations. Normalized in pervasive gender codings, protectionist ideologies are always already available and readily deployed to justify masculinist presumption and aggression. In an international order of hierarchical states premised on "sovereign power," real and/or perceived threats to national honor, status, or security are understood as emasculating (read: feminizing). As detailed in these studies, the stigma of feminization may result from a decline in geopolitical power, the humiliation that haunts postcolonial states, the "unraveling of patriarchy" due to globalization, or the purported "unmanning" of a nation where feminist and queer politics gain traction. Whatever the impetus for defensiveness, the stakes are high enough for states to typically act, in whatever way they can, to project a "more sufficiently masculine" profile. The futility of pursuing "unquestionable masculinity" and the fragility of such claims entail frequent resort to protectionism as "necessary" for sustaining or re-establishing national honor, status, and security.

Historically familiar and also novel uses of protectionism thread through these chapters. Some depict how long-standing nationalist tropes of the "motherland" retain emotional and militarizing force, spurring citizen allegiance, service, and sacrifice. Others reveal the top-down manipulation and popular embrace of *both* maternal and masculinist imagery. The text offers fascinating examples. In Russia, Putin literally "bares his chest" to project an (apparently very popular) embodiment of manliness, presumably underpinning and projecting the state's protective and powerful capacities. Demonizing feminists and homosexuals, Putin remasculinizes Mother Russia by promoting (protecting) the hyperfemininity of the "domestic woman" and her procreative, heteronormative family. India presents a different (gendered) narrative. While the Indian state (re)claims hypermasculinity through violent repression of internal rebels, its emotional language uses the "exalted status of mother" to retain a nurturing (protecting) narrative of the maternal state. And in the Middle East, in spite of its claimed rejection of statehood, Daesh / Islamic State promotes gendered identities—the "Muslimwoman" sharply distinguished from and subservient to the "warrior-monk"—and governing practices familiar in conventional nation-building projects.

My brief comments cannot convey the range of insights so richly presented in this volume on the "gendered state." Contributors ask stimulating questions, challenge conventional analytics, tackle enduring problems, and produce exciting research. We are reminded that processes of (re) masculinization entail appropriate performances not only of state and military manliness, but also feminized domesticity: females and families/ households committed to social and heterosexual reproduction in service to national priorities. These thoughtful studies convey the tenacity of gendered imagery, identities, practices, and emotional investments in creating and/or reclaiming sufficiently powerful (read: masculine) "stateness." This is daunting confirmation of continuities in how gender coding produces and normalizes interrelated inequalities. Yet that is only a portion of what we learn. The contributors document and urge us to be more aware of the extraordinary variation and differentiation in how states "do" gender. They remind of us that much has changed, not only in "what is going on" but perhaps more importantly, in "how we think."

As contributors to this timely volume show, the study of "gendered states" continues to be vital and productive: it exposes patterns of inequality, expands our understanding of power, and advances our knowledge of national and international politics. Perhaps most important, it reveals how gendered codes pervade our worlds and work to normalize multiple inequalities and their corollary in/securities.

ACKNOWLEDGMENTS

The idea for this volume originated in a workshop held at Monash University and the Institute of Postcolonial Studies (IPCS) in Melbourne, Australia in November 2014. The two-day workshop was planned to coincide with the visit of Ann Tickner to Monash. Ann Tickner had convened one of the early conferences on the then nascent field of Feminist International Relations held at Wellesley College, USA in 1990. Papers from that conference were published in Spike Peterson's 1992 edited volume *Gendered States: (Re) Visioning International Relations.* To mark the twenty-five years since that founding conference, it was decided that the theme of the Monash workshop should be "Gendered States Revisited." We would like to thank the School of Social Sciences, Faculty of Arts at Monash University for financially supporting this workshop. We would also like to thank the IPCS and its Director, Phillip Darby for their generous support and hospitality in hosting this workshop.

This volume would not have been possible without the support and encouragement we received from Laura Sjoberg as editor of the OUP book series on Gender and International Relations, and Angela Chnapko and the OUP team who helped us at each stage of the publication process. Most of the authors in this volume were participants in the 2014 Monash-IPCS workshop and we would like to thank each one of them for their scholarly contributions, and for patiently working with us as we sent them comments on their various drafts. We are also grateful to Spike Peterson for the insightful foreword and to Christine Sylvester for the thought provoking 'afterwards' to the volume. We appreciate the assistance of Janet Andrew Shah with proof reading and references.

Swati, Ann, and Jacqui would like to celebrate the collective effort that went into this book project. They have accumulated a lifetime of wonderful memories while working on this book. Swati would like to acknowledge the Centre for the Study of Developing Societies (CSDS) Delhi, where she was a Visiting Fellow in 2016. The time spent at the Centre was invaluable in discussing the ideas in the book and her own chapter, with the faculty members and other visiting scholars. Her parents, Uma Jha and Arvind Kumar Jha, always proud of her achievements, have never been found wanting in support and encouragement. She would like to thank her husband, Ravi Bajpai, for his intellectual inputs and constant support during the preparation of this manuscript. Ann would like to thank her family for encouraging her travels to faraway places, and Jacqui and Swati and their families for being such gracious hosts in Melbourne—lovely dinners, family concerts, and visits with koalas and kangaroos. Ann is grateful to the Faculty of Arts at Monash University which has made her annual visits to Australia possible. Jacqui would like to thank her family for their support—gendered states are a frequent topic of conversation around the dinner table as a result and have sometimes been robustly rebutted even in the company of the esteemed Ann Tickner! ("Men fight in all the wars and do all the work, so why shouldn't they make all the decisions?!") She would also like to recognize the Australian Research Council under the Future Fellowship Scheme Award for making her time on the project possible.

This book is an example of what feminist intellectual collaboration can achieve and why it remains extremely important in these times. We dedicate this book to all those who are resisting the tyranny of masculine states and those working hard to make states inclusive and responsive to the needs of women and other gender minorities. We hope that others will take up the myriad frameworks developed here, for making sense of how gendered states, despite their diversity, tend to exacerbate insecurities and inequalities in a world of rapid changes even as they portend to alleviate them.

ABOUT THE CONTRIBUTORS

Christine Agius is Senior Lecturer in Politics and International Relations at Swinburne University of Technology, Melbourne, Australia. Her research interests cover Nordic politics and security, identity, and critical security studies. Publications include *The Social Construction of Swedish Neutrality: Challenges to Swedish Identity and Sovereignty* (2006, Manchester University Press), *The Politics of Identity* (edited with Dean Keep, Manchester University Press), *The Persistence of Global Masculinism: Discourse, Gender and Neo-Colonial Re-Articulations of Violence* (with Lucy Nicholas, Palgrave) and articles in *Cooperation and Conflict, Security Dialogue*, and other journals. She is the director of the Identity Research Network (IRN), which brings together interdisciplinary research on the theme of identity.

Katherine E. Brown is a Lecturer in the Department of Religion and Theology at the University of Birmingham, specializing in gender, jihad, and counterterrorism. She has published widely in academic journals and blogs, and is currently working on a monograph on antiradicalization policies and gender from around the globe. Her expertise has been sought by a number of academic, policy, and media outlets in the United Kingdom, United States, Tunisia, Canada, Australia, Norway, and Austria, including, for example, the 9/11 Memorial, the European Parliament, and UN women.

David Duriesmith is a Development Fellow in the School of Political Science and International Studies at the University of Queensland. He was formerly a Postdoctoral Fellow for Conflict, Justice, and Development at the University of Melbourne. David researches masculinities, armed conflict, and violence prevention. David's work has been published in the *International Feminist Journal of Politics*, the *Australasian Review of African Studies*, and in his 2016 book *Masculinities and New Wars: The Gendered Dynamics of Contemporary Armed Conflict* (Routledge). David's current research focuses on the construction of masculinities and the "local turn" in peacebuilding.

Samanthi J. Gunawardana is a Lecturer in Gender and Development in the Faculty of Arts, Monash University. The Director of the Master of International Development Practice, she has a PhD in Economics and Commerce from the University of Melbourne. Samanthi's research examines the impact of development policy on employment systems, labor, and livelihoods among rural women in South Asia, with a particular emphasis on gender, development, and labor in Sri Lanka. She is the editor of *The Global Political Economy of the Household in Asia* (with Juanita Elias, Palgrave, 2014), and the author of several book chapters and articles in journals such as *Globalisations*, and *Work, Employment and Society*.

Katrina Lee-Koo is a Reader in international relations at Monash University, Melbourne and Deputy Director of Monash GPS (Gender, Peace and Security Research Centre). She teaches and researches in the fields of gender, security studies, and children and global conflict. She is also recently the coauthor of *Children and Global Conflict* (with Kim Huynh and Bina D'Costa, Cambridge University Press, 2015) and *Ethics and Global Security* (with Anthony Burke and Matt McDonald, Routledge, 2014).

Swati Parashar is Associate Professor in Peace and Development at the School of Global Studies, University of Gothenburg, Sweden. During 2016 she was a Visiting Fellow at the Centre for the Study of Developing Societies, Delhi. Her research engages with the intersections between feminism and postcolonialism, focused on conflict and development issues in South Asia. She is the author of *Women and Militant Wars: The Politics of Injury* (Routledge: London, 2014) and of several books chapters and articles in journals such as *Postcolonial Studies, Cambridge Review of International Affairs, Studies in Conflict & Terrorism, International Studies Review, Security Dialogue* and *International Studies Perspectives*.

V. Spike Peterson is Professor of International Relations at the University of Arizona, with courtesy appointments in the Department of Gender and Women's Studies and the Institute for LGBT Studies. Her book *A Critical Rewriting of Global Political Economy: Integrating Reproductive, Productive and Virtual Economies* introduced an alternative analytics for examining intersections of race, class, gender, and national hierarchies in the context of neoliberal globalization. She also coauthored, with Anne Sisson Runyan, *Global Gender Issues in the New Millennium*. Her cross-disciplinary research interrogates the sex/gender and racial dynamics of informalization, transnational householding, and global insecurities in the context of critically analyzing global political economy, and generates long histories and critical queerings of state formation, marriage, citizenship, and nationalism.

Lesley J. Pruitt is a Senior Lecturer in International Relations at Monash University and a member of the Monash GPS (Gender, Peace and Security) Centre. Lesley's research focuses on peace and conflict studies, especially recognizing and enhancing youth participation in peacebuilding and advancing gender equity in peacekeeping. A Truman Scholar and Rotary Ambassadorial Scholar, Lesley received her master's and PhD from the University of Queensland. Lesley's books include *The Women in Blue Helmets: Gender, Policing and the UN's First All-Female Peacekeeping Unit* (2016, University of California Press) and *Youth Peacebuilding: Music, Gender and Change* (2013, State University of New York Press).

Christine Sylvester is Professor of Political Science at the University of Connecticut, and professorial affiliate of the School of Global Studies, Gothenburg University. Her latest book is an edited collection of essays, *Masquerades of War* (2015), related to the Experiencing War Project she facilitates. She is currently a fellow of the Humanities Institute at the University of Connecticut, working on a book manuscript contracted with Oxford University Press: *Curating and Re-curating America's Wars in Vietnam and Iraq*. Related books include *Art/Museums: International Relations Where We Least Expect It* (2009) and *War as Experience: Contributions from International Relations and Feminist Analysis* (2013).

J. Ann Tickner is Professor Emerita in the School of International Relations at the University of Southern California, Distinguished Scholar in Residence at the School of International Service at American University, Washington, DC, and Professor of Politics and International Relations in the Gender, Peace and Security Centre at Monash University in Melbourne. Her principal areas of research include international theory, peace and security, and feminist approaches to international relations. Her publications include *Gendering World Politics: Issues and Approaches in the Post–Cold War World* (2001) and *A Feminist Voyage through International Relations* (2014). She is a past President of the International Studies Association. She was named as one of fifty key thinkers in Martin Griffiths, *Fifty Key Thinkers in International Relations*.

Jacqui True is Professor of Politics and International Relations and Director of Monash University's Centre for Gender, Peace and Security, Australia. She is also an Australian Research Council (ARC) Future Fellow and a Global Fellow, Peace Research Institute (PRIO), Oslo. Her current research is focused on understanding the political economy of postconflict violence against women and the patterns of systemic sexual and gender-based violence in Asia Pacific conflict-affected countries. Recent publications include

The Political Economy of Violence against Women (Oxford University Press, 2012), and *Scandalous Economics: The Politics of Gender and Financial Crises* (Oxford University Press, 2016), edited with Aida Hozić. She is a coeditor with Sara Davies of the *Oxford Handbook on Women, Peace and Security* (Oxford University Press, 2018).

Cai Wilkinson is a Senior Lecturer in International Relations at Deakin University, Australia. Her research focuses on societal security in the post-Soviet space, with a particular focus on LGBTQ human rights and "traditional values" in Kyrgyzstan and Russia. Recent publications include a guest-edited special issue of the *Journal of Human Rights* on resistance to LGBT human rights (with Anthony J. Langlois), a guest-edited interventions symposium on queer/ing in/security in *Critical Studies on Security* and co-authored publications on LGBT human rights in Southeast Asia. She has also contributed chapters to volumes on securitization theory, LGBT activism in Central Asia, and fieldwork-based research methods, and is currently working on a monograph about the politics of LGBT rights in the post-Soviet space.

Revisiting Gendered States

CHAPTER 1

Introduction

Feminist Imaginings of Twenty-First-Century
Gendered States

SWATI PARASHAR, J. ANN TICKNER, AND JACQUI TRUE

In spite of many contradictions, it is widely accepted that the state is the only political institution that has survived in Europe for more than three hundred years, and in Oceania, the Americas, Asia, and Africa, since independence from colonial rule. It is a paradox that while the sovereign state was the institutional ideal and form of freedom in anticolonial movements, many of these postcolonial states became perpetrators of gross human rights violations, particularly against women and minorities, violations that have been largely unseen or silenced, neither reported, recorded, nor recognized.[1] Today, violent armed conflicts are raging in parts of Africa, Asia, and the Middle East, where various political groups are claiming full-fledged statehood and/or are challenging the authority of existing states. Meanwhile European states are in turmoil due to the unprecedented refugee crisis, resulting in xenophobic nationalism and the rise of far-right political factions. Many states in both the global North and South, including those that claim to be democracies, have lacked the political and social will to enforce human rights, while others have committed war crimes against their own citizens.[2]

If state power and influence were on the decline after the end of the Cold War and altered by the social forces of globalization, their ascendance is visible once again in the twenty-first century, when the "security" state and the "developmental" state have gained prominence in global policy and discourse. The state's revival was particularly visible in the wake of the global financial crisis in 2008–2009, as states have been rescued even at costs to individual citizens. The United States and Europe have bailed out investment banks and imposed harsh austerity on citizens with disproportionate impacts on women, especially women of color and migrants (Hozic and True 2016).

The state continues to be reinvented and sought after as an aspirational and powerful political entity, even by women and minorities, even as the sovereignty of the state is challenged in multiple ways from both inside and outside. Despite the commonly held view that "there is something rotten in the state of the state" (Nandy 2003, 14), no alternatives have captured the public or political imagination. Postcolonial thinker Ashis Nandy powerfully reminds us that "no system becomes morally acceptable merely because human imagination has failed to produce an alternative to it at any given point of time" (2003, 14). Yet the idea of the state continues to fascinate social scientists, writers, poets, artists and litterateurs.

The state as the dominant political actor in everyday life, as well as in international politics, has been a consistent focus of feminist scholarship across the humanities and social sciences (Peterson 1992b; Brown 1995; Anthias and Yuval-Davis 1987; Stetson and Mazur 1995; Hooper 2001; Htun 2003). Feminist scholars have vacillated between embracing the state as the only institution that can realize women's human rights and redress patriarchal structures, and critiquing the state as a site of masculinist power that legitimizes these patriarchal structures through domestic and foreign policies (e.g., Sawer 2003a; Jaquette 2009; cf. Young 2003; Pateman 1988). *Revisiting Gendered States: Feminist Imaginings of the State in International Relations* offers a further contribution to this literature by examining the various ways in which gender affects the construction and interplay of states in contemporary global politics. It investigates how the neoliberal, Western, postcolonial, or religious states affect the everyday lives and security of their citizens. We believe that this book is a timely contribution to theorizing the state and understanding its various gendered nuances in these deeply troubled times of the twenty-first century.

Using a variety of feminist approaches, the volume surveys the intellectual landscape of existing debates about the gendered nature of the state, still the most important political actor in international relations. Most of the contributors to this volume are from a new generation of scholars who have been trained to analyze and critique the state and global politics using a gender lens. The volume challenges the dominant narratives of the state as a gender-neutral political entity whose function and achievements include the safety and security of women and all gender minorities. It also challenges the claim that, for real gender equality to emerge, the state is an anachronism or must cease to exist. In spite of the failures of many states to guarantee the security of their citizens, in some cases, the state may be the only guarantor of human rights and gender justice.

The volume revisits the analyses and arguments put forth in *Gendered States: Feminist (Re)Visions of International Theory* (1992a). However, it goes further, drawing on a rich array of feminist international relations (IR) scholarship that has emerged over the last twenty-five years. Certain authors draw on masculinity studies and postcolonial theory and on more recent interventions, such as queer theory. Many of the authors have engaged in field research in both the global South and North and bring in-depth and diverse gendered analyses of a wide variety of states and issues such as the religious proto-state in the Middle East, the emotional and peacekeeping state in India, the social democratic, protection state in Sweden, and the crisis state in Indonesia. We aim to provide a wide-ranging, if not comprehensive, feminist account of how the state might be changing while remaining gendered in more ways than ever imagined.

THE STATE RETURNS

It has been more than two decades since *Gendered States: Feminist (Re) Visions of International Relations Theory*, edited by V. Spike Peterson (1992a), was published. That volume, one of the first in what was then a relatively new and emerging field of feminist IR, provided an important critique of IR theory. The contributions to that book explored how gender shapes security, sovereignty, and revolution; it highlighted how the state is gendered in its constitution and practices that, throughout history, have privileged men and hegemonic masculinity while subordinating women in myriad ways. All the contributors to that volume persuasively claimed that feminist theorizing of the state was essential to understanding the new emerging post–Cold War world order.

Subsequent to the publication of *Gendered States*, feminist IR turned its attention away from the state, looking at the gendered dimensions of issues such as human rights, peace and conflict, nationalist movements, development, and economic globalization (see Tickner 2001; True 2003; Yuval-Davis 1997; Pettman 1996; Marchand and Runyan 2000). The 1990s provided a brief moment when cooperation among states with respect to political, economic, and environmental issues seemed to be on the rise, with hopes for a more consensual global community. There was even talk of the withering away of the state (Ohmae 1991). The 1990s was also the decade when IR theory opened up to post-positivist theoretical perspectives such as critical theory, poststructuralism, and postcolonialism, theoretical perspectives more conducive to answering the kind of questions that IR feminists were asking (e.g., Booth, Smith, and Zalewski 1996).

However, this optimism underwent an abrupt change after the terrorist attacks of 2001. The discipline of IR turned its focus back to security studies and the state's role as a bulwark against violent extremism; neorealist explanations for the new types of wars were redeployed. Feminist IR, which had previously been reluctant to engage security issues, began to focus its attention on international security, forging a new subfield of feminist security studies that revisited more traditional IR topics such as war, militant movements, and national security, albeit from very different critical gendered perspectives (Wibben 2011; Sjoberg 2009; Parashar 2014). While security is inevitably one of our foci in this volume, we engage more broadly with rethinking the state as an assemblage that works through economic, as well as political, processes to further, not only its security interests, but its economic interests also, such as labor migration and capitalist accumulation (Elias and Gunawardana eds. 2014; True 2012).

Following transformations in the aftermath of the 2008–2009 global financial crisis (Hozic and True eds. 2016), feminist political economy perspectives on the state revealed an interface between the "security state" and the "neoliberal state." Both forms of state are legitimated through gender relations. Like the security state, the neoliberal state values masculine qualities of rationality, competitiveness, and risk-taking; in this way they support one another. But as political economists argue contra ideologies of the free market (see Held et al.1999; Bruff 2014), neoliberalism does not involve *less* state but often *more* state orchestration of the kinds of activity that are feasible and appropriate for market and public institutions to engage in (True 2015a, 423). With this edited volume, we hope to take forward earlier debates about the meaning, practices, and salience of the gendered state, as we move into an increasingly marketized and securitized world.

The idea for this volume originated in a collaborative workshop held at Monash University and the Institute of Postcolonial Studies in Melbourne, Australia, in November 2014. The workshop coincided with Ann Tickner's professorial appointment at Monash. Tickner had convened one of the early conferences in the nascent field of feminist IR, held at Wellesley College in the United States in 1990. The papers from the 1990 conference were the foundation for the edited volume on *Gendered States*. To mark the twenty-five years since that founding meeting, the Monash-IPCS workshop theme was "Gendered States Revisited." Many, but not all, of the contributing authors in this volume were participants in the 2014 workshop. They are a group of scholars with diverse methodological orientations—whose work employs gender-informed analyses in IR and is influenced by development, cultural, and critical theories as well as postcolonial studies; most, but not all, do empirical work in South Asia, the Middle East, and the Asia-Pacific region.

Bringing a rich array of feminist analyses and understandings to an examination of multiple modes of "being a state" can provide crucial new insights not only about gender injustices (in relatively stable states) but also about political, economic, social, and cultural inequalities in all states. These inequalities have produced violent conflicts that challenge and threaten certain states' sovereignty and even produce new territorial states with difficulties of state building. We argue that feminist IR scholars have been more engaged with critiquing the state than in theorizing states and understanding their gendered origins. Most feminist critiques of the state have addressed the exclusion and marginalization of women and gender minorities, its inherent inequalities, patriarchal character, and violence (Peterson 1992a). We ask, in this volume, to what extent the state speaks a gendered language, behaves like a patriarch, and enables gendered politics, citizenship, and policies at different levels. We hope this volume will enable renewed attention to feminist theorizing about states and their imbrication in global politics.

Gendered States was primarily concerned with the Western liberal state, as was much of the early feminist scholarship on the state. Certain liberal feminists saw the state as the primary provider of women's rights, while those who were more critical pointed to its subordination of (certain) women and other identities. With this volume, we engage with the state as a concept and practice more broadly, focusing our attention not only on the liberal state, but importantly, on the postcolonial state. We build on past feminist analysis by interrogating how the modern state is gendered at the intersections of globalization, postcolonial nation building, and conflict. We consider how the concept of the "gendered state" can usefully advance our theoretical and empirical understanding and analysis of contemporary political, economic, and social dynamics within and across societies. We question how far and in what ways all states are gendered and whether some states are particularly gendered in their identities and interests and with implications for citizenship, society, and international security. We also examine the distinctively gendered practices of postcolonial states set against the norms of metropolitan/core states, asking which voices are still unheard and silenced in postcolonial states.

Theorizing the state has not been the main focus of mainstream IR theory; since the publication of Waltz's 1979 *Theory of International Politics*, mainstream IR has focused on the structural level of analysis. Theorizing the state has largely been left to foreign policy analysis, an approach that has tended to focus on decision-makers. However, historical sociologists, critical theorists, poststructuralists, and feminists have been more willing to engage the state (see Brown 1995). Feminist IR theory is well positioned to theorize the state in all its dimensions. Feminism generally employs bottom-up, rather than top-down, analysis; starting its investigations from the perspectives of individuals and groups, it asks how the state and the international structures in which it is embedded impact people's lives. Feminist methodologies look for connections between the local and global—how the local impacts and transforms world politics and vice versa.

Feminists' challenges to claims that states are gender neutral are rooted in their examination of the history of the states system. The foundational structures of the Eurocentric Westphalian state system, which originated in the seventeenth century, were deeply gendered. Women were consigned to the private space of the household and denied rights of citizenship. While these gendered foundations have shifted and evolved, women are still denied equal rights in many societies and gendered expectations and identities impede women's access to political and economic power even in states where formal equality has been achieved. Imperial powers imposed these same gendered structures of inequality on their colonies, structures that have persisted in postcolonial states even after independence. While these gendering processes are constantly changing, they have acted in ways that have denied rights and voice to certain women, as well as to racial and ethnic minorities more generally while empowering and according privilege to others.

Social scientists may argue that if gender is everywhere, what gives analytical purchase to the concept of gender to be able to understand and explain state behavior? We see gender as a practice that is fluid and constantly changing with implications for people's everyday lives. Importantly, gender is a relationship of unequal power that intersects with other forms of oppressions such as race, class, caste, and ethnicity. Accordingly, gendering practices impact different groups in different ways at different times. Because of these intersections, which reflect distinct political and social histories, every gendered state is unique in terms of the forms and expression of gender identities, structures, and symbolism, while sharing some general features. Methodologically, it is incumbent upon us as feminist scholars to disaggregate among gendered states, that is, to distinguish the degree of gendering in any given state, even while acknowledging that all state projects necessarily involve forms of gendered inclusion and exclusion. Crucially, the concept of the gendered state should be used to highlight when the gendered dimension of state identity becomes most salient and visible as a way to forge or legitimize unequal or unjust power relations and as a means for mobilizing and/or justifying state violence either inside vis-à-vis minority groups or outside vis-à-vis rival states or nonstate enemies.

Gender identities and symbolism, for instance, are frequently used to legitimate state authority, particularly around war and conflict. For instance, war is often justified as necessary to protect women and children, while the protection of these defenseless citizens is used to mobilize men to fight. State-making is achieved through war-making (Tilly 1985), the outward projection of power and identity set against dangerous others who are often feminized. And making states also involves "making sex" (Laquer 1990) through the ordering of heterosexual norms and gender hierarchy, which suppress or subordinate dangerous differences within. For example, Sweden, which is seeking to craft a feminist foreign policy, is engaged in an identity-building project that relies on the use of force and the exclusion of difference. And in Russia, the hypermasculine state that supresses homosexuality and promotes the cultural concept of "Mother Russia" which has long played a crucial role in the articulation of Russian statehood.

At the heart of the states/statehood debate is the question about gendered citizenship. How does the state gender its citizens? Who can stand symbolically for the nation and who has access to real power and resources? The state is known (particularly in postcolonial contexts) to protect certain majority or dominant groups and individuals and is a source of insecurity for others (whose identities do not fit the state narrative). Indigenous women and women with minority status are particularly threatened and mark the boundaries of the state with their bodies. Would the state survive without gender, and can we ungender the state? We need to understand how the state is produced through gender binaries in order to undo it—and open up alternative political forms and opportunities for the political expression of all peoples.

Postcolonial states have demonstrated more faith in the nation state than their Western counterparts. This has typically been the case in their much-cherished transition from colonial rule to self-rule and the degree of optimism that emerged with the embracing of modernity. The state was seen in an "idealized form—as an impartial, secular arbiter among different classes, ethnicities and interests" (Nandy 2003, 3). All types of political arrangements in the postcolonial world had to conform to the European nation state model. Premodern versions of the state were discarded with the idea that these ancient systems of governance were neither universal in their legitimacy nor adequate for addressing structural inequalities in society (Kaviraj 2000). The antistate rhetoric of Marxists and insurgent Maoists is also rooted in the notion that the European nation state must first be established in an ideal form, before the state withers away. The Maoists in India, for example, want to overthrow the modern state but with the view that they can replace it with their own state and systems of governance. One could also argue that if the gendered colonial encounter had feminized these non-Western societies and also their colonizers (Nandy 1983), the faith in the newly founded postcolonial state was essential to reclaim masculinities of traditional societies.

This unwavering faith in the nation state as the end product of anticolonial nationalisms, has caused anxiety and suspicion among postcolonial scholars. Nandy (2003) calls the state a colonial institution that shares the "white man's burden" in the civilizing mission. The state controls and civilizes societies to usher in modernization through development, security, and technology; and appears like some kind of "specialized coercive apparatus or private business venture" (Nandy 2003, 1). Leela Gandhi sees "generic conformity" between anticolonial nationalism and the European empire as the paradigmatic moment of the foundation of the postcolonial nation state (Gandhi 1998, 119). There is a Western universalism (of statehood) that postcolonial states adopt over the heterogeneous nationalisms that define their identity. The transfer of power (state machinery) is often a change of bureaucratic control from the colonial rulers to the nationalists. It is this continuity of the state system and the legitimization of violence and totalitarianism that postcolonial nationhood must reject; statehood does no good to the national consciousness as enunciated by Gandhi, Fanon, Tagore, and others (Gandhi 1998).

Two distinct processes mark postcolonial states, where the idea of statehood is both entrenched and highly aspirational for all identity groups. These processes are distinctively gendered by contrast with metropolitan/ core states. When the ruling elite, in order to perpetuate and protect the state, extract new kinds of political and economic surplus and continue to unleash new forms of violence on resisting citizens (Nandy 2003, 7), both that violence and resistance to it are gendered in their discursive and physical manifestations. Chapters in this volume explore the gender dynamics in postcolonial states that are already troubled by ethnic, religious, and ideological armed conflicts and violence. They also highlight how gender is crucial to the strategies, language, emotions, and responses these states adopt to address their internal conflicts and reclaim their power and sovereignty. We cannot think of the state or analyze globalized politics within and among states without accounting for both their gendered and their postcolonial dynamics. In this sense, this volume is a departure from earlier IR feminist scholarship on gendered states.

OUTLINE OF THE VOLUME

Part I of this volume, "Stating Gender and Gendering States," traces the genealogies of the modern gendered states system, delineating some of its key features and suggesting possible transformations. The authors demonstrate how gender is intrinsic to the constitution of all states and the international society of which they are a part. In chapter 2, Ann Tickner revisits some of her early research on two postcolonial states, the United States from 1776 to 1829 and India from 1947 to 1980, examining the types of state-building strategies they followed to build national power and avoid dependence on an international system dominated by the hegemonic states of the time. These strategies are contrasted with two very different nation-building models, both of which were designed to satisfy the basic needs of their citizens rather than build national power. Drawing on the work of feminist historians, Tickner uses a feminist lens to critically reassess her early work on national development in postcolonial states, concluding that we are in need of new transformational models that take us beyond a world of states. Illustratively, she draws on some indigenous scholarship that, like feminist scholarship, suggests some possibilities for less statist and less hierarchically gendered futures (e.g., Stewart-Harawera 2005). Advocating a multilevel view of governance and a very different concept of state sovereignty, indigenous peoples are often bypassing the state and appealing directly to the international community in pursuit of their rights.

In chapter 3, Jacqui True claims that gender is *central*, not peripheral, to the constitution of the state and to change "in" and "of" the interstate system, contra conventional IR theories. Diverse patriarchal structures in both Western and non-Western societies shape and constrain what states are, what they do, and how. These structures have always played a crucial role in the constitution of state identities, diplomatic practices, and the maintenance, transformation, and expansion of the society of sovereign states. This chapter argues that bringing back the concept of "gendered states" and its political, economic, and social dimensions can help us explain the intensely gendered violence playing out in globalized conflicts today and the unraveling of patriarchal structures, practices, and norms in many parts of the world, in part due to processes of economic globalization. The breakdown of patriarchal social contracts, True argues, is fueling a backlash of gendered violence at all levels within and across states, including the explicit targeting of women and girls in intrastate and international conflicts. This phenomenon is at once an embodiment of, and a threat to, sovereign statehood and political order.

Part II, "The Making of the Gendered State," features chapters that engage with the ontological foundations of gendered states by looking at specific case studies of both liberal and postcolonial states. Focusing on masculinity, sovereignty and securitization, and labor migration, the chapters demonstrate the constituent gendered factors that go into the "making" and sustaining of the state and/or claims to statehood.

In chapter 4 David Duriesmith revisits Mona Harrington's (in Peterson 1992a) defense of the liberal state as an agent of change in light of twenty-five years of subsequent feminist scholarship. Since the publication of *Gendered States*, considerable theorization has gone into the role of masculinity in constructing the liberal state. By looking at recent state attempts to pursue profeminist policies in the international arena, Duriesmith asks if the manly liberal state can be an agent of meaningful international change. Building on masculinities scholarship, he analyzes the relationship between masculine modes of state action and profeminist activism. Through an exploration of the United Nations' HeForShe campaign, the chapter argues that the use of the liberal state as an agent of change risks a quixotic search for a "good" or "profeminist" notion of masculinity as a basis for state action. Duriesmith challenges the notion that states can break free from their masculinist expressions without first disrupting the gender hierarchies that underpin them. He suggests that states should adopt the position of reflexive allies to feminist causes as a way to contribute to ending oppression without reinforcing the hegemony of masculine state structures.

The concept of protection has been an important, and often-criticized function of the masculinist state. In chapter 5, Christine Agius uses a gendered approach to examine the intersection of sovereignty, security, and the politics of protection. She demonstrates that responses to wider globalizing tendencies have produced divergent readings of sovereignty and security across states. By examining two middle powers, Sweden and Australia, Agius explores how the politics of protection has been deployed in different ways. Sweden's efforts to remake the state in order to disentangle itself from its past policy of neutrality can be viewed using a gendered concept of security, rearticulated through more robust military applications, while embodying a peaceful self-narrative linked to military nonalignment, active internationalism, and, more recently, a "feminist foreign policy." She then explores efforts to *reclaim* a bounded concept of the sovereign state in Australia's masculinist and militarized approach to securing its borders with respect to asylum seekers and boat arrivals. What is being reclaimed in the case of Australia is a more traditional imagining of the state, or a return to "restoring" state sovereignty perceived to be under threat by globalizing forces. The chapter explores the sites through which this reclamation takes place, focusing on the relationship between security, identity, and sovereignty through masculinist approaches to violence, order, and borders. Both case studies explore the gendered and securitized reworking and revisioning of the state, and the inherent tensions and contradictions that emerge in questions of security, sovereignty, and identity.

The issue of borders has become a crucial if contested site as the state attempts to control, but also promote, its citizens' movements across international boundaries. In chapter 6, Samanthi Gunawardana develops the concept of "assemblage" to understand how the post-colonial, developmental state produces and reproduces gender. Gunawardana builds on Saskia Sassen's (2006) analysis of global restructuring as a process of disassembling the territory, authority, and rights of the modern nation state, to explore how often-contradictory state practices facilitate feminized, transnational labor migration. Using Sri Lanka as an illustrative case, she argues that three distinct but interrelated regimes, the regulatory, the protective, and the brokerage, constitute the postcolonial gendered state as an assemblage rather than a unified agent or structure. Although this assemblage state attempts to protect workers and regulate against harm, the production and reproduction of gender through brokerage, protection, and regulatory agencies and discourses ensures that labor migration is sustained even in the face of significant harm, especially to women citizens and workers.

Modern states are troubled by queer populations, by conflicts and disasters, and by the international demands of peacekeeping. Part III, entitled "Troubling the Gendered State," includes chapters that explore these globalized processes and how they pose significant challenges and opportunities to gendered states.

Drawing on Peterson's use of the "lens of protection" (1992a, 50) in chapter 7, Cai Wilkinson interrogates how "Russia as Motherland" has been utilized by the Kremlin to help construct a neopaternalist and heterosexist gender regime that is central to the promotion of "traditional family values." While in both pre-Soviet and Soviet periods Mother Russia served as an aspirational ideal for proud womanhood that is to be revered and defended, in the post-Soviet period she has frequently been portrayed as humiliated and in urgent need of protection against a "queer peril" of feminists, homosexuals, and other Western deviants who wish to see her fall. In tracing the construction of this narrative of existential threat to Mother Russia, the chapter highlights the state's continued dogmatic adherence to binary, essentialist, and highly normative understandings of gender and sexuality that can conceive of the queer as an existential threat both to itself and the body politic that must be eliminated. The chapter concludes by considering the implications of this stance for practices of statecraft, arguing that while, in many ways, "queer" presents a threat to the modern state, queering institutional understandings of gender and sexuality remains crucial for the success of postmodern states in a queer world.

In chapter 8, Leslie Pruitt focuses on the introduction of the first all-female formed police unit (FFPU) in UN peacekeeping, a unit that, by virtue of its all-female composition, troubles the traditional notion of peacekeeping; it also unsettles the notion that it is states in the global North that have made the most progress on women's equality. Deployed from India to Liberia in 2007, the FFPU offers a lens that can inform a broader critical analysis of approaches to pursuing gender equity within and through peace and security initiatives. The FFPU has led to important outcomes around women's participation in peacekeeping and responsiveness to women's claims for their rights and access to justice. The potential for such international contributions by postcolonial states or global South states should not be overlooked. Investigating the FFPU suggests that this approach may offer useful insights while providing significant opportunities for women in India and abroad. It argues that effective moves toward implementing UN Security Council Resolution 1325 and the broader women, peace, and security agenda will not be served by assumptions that only some states, or only certain kinds of (Western) states, ought to be able to credibly contribute.

Chapter 9 turns to a different kind of threat to the state—that of natural disasters. Crises, brought about by disaster, conflict, or political transformation, can also bring opportunities to reconstitute states. As states emerge from crisis with a national focus upon rebuilding, new or renewed agendas and perspectives can be integrated into their design. This can include programs advocating for the inclusion and participation of women. Issues such as women's participation in peace processes, gender sensitivity in disaster response, and gender inclusiveness in governance structures become central to building foundations for women's empowerment in states emerging from crisis. Katrina Lee-Koo explores efforts to reconstitute the state after crisis and conflict. Using the case of Aceh, the northernmost point of Indonesia, she examines the role of gender within the competing discourses of "crisis and urgency" on the one hand, and "renewal and opportunity" on the other. Aceh became a semiautonomous state in 2006 in the wake of a three-decades long conflict and the devastating 2004 tsunami. At that moment, local and global actors working in Aceh had an opportunity to infuse values of women's rights into the foundations of the newly emerging political arrangements. However, efforts to "build back better" in Aceh were devoid of practices to promote this agenda. Instead, political power brokers allowed familiar and formidable patriarchal agendas and practices to dominate the rebuilding process. The gendered state was resurgent, and gender equality became a "missed opportunity." Reflecting on this case, the chapter concludes with a consideration of the opportunities for reshaping gendered states more generally in the aftermath of crisis.

Part IV, "Gender in Troubled States," focuses on states that are already troubled by ethnic, religious, and ideological armed conflicts and violence. Looking at examples of India and the ISIS, a nonnormative state in the Middle East, the chapters in this part highlight how gender is crucial to the strategies that these states adopt to address their internal conflicts and reclaim their power and sovereignty.

In chapter 10, Swati Parashar uses a feminist perspective to argue that the state conscripts gendered emotions in its efforts to seek/retain legitimacy and to police citizens to conform to its ideological and developmental moorings. Postcolonial statehood itself is a product of gendered emotional encounters, she argues. The chapter asks how the state manifests and constitutes gendered emotions through "affective citizenship" and whether it can claim an emotional existence as much as a political and cultural one. The chapter draws on the Naxalite/Maoist insurgency in India to highlight the gendered emotional language of the postcolonial state in violent conflict with its own marginalized citizens who challenge its legitimacy and violence. The state confers citizenship rights on individuals who demonstrate allegiance to the dominant affective language of the state and its nationalism. Those (Dalits and Adivasis in this case) whose emotional journeys are at variance with the state's narrative are considered extremists or insurgents who have strayed from the path of righteous citizenry. While they are obliterated in military encounters, emotional appeals are made to the insurgents to abandon their path of violent resistance and join the "mainstream," to embrace affective citizenship and legitimacy of the state. Parashar demonstrates that the Indian state navigates both maternal nurturing emotions and violent masculinity in its efforts to deal with its insurgent population.

In chapter 11, Katherine Brown explores conflict and legitimacy in a very different kind of state that she calls a "proto-state," the so-called Islamic State, also known as Daesh. A proto-state not only operates in an environment of extreme instability, but, like the nucleus of an atom, exists in a permanent state of flux and tension while, at the same time, managing to generate cohesion or structural integrity. Despite rejecting both statehood and nationalism in its rhetoric, Daesh remains paradoxically dependent upon both. The chapter shows how the instability and insecurity characteristic of a proto-state such as Daesh generates extreme attempts at control through three key mechanisms. The first is the construction of a "Muslim woman" dependent upon a religious nationalism. She is defined by purdah, piety, and nonviolent jihad. She transcends local culture and race, paradoxically utilizing transnational ideals to create a nationalist framework of the proto-state. The second is the creation of the "warrior-monk" built upon a militarized nationalism. He overcomes preexisting tribal allegiances for the "brotherhood." These two figures operate in gender-segregated but codependent imagined spaces (the latter in the battlefield, the former in the home), but they are brought together through Daesh's public demonstrations of organized gendered violence in a third space: the street. This third mechanism of highly symbolic and organized street violence redefines access, acceptable conduct, and governance of the so-called caliphate across the public and private spheres. In so doing it enforces order and cohesion by creating new centers of power that affect all lives. These complex gender maneuvers that hold together in tension both the rejection and the desire for nationalism and statehood are necessary because Daesh remains trapped as a proto-state. The chapter reveals how gender is essential to understanding how the mechanisms of extreme control both transcend and depend upon nationalism and statism, and through them create fluctuating forms of authority and legitimacy.

THE WAY FORWARD

Intense global and local contestations are a trademark of gendered states in the twenty-first century. The sovereignty and autonomy of states is under serious scrutiny perhaps more so than at any other time during the modern era. However, this sovereignty and autonomy is also asserted and manifested in many different ways, making it pertinent to revisit the idea of states as gendered political entities with distinct and differentiated gendered ways of behaving and identifying, especially as they are under threat.

We recognize the limitations of this volume and are particularly mindful of the absence of a chapter on the gendered state and the environment on which feminists have pushed new boundaries (Detraz 2016; Backstrand and Kronsell 2015). However, in a book project like this due to resource and time constraints not everything can be included. Moreover, we also hope that this book will be a conversation starter and will inspire further conceptual and empirical investigations of gendered states in the future. In that conversation, ours will be one of the many voices and certainly not the last. For now, we believe that the chapters in this volume illustrate new conceptual, methodological, and empirical paths that feminists are constantly navigating to make sense of the gendered world of states.

NOTES

1. For example, Cambodia, Myanmar, Argentina, Chile, Zimbabwe, and Sri Lanka.
2. Gender and religious minorities continue to be oppressed, marginalized, and threatened in Myanmar, Pakistan, Sri Lanka, and in other countries in the Asia Pacific region. Sudan, Israel, Congo, and Cambodia have committed serious human rights violations against their own citizens.

PART I

Stating Gender and Gendering States

CHAPTER 2

Rethinking the State in International Relations

A Personal Reflection

J. ANN TICKNER

In 1979, Kenneth Waltz's published *Theory of International Politics*, and his shadow loomed large in the Department of Political Science at Brandeis University, where he had previously been a faculty member and where I was pursuing a PhD. His concept of states as billiard balls clashing in an unregulated space called anarchy made little sense to me (Waltz 1979). Well before my feminist consciousness was raised, international relations (IR) theory and its assumptions about states as unitary power-seeking rational actors seemed narrow and unreflective. Realism, the dominant theoretical approach during the Cold War, was concerned with the structure of the system rather than with examining the different compositions of states themselves. Emphasizing order over justice, realists sought to understand what factors increased the stability of the system rather than whether states were meeting the basic needs of their citizens.

My return to graduate school to study international politics was motivated by my concerns with peace, social justice, and inequality—particularly between the Third and First Worlds.[1] Nothing I was learning seemed to speak to these issues. Therefore, I chose an unconventional dissertation topic—self-reliance as a development strategy for newly independent, postcolonial states, a topic that several of my professors tried to dissuade me from pursuing. My dissertation was completed well before I embarked on my feminist journey through international relations and, indeed, before there was any feminist research in the field. Nevertheless, the extent to which its themes parallel some of my, and other IR feminists', subsequent writings on gendered states is remarkable. Feminist analyses usually start, not with the structure of the system, but by examining the composition and behavior of states in terms of their ability to increase the security of their citizens in both physical and economic terms.

My dissertation, *Self-Reliance versus Power Politics*, published in 1987, examined the development paths of two postcolonial states, the United States from 1776 to 1829 and India from 1947 to 1980, a comparison that would draw criticism from those with strong beliefs in American exceptionalism (Tickner 1987).[2] Contrary to liberal strategies of open development as the best route to modernization, which were promoted by the West for the Third World in the post–World War II era, the early United States and postindependence India both chose protectionist strategies designed to build national economic strength and decrease external dependency; these strategies were devised in order to resist penetration by the hegemonic powers of their time. I explored these strategies through the writings of Friedrich List, Alexander Hamilton, and Jawaharlal Nehru, each of whom proscribed a protectionist strategy in order to build national power and decrease dependence on an international system dominated by Britain, whose influence on its former colonies would not cease with independence.[3] In contrast to this mercantilist model, a parallel examination of the works of Mahatma Gandhi and the early Thomas Jefferson revealed a model of agrarian self-reliance more in line with satisfying the basic needs of people than with building national power, a model seemingly more compatible with certain subsequent feminists' analyses of state building, but one that lost out in both cases.

Although his concept of a property-owner did not extend beyond white males, Thomas Jefferson, one of the authors of the US Declaration of Independence, believed that the right to own property should be distributed as widely as possible, so that each individual could be as self-reliant as possible and satisfy his (*sic*) own basic needs, producing a surplus only to the extent that it could be traded for necessary goods. He also suggested that those without property should be given land from the vast tracts available in eighteenth-century North America (Tickner 1987, 75).[4]

Gandhi also promoted a rural decentralized democracy, but one quite different from Jefferson's individualist form of liberal democracy that was built around self-reliant male property-owners. While he strongly believed in the centrality of the individual in shaping his or her own environment,

Gandhi claimed that each individual is part of an integrated whole and has an obligation to build a kind of society in which exploitation associated with colonial rule could not be reproduced. State building must be bottom up—with the central government responsible only for tasks, such as education, that enabled people to better themselves. Ahead of his time, Gandhi favored equality for women, whose exclusion was constitutive of the institutional structures of the early Western liberal state.[5] Unlike Jefferson, who became president of the United States, Gandhi never held political office, so he was never confronted with compromising his vision of a postcolonial state that would not be an end in itself, but rather one that would enable people to better their lives.

My prefeminist analysis pointed to the tensions in the early development strategies of these postcolonial states between state building and survival in a competitive international system and meeting the basic needs of citizens. When I reflect on my conclusions in light of my subsequent feminist writings on the state, I have come to recognize the gendered implications of the two models for postcolonial states analyzed in my dissertation and to see their connection to my later thinking. Most other feminists have also claimed that postcolonial states have too often served their own reproductive/security needs rather than the needs and interests of their citizens. Nevertheless, in spite of the obviously gendered nature of these differing development strategies—building national power versus satisfying basic needs—it was the realities of my having entered a field almost entirely populated by men writing about men's experiences, as well as the heavy focus on warring states and national security, that first aroused my feminist consciousness some years later when I began to analyze the explicitly gendered nature of international relations theory, particularly its depictions of states.

In this chapter, I will discuss some of my later thinking about the state. I will situate this within a more general discussion of feminist analyses of the state, focusing on some of the work presented in *Gendered States*, the first feminist IR text to engage the state (Peterson 1992a). It has usually been the case that IR feminists, particularly those from the United States, have assessed the liberal state negatively, particularly with respect to its association with war and conflict as well as the gendered structures of social and economic inequality built into its historical foundations. I shall also discuss some feminist work that has presented a more positive view of the state. Drawing on these feminist analyses, I will further reflect on and critique my own prefeminist work on self-reliance, suggesting some positive feminist visions for postcolonial states, as well as some obstacles to their realization.

My early feminist thinking on the state led me to an analysis and critique of Hans Morgenthau's six principles of political realism, a much-cited early statement of post–World War II realism. I used feminist analysis to challenge Morgenthau's assumptions about unitary states in an anarchical world where security is defined in terms of the security of the state to be achieved through building power and autonomy (Tickner 1988). The world that Morgenthau was describing was a masculine world, a world of power and conflict in which the possibility of war is an ever-present reality. Power and autonomy, desirable traits for successful states, are words we also associate with masculinity. I argued that states also engage in more cooperative behavior, usually ignored by realists, and that many problems in today's world demand cooperative rather than zero-sum solutions. It was in this piece that I first introduced my feminist redefinition of a more comprehensive notion of security that includes the security not only of states but also of individuals, both physical and structural, as well as of the natural environment.[6]

Morgenthau and other classical realists writing in the post–World War II period focused on the behavior of great powers and their decision-makers, who sought to maximize power in a hostile international system where conflict was an ever-present possibility. Waltz's *Theory of International Politics* (1979) marked a shift, not in assumptions but in methodology, putting IR theory on a more "scientific" footing. Waltzian "neorealism" removed foreign policy decision-makers, as well as people more generally, from its theoretical constructions: instead, Waltz chose to focus on the structure of the system in order to explain the behavior of its constituent parts. Rejecting what he called "reductionist theories," Waltz claimed that only at the level of the international system could we discover laws that can help us explain the international behavior of states and the propensity for conflict (Waltz 1979, ch. 6). Waltz used microeconomic analysis, projecting the behavior of rational economic man in the market onto the behavior of states.[7] It was notable the extent to which Waltz's writings, works that had featured so prominently in my own graduate education, influenced early ventures into feminist IR more generally.

Echoing Waltz, one of the first conferences, held at the University of Southern California in 1989, that brought together feminists and IR scholars was called "Women, the State and War: What Difference Does Gender Make?"[8] A year later, papers from a similarly structured conference at Wellesley College, Massachusetts, funded by the Ford Foundation, were published in the volume *Gendered States: Feminist (Re)Visions of International Theory* (Peterson 1992a). The end of the Cold War presented an opportunity to open the black-boxed state, typical of Waltzian neorealism.

In response to this moment, contributors to *Gendered States* focused on issues such as the gendered meaning of national security, the connection between masculinity, autonomy, and state sovereignty, the state as embodied in the notion of (male) warriors self-sacrificing to protect the (female) nation, and the relationship between masculinity and citizenship.

In her chapter in *Gendered States*, Spike Peterson claimed that national security, centered on the security of the state, is profoundly contradictory for individuals, particularly for women, a claim similar to the conclusion of my dissertation. Working from a broad multidimensional definition of security similar to mine, Peterson argued that an emphasis on military security and the prioritizing of national defense by certain states generates system wide insecurity. She also argued that state-centric management is unable to address global processes of environmental insecurity or structural inequalities created by a capitalist world system (Peterson 1992b, 32). She claimed that we must get beyond state security and begin to think in terms of world security.

Christine Sylvester examined the meaning of autonomy that, in liberal theory, translates into social contract theory. Drawing on psychoanalytic theory, she claimed that the separation of boys from their mothers— what she called reactive autonomy, a separateness and independence from others—describes only male behavior. This, she argues, translates into social contract theory whereby realist theory sees states as primitive (male) individuals separated by the rights of sovereignty (Sylvester 1992, 157). Revealing women's various roles in international politics (as well as individuals more generally) complicates this story and challenges assumptions about unitary states. She argues for a feminist standpoint that challenges the timelessness of realist theory and contextualizes autonomy.

Rebecca Grant claimed that the tools of political theory that are used to explain the behavior of states are based on men's experiences. Rousseau's metaphor of the stag hunt is based on male behavior and is used by realists such as Waltz to explain that cooperation is impossible in a world where the likelihood of defection from cooperative solutions is high. IR theorists, she asserts, have been uncritical and unreflective about the social relations that support the international role of the state (Grant 1992, 85). Grant calls for better theories that expose gender bias and offer us a more complete picture of human behavior, something I also tried to do in my Morgenthau piece.

Jean Elshtain's chapter takes up the issue of protection. She claims that war should not be understood as the result of men's aggressiveness but rather as a "will to sacrifice" and die if necessary for the "mother" country. Our war stories center on "manly" states sacrificing for the female nation.[9]

Given this will to sacrifice, Elshtain concludes that with the state comes the inevitability of war (1992, 143). She also concludes that the state cannot be willed out of existence since we need the outside "other" to define ourselves (150).

All of these contributors to *Gendered States* emphasize the partial theorization of the state, incomplete because it is based only on a male model of behavior. All raise the gendered concept of protection, the notion that males (usually soldiers) must protect vulnerable women not able to protect themselves. The association of the state with national security, war, and protection has been a dominant one in IR feminist analyses since the early 1990s, as has the critique of social contract theory, upon which so much of Western IR theory is based. The Leviathan—portrayed in Hobbes's famous text as a sovereign king sitting on a throne, with a crown on his head and a sword in his hand protecting his people from danger—has become a founding metaphor for IR realists and a powerful one for feminists also (Tickner 1996, 152). Danger is associated with those others on the outside, often portrayed in feminized terms, as either irrational or weak.[10]

As many feminists have pointed out, the masculinity of war has always depended on the myth that strong men are protecting women, children, and the more vulnerable who are too weak to protect themselves. Ten years before *Gendered States* was published, Judith Stiehm wrote a much-cited article examining this relationship. Stiehm argued that the myth of women needing protection has been sustained by two claims—that women are too valuable to fight and that they would be ineffective if called upon to do so. Women's patriotic duty is to produce male warriors ready to sacrifice their lives for the state. This sets up an unequal dichotomous relationship in which women are perceived as vulnerable, dependent, and lacking in agency and sends a powerful message that is hard for women to overcome (Stiehm 1982).

Elaborating on the theme of protection, Jonathan Wadley claims that while IR theorists often personify the state, presenting it as a person, they rarely acknowledge that that person is gendered, thereby elevating the masculine to universal status (Wadley 2010, 39). Drawing on Judith Butler's concept of performativity, Wadley asserts that states perform as masculine protectors, thus enabling them gain legitimacy from domestic audiences and respect from international ones (Wadley 2010, 40). Protection is central to the production of the state, and war allows leaders to perform in ways that accord with masculine ideals.

If the state has been portrayed as the masculine protector, the identity of the nation has often been portrayed as female. During war, and in times of crisis more generally, states exhort masculine protectors to fight for the defense of the "mother" country (Tickner 1996, 154). Just as families have been patriarchal institutions of hierarchy, so too these family metaphors denote hierarchy in which men's roles are privileged over women's (Tickner 1996, 153).

The personification of the state as masculine has been a central theme of feminist analyses. Elaborating on the theme of "hegemonic masculinity," a term used to describe the type of masculinity associated with the gendered state, Jennifer Heeg Maruska introduces the concept of "hypermasculinity"—what she defines as "extreme behavior within gender roles brought about by a reaction to some internal or external threat" (Heeg Maruska 2010, 241).[11] She claims that hypermasculinity has taken on different forms at various points in US history when the state has seen itself as experiencing a domestic or international threat. The three examples she uses are the closing of the American frontier in the 1890s, the start of the Cold War in the 1950s, and the period following the September 11, 2001, attacks. The closing of the frontier in the 1890s led to what she terms "restlessness and hopelessness" and a call for imperialist designs beyond the borders of the continental United States (Heeg Maruska 2010, 241). Both internal and external threats caused a similar surge of hypermasculinity at the start of the Cold War, when both homegrown communism and the ideology and power of the Soviet Union threatened, as did Muslims, both inside and outside the United States, in the wake of the 2001 attacks.

Gendered concepts, such as sovereignty, protection, and anarchy, that were first analyzed in *Gendered States* have been reformulated and elaborated upon by feminists over the past twenty-five years. Rarely acknowledged as such by conventional IR scholars, particularly security specialists, these concepts, feminists have pointed out, not only have negative effects on women but also privilege war and conflict. Feminists have traced gendered militarism to gendered notions of sovereignty, since state sovereignty sanctions the legal use of force (Sjoberg 2013, 142). The privileging of concepts such as protection sanctions an unequal gender hierarchy where women are seen as helpless victims without agency and the anarchy assumption leaves little room for assumptions about cooperative behavior, also a feature of the international system.

My review of some feminist analysis of the state, first articulated in *Gendered States* and further elaborated on in later analyses, has generally presented the state in a fairly negative light. I will now turn to some writings by feminists who have offered a more positive view of the state. I begin with reference to a unique chapter in *Gendered States* by feminist international lawyer Mona Harrington that offers a nonconventional view of the state and a more positive assessment of the possibilities for a restructured state that would promote the interests of its citizens over the priorities of national security. Examining the post–World War II period, Harrington portrays an isolationist streak in small-scale agricultural interests in the western United States as well as in American small businesses of the same era. She contrasts this ideology with that of multinational corporate managers and professionals who favored a form of international openness that would enable them to move billions of dollars around the globe irrespective of state boundaries (Harrington 1992, 70). While not necessarily agreeing with the political ideology of these isolationist groups, Harrington claims that the strongly bounded state is the political form preferred by the relatively powerless, a point that seems even more relevant with respect to today's unregulated global economy. While endorsing feminist critiques of liberal individualism, Harrington laments feminists' lack of attention to what she called nonatomistic forms of liberal theory such as social democracy and the welfare state (Harrington 1992, 72). She suggests that feminists might do well to examine the more women-friendly policies of the Nordic states, states that not only do well on redistributional social benefits but also have a large majority of women in government.[12] Harrington was not advocating a dichotomized, "feminized" state but rather one in which there would be dissolution of the public/private divide, a founding principle of the liberal state, with the public sphere assuming more responsibility for day care and parental leave and with reformulated roles within marriage and families in the private sphere (Harrington 1992, 74). She postulated a world of what she called "an international system of inward-turned feminist states, a world that is still contentious but one in which there could not be legitimate national interests that cause states to respond to tense situations with aggressive or imperial action" (Harrington 1992, 77).

Ten years after the 1990 Wellesley conference, where Harrington's and the other papers that were published in *Gendered States* were first presented, a second conference, also funded by the Ford Foundation, was held at the University of Southern California. Titled "Gender in International Relations: From Seeing Women and Gender to Transforming Policy Research," the agenda was more expansive, reflecting not only the proliferation of feminist research but also the feminist goal of engaging those in the policy community and the activist world. A conference paper delivered by Jane Jaquette sympathized with feminists' unease with the liberal democratic state that, at its foundation, was neither liberal nor democratic due to its failure to recognize the citizenship of women, slaves, and individuals without property. Nevertheless, she chastised feminists for failing to recognize that the state is the only social institution with the legitimacy and scope to deliver any of the goods that feminists seek, such as reproductive rights, redistributive benefits, and meaningful engagement in the public sphere (Jaquette 2003, 342). Quoting Drude Dahlerup, Jaquette asserted that feminists would have to learn to live with the state (Jaquette 2003, 343). Commenting on Jaquette's subsequent publication, Jane Mansbridge went further, claiming that feminists would not only have to learn to live with the state, they would also have to learn to work with the state (2003, 360).

Clearly, feminists in a variety of countries, especially those in policy circles and women's movements, have been doing just that, even before the suffrage movements of the early twentieth century. The more recent use of gender quotas and gender mainstreaming have been important tools for ensuring women's greater political participation and have met with some success in certain states, although they have been less successful at the international level due to the lack of enforcement. Marian Sawyer, one of the Australian "femocrats" who were quite successful in promoting women's agendas, reinforces this more positive stance.[13] She argues that the case against the state does not accord with women's historical agency in creating welfare states (Sawer 2003a, 363). She suggests that just as many groups have been created to promote state intervention as have arisen in opposition to it. She cites feminists in the European Union, Scandinavia, and New Zealand who have led political campaigns to defend the welfare state (Sawyer 2003, 364). She concludes that hostility to the state may be more prevalent among US feminists, given the weak development of social liberalism and the welfare state in the United States, an issue to which I shall return later.

So, given that we still live in a world of states, how can feminists work with, or beyond, the state to promote feminist agendas that function in the interests of all its citizens—women as well as other less privileged individuals? In attempting to offer some answers to this question, I return to my dissertation, this time using a critical feminist lens, to think about some possibilities for, and obstacles to, postcolonial "feminist friendly" states.

While describing them in somewhat different terms from mine, feminist historians Joyce Appleby, Lynn Hunt, and Margaret Jacob, in their text *Telling the Truth about History*, also point to two different underlying models of the early American state: the first, elitist direction from the center by ruling elites holding themselves aloof from the people, similar to my Hamiltonian model; the second, a Jeffersonian model of participatory democracy that drew inspiration from the French Revolution of 1789, somewhat similar also to Harrington's isolationist agrarianism. Appleby et al. claim that, out of this Jeffersonian republican version of the history of the pioneering American West with its promise of freedom and equality of opportunity, came a new model of human behavior—man the doer (Appleby 1996, 95). However, as they note, this model was built on stereotypical white male behavior and was associated with taming and working the land. Indians were placed outside the circle of progress, the emphasis on progress being the rationale for their displacement. This heroic history also omitted any discussion of slavery (Appleby 1996, 114–135).[14]

This vision of autonomous man depended on the availability of vast tracts of land in the American West or, in the South, on the labor of slaves. In both cases, the unrecognized caring labor provided by women was also essential. The myth of unoccupied land not only depended on the removal of indigenous peoples, but also fostered the American belief in the superiority of capitalism and private ownership and an aversion to social planning (Appleby 1996, 157). Notably, this has contributed to Americans' ambivalence about the welfare state and the strong belief in individualism that, as I mentioned earlier, may contribute to US feminists' negative view of the state.

Reading Appleby's critique thirty years after I completed my dissertation, I have come to appreciate not only the gendered dichotomy between the more feminized decentralized agrarian self-reliance of the Gandhian and Jeffersonian models and the masculinized national power-building model adopted by postcolonial India and the United States, but also the gender inequalities inherent in the models themselves. As feminists have pointed out, building national power runs the risk of excessive focus on national security at the expense of social welfare programs that benefit the less privileged, often women. It also legitimates the use of force through the deployment of the protector myth and the notion that women are not first-class citizens due to their need for male protection. And while the Jeffersonian model of local self-reliance is more compatible with feminist sensibilities, it carries with it the same unequal gendered and racialized foundational structures that feminist historians and political theorists have found so troubling in the development of liberal states.

Gandhi's version of self-reliance, less dependent on the gendered foundations of Western liberal individualism, has the potential to be more communal and feminist and more compatible with Mona Harrington's caring social democratic state, where dichotomies between a privileged masculinized public sphere and a private sphere occupied by women in caring and reproductive roles are broken down. Lessening the unequal gendering of the public/private divide is essential to building feminist-friendly states. Only when care work is valued to the same extent as national security can we hope to realize a vision of a state that recognizes the agency and satisfies the needs of all its citizens.

In conclusion, we must ask if Harrington's vision of an inwardly turning caring state is relevant in today's world even as a normative model. States that score high on human development indicators tend to be relatively homogeneous. Most postcolonial states in the Third World are ethnically diverse; many struggle to contain conflicts exacerbated by state boundaries imposed by imperial designs that do not accord with the ethnic or national identities of their citizens. And as more affluent states, some of them former imperial powers, contend with increasing numbers of refugees made homeless by these conflicts and discriminatory practices, state borders are becoming barriers of oppression preventing people from fleeing from various forms of violence. Today, the most powerful are not always those discriminated against within states but the 60 million refugees and asylum seekers displaced by these conflicts, many of them women and children. And of those who travel across national boundaries to seek income to support their families left behind, many of them are women caregivers or sex workers who are among the most exploited of today's waged labor.

So perhaps we are in need of new models that look beyond our contemporary world of nation states with its masculinized notion of sovereignty that feminists have found so problematic. I will conclude by offering a vision of a world order that is different from the statist one in which we presently live and which has a number of parallels with feminist visions of a less gendered world order. I have learned from my recent examination of indigenous knowledge that indigenous people, while contending with a state system that has imposed terrible costs on them, see the world very differently. Their "nations" have never conformed to state boundaries imposed on them, and they have never been formally recognized as states. Indigenous politics originates in forms of governance constituted outside and before the modern state. Indigeneity is a useful tool for examining the diversity of political configurations differing from state-centrism, an order imposed on the world through imperialism. Since they do not possess the attribute of sovereign equality that enables even the poorest states to participate in the global discourse affecting their future, indigenous peoples are bypassing the state and making claims about world order directly to the international community, in some cases with some measure of success (Tickner 2015).

Using the case of Kichwa women in Ecuador, feminist Manuela Picq shows how these women took international law as the main tool to advance their rights within their ancestral systems of justice. Their goal was to bypass the legal sovereignty of the state and to make subnational systems of indigenous justice accountable to international women's rights, thereby pressuring the state to adopt language on gender equality within the framework of collective rights and cultural autonomy (Picq 2013, 131). Picq suggests that this articulation of multiple scales of legal authority makes homogenous forms of state sovereignty obsolete and, instead, offers possibilities of sovereignties in the plural (Picq 2013, 133).

Similarly, Peruvian anthropologist Marisol de la Cadena tells of a process called "the return of the Indian" that began in the Andean countries in the late twentieth century, a process whereby social movements started to articulate their demands around indigenous issues and ethnic claims. Among their demands was the concept of indigenous citizenship, a pluriethnic or pluricultural ideal that had as its goal the transformation of the modern state and its principle of exclusive national sovereignty. The most widespread expression of this ideal is a political project, most prominent in Ecuador, Peru, and Bolivia, known as *interculturalidad*, a project that proposes, in part through bilingual education, to create a plurinational state that recognizes the diversity of its peoples and does not require cultural renunciation as a condition for citizenship (Cadena 2005, 24).[15]

Both these authors are advocating for multilevel systems of governance that accord with feminist sensibilities for achieving global security. Pluriethnic citizenship has some similarities with feminist goals of getting beyond rigid gender hierarchies denoting insiders and outsiders, whether they are designated by race, gender, or national identity. And feminists have worked hard at the global level to establish UN conventions to address women's human rights and sexual violence.

Clearly, we are far from living in a world that is not statist. Just as the early United States and postcolonial India built national power as a way to survive and prosper in a statist world, postcolonial states have been eager to join a state system that, while it may have been imposed by the West, has provided them with a voice and some measure of independence in the current world order. And feminists have demonstrated that development strategies that are inclusive of women are the ones most likely to build states with the ability to satisfy the basic needs of all their people. While feminist scholarship on the state has rightly pointed to the injustices of the present system, it has also suggested some possibilities for a less hierarchically gendered future.

NOTES

1. I have chosen to use the term "Third World" over the now more widely used "global South." Third World was originally coined by members of the unaligned

bloc at the United Nations to distinguish themselves from the First and Second Worlds, the Western and the Eastern blocs.

2. American exceptionalism is a theory that claims that the United States is inherently better than other nations. It can be traced back, as early as the 1640s, to English colonists evoking the metaphor of a "City upon a Hill." However, it was Alexis de Tocqueville who first wrote about it in 1835, calling the United States an exceptional country. Today, conservative writers promote its use, while critics claim that the United States remains rooted in its European origins, with its history of imperialism and war as well as class and racial inequalities. See Lipset (1996). It is also associated with "Manifest Destiny," a term coined in the 1830s to justify US westward territorial expansion.

3. Nehru was a leader in the call for a New International Economic Order (NIEO), a term derived from the Declaration for the Establishment of the New International Economic Order, introduced by a group of Third World countries and adopted by the UN General Assembly in 1974. It called for the restructuring of the global economy to promote greater participation and benefits to Third World countries. Advocating mercantilist policies over open markets, it was never endorsed by the richer and more powerful northern states. See Murphy (1984).

4. The term "available" completely ignored the fact that native peoples had inhabited these lands for hundreds of years. Initially Jefferson believed that white men should not encroach on Indian land without their consent. After he became president, his views changed to one of paternalism toward the Indians. He advocated that they should give up their nomadic existence, adopt a more sedentary lifestyle, and participate in the benefit of white man's government and civilization (Tickner 1987, 78). For a fascinating account of Cherokee resistance to the policy of incorporation and conquest in the early nineteenth century, see Inskeep (2015).

5. As political theorists such as Carole Pateman have pointed out, women were completely excluded from the original social contract, postulated by seventeenth- and eighteenth-century European social contract theorists hypothesizing on the origins of states. Only men were seen as political actors, whereas women were excluded from the social contract. Men's freedom depended on women's occlusion in the private sphere, which was not deemed politically relevant (Pateman 1988, especially ch. 1). This creation of the public/private divide has been a defining feature of the Western state and one imposed on postcolonial states through imperialism.

6. While this has changed somewhat since 1988 when this piece was published, there are still relatively few women in the top ranks of the US Foreign Service, the military and the US Department of Defense, and in the academic discipline of international relations, particularly in security studies. There is, however, a growing and thriving field of feminist security studies.

7. Neorealists were attempting to construct a "positivist" science of international relations, using game-theoretic and rational choice models in order to introduce more "scientific rigor" into the field.

8. This title is taken from one of Waltz's earlier books, entitled *Man, the State and War* (1959). Here Waltz situated his explanation for conflict at three levels of analysis, the individual, the state, and the international system. By the time he wrote *Theory of International Politics*, levels 1 and 2 had dropped out. Labeling second-level explanations of states' behavior as "reductionist," Waltz, in his later work, focused his attention entirely at the level of the structure of the system.

9. This is a theme I take up in Tickner (1996).

10. This is especially true of racialized enemies. Whereas the Russians were perceived as "dangerous" and labeled as the "Evil Empire" during the Cold War, they were not seen as "irrational," such terms being usually reserved for racialized others such as Saddam Hussein. For an interesting comparison between differing discourses about Germany and Japan during World War II that makes a similar point, see Dower (1986).

11. The term "hegemonic masculinity" was first introduced by R. W. Connell (1995). It has been used in feminist IR by various authors, including Charlotte Hooper (2001).

12. Since Harrington wrote this chapter, feminists have written a great deal about Scandinavian states and their women-friendly policies. It should be noted, however, that Sweden is a major arms exporter, this being a source of revenue that helps make possible its generous spending on social welfare. Sweden's business and financial sectors are still male dominated.

13. Hester Eisenstein employs this term in the title of her 1996 book, *Inside Agitators: Australian Femocrats and the State*. Echoing Harrington she asks: is a "woman-friendly state" possible? She demonstrates how Australian feminists succeeded in making women's issues, such as childcare and domestic violence, part of the mainstream agenda in the 1980s and 1990s. Femocrats emerged in response to the UN Decade for Women (1975–1985), but women-friendly policies have generally been more successful at the state rather than at the international level.

14. In theory but not in practice, Jefferson was in favor of emancipation, although his support was based on the view that any society is corrupted by the existence of slavery. He believed that blacks were inferior to whites and should be sent back to Africa or the West Indies (Tickner 1987, 78).

15. For a fuller elaboration of indigenous knowledge from which this brief discussion is taken, see Tickner (2015).

CHAPTER 3

Bringing Back Gendered States

Feminist Second Image Theorizing of International Relations

JACQUI TRUE

Feminist scholars of international relations argue that gender is *central* to the constitution of the state and to change "in" and "of" the inter-state system. The domination of masculinity over femininity is a structural pattern that may have existed prior to the development of the states system. However, the gender division of masculine public and feminine private spheres submerged within civil society is one of the foundations upon which modern European states were built and postcolonial states beyond Europe were subsequently established. This public-private division takes particular forms with specific manifestations in different Western and non-Western contexts. However, gender structures similarly differentiate male and female, masculine and feminine, rational and emotional, public and private in mutually constitutive ways, shaping and constraining what states are, what they do, and how they do it. These structures continue to play a crucial role in the constitution of state identities, diplomatic practices, and the maintenance and transformation of international relations.

This chapter argues that bringing back the concept of "gendered states" in its political, economic, and social dimensions can help us to explain the gendered nature of violence and conflict and the unraveling of patriarchal structures, practices, and norms in many parts of the world, in part due to the forces of economic globalization. To the extent that increased gender equality and social change is occurring alongside the continuation and exacerbation in some contexts of gendered violence, we could interpret the backlash against gender emancipation and the breakdown of traditional patriarchal social contracts as fueling gendered violence at all levels, including the explicit targeting of women and girls in intrastate and international conflicts. Changing gendered social relations are at once an embodiment of, and a threat to, sovereign statehood and political order. If patriarchal society in Europe, and its demarcation of public-private boundaries, once consolidated the modern states-system, now resurgent, often tribal patriarchies challenge Western and non-Western states from within and without.

There are three main parts to the argument presented in this chapter. The first part considers how traditional patriarchal relations are a historical feature of gendered state identities and interstate behavior. The next part examines the current situation where traditional patriarchal structures and norms in the many parts of the world are being transformed. The third part of the chapter explores the implications of these changes in the gendered nature and dynamics of states for global politics. The chapter argues that the apparent unraveling of patriarchy has at least three significant implications for the state in international relations. First, because patriarchal relations are a constitutive principle of the formation of states, their undoing also undoes a significant, albeit often ignored, cultural foundation of international relations. Second, to the extent that gendered states have played a positive role in unraveling of patriarchal relations, promoting gender equality and women's integration into the workforce and public realm, it is incumbent upon them to address the effects of that unraveling within societies. Third, reactions to patriarchal unraveling may take unusual and violent forms, threatening the stability of international order and the values upon which it has rested.

Above all, if we take patriarchal relations seriously as a constitutive part of the evolving world order, then it is possible to see both positive and negative effects of the unraveling of local and global patriarchies on gendered states in international relations. It is also possible to see that a stable world order will not be constructed without gender justice, together with social and economic justice, for all subordinated groups.

THEORIZING THE PATRIARCHAL FOUNDATIONS OF GENDERED STATES

Sovereignty is a structuring principle of international order—and one of the most enduring features of modern world politics. Patriarchy is also a structural relationship—defined as the gender hierarchy that privileges masculinity over femininity, creating and reinforcing the divisions between public and private (family/home) spheres, reason and emotion, men and women. Both feminist and nonfeminist international relations scholars seek to theorize these globalized structures that are not visible per se but are revealed when we analyze patterns of behavior across many interactions. Because violence is patterned along gender lines, with men historically fighting wars and women largely supporting their efforts on the home front (across diverse states and social formations), examining the gender social order is essential to theorizing international relations.

Patriarchy is a pattern of social arrangements that are grounded in women's and men's negotiations or "bargains" set within institutional and structural contexts that reinforce gender hierarchy (Kandiyoti 1989; Hunnicutt 2009; Mies 1986). Like the interstate order, patriarchal relations are readily obscured precisely because masculine domination is so pervasive and taken for granted. For example, the everyday practices of chivalry, some of which still thrive today in Western societies, such as opening doors for women to go through first and shaking hands among men (but not with women), effectively entrench masculine protection and women's status as the weaker sex. No one dictates them from above or coerces individuals to follow them. They are, rather (or were once), appropriate standards of behavior.

Importantly, patriarchal and interstate relations may not always require violence to uphold them—to the extent that their practices are self-reproducing (Hunnicutt 2009, 9). Those who are not the architects of these institutions and/or do not have access to systems of law and justice may use violence because legitimate or institutional means are not available or effective (though this is clearly not the case for the most part with women). Violence may be needed especially when consensual, hegemonic orders break down (Gramsci 1971), that is, when international and patriarchal societies no longer appeal to their weaker members and confront contending goals and values.

The concept of gendered states captures the ways in which gendered social relations constitute the meaning of sovereign statehood historically and in the present. Specifically, the gender hierarchy that privileges subjects that accord with masculine, competitive, rational, and autonomous attributes over feminine, caring, emotional, and relational attributes is manifest in the relations between states within international relations. There are myriad ways in which these gendered relations affect the governance of international order. Underpinning international relations is an implicit gender hierarchy among states, from strong to weak, rational to

irrational, powerful to powerless, dominant to subordinate, manly to fragile or deviant (Sjoberg 2012). For instance, one of the ways of determining
membership in international society or "governing" states on the margins
of international society is to categorize them as "weak or fragile states"
and/or to refer to them with feminine or nonrational qualifiers, such as
rogue or *deviant*, and so forth.

However, Carole Pateman argues that the problem of patriarchy is
repressed within the structure of the state and state system (1988, 1;
1989, 2). In her major work, *The Sexual Contract* (1988), Pateman sub-
stantiated how modern European states emerged from absolutist patriarchal states and were founded on a "fraternal sexual contract" that upheld
the equal rights of male individuals in the public sphere, while relegating
wives and daughters as property to the private family household sphere.
Patriarchal relations within the households of modern European states
were both created and reinforced through the material changes that
ensued with the Industrial Revolution, which, in turn, enabled capital
accumulation to fuel the war and gender-making capacities of states in
formation (Mies 1986; Tilly 1985; Peterson 1992a). That order within
states was extended and diffused across states. Accordingly, the state system and international society have been made possible by normalized
gender divisions of labor that have produced and reproduced the identities and war-making capacities of states. These gendered relations have
further helped to cement the sovereignty principle shared and diffused
by modern states, which has upheld the prerogative of individual states
to determine the distribution of power and resources among individuals,
maintaining unjust and unequal gendered relations of domination.

Though patriarchal relations have been "repressed" or hidden within
states, they are fundamental. Indeed, international membership has been
based on conformity with modern standards of civilization that include
gender-appropriate conduct. Ann Towns recounts the directive in the
nineteenth-century European society of states to officially exclude women
from politics and public life, consistent with bourgeois notions of respectable behavior at the time (2010). Accordingly, Japan and China through
legislation "barred women from political participation for the first time
upon formally entering the civilized society of states" (Towns 2010, 187).
This arrangement was then seen as a progressive feature of Western civilization. The struggle against this norm has involved more than a century
of transnational politics. Only recently, in the last two to three decades,
have we seen gender justice or formal equality become part of the practices
of diplomacy and war, being stated as a condition for international recognition and legitimacy of a state, and as a justification for international

intervention. Though gender and state identities are not fixed, what has remained constant is the notion that women's political status is linked to the progress of states, their international ranking, and to the "othering" of poorly performing states. That is, the division between states belonging to the international community and those state and nonstate actors outside or on the margins of this community reflects a gendered ordering (Ling and Agathangelou 2004).

To argue that states are gendered does not imply that gender is the dominant social relation. Rather, patriarchal relations are bound up with other systems of domination based on race, ethnicity, nationality, sexuality, class, and age for instance, which are both cross-cutting and aligned. This is why some women, men, and states behave to maintain the system of gendered power even when it ensures their subordination. It may advance their status along another axis of power. The next part of the chapter explores transformations in the structures and practices of modern and postcolonial gendered states.

CONTEMPORARY CHANGE IN GENDERED STATES

There have been visible transformations in patriarchal gender relations over the past half-century, including changes in the social roles of women and men and the rise of global women's and feminist movements and women political leaders. To what extent can we still speak of states as gendered therefore? What implications have changes in gender relations had for international relations, and to what extent are they shared beyond the West?

Theorizing the relationship between social relations and international order is crucial to understanding change in world politics, change that is not likely to come from within existing institutions. Historical patriarchal structures established within modern states are unraveling in many parts of the world due, in part, to the material changes wrought by globalization. For example, powerful states increasingly promote the cause of gender equality because it is in their national interest to do so. A key source of the competitive advantage of states today is their capacity to harness the talents and potentials of their population in tradable economic activity and in the defense of the state via the military and broad security apparatus. Even states like Japan are becoming advocates for gender equality and major supporters of the United Nations' women, peace, and security agenda, which promotes women's participation in peace and security institutions and national and international decision-making. The achievement of state goals requires them to close gender gaps between the public and market-based participation of men and women and, in so doing, increase the numbers of women available for these activities. Powerful states may also be able to shore up the legitimacy of their position at the top of the international hierarchy by pointing to the gender equality or "gender inclusiveness" in their society. Through visible women leaders serving as their representatives, they may justify coercive policies vis-à-vis state or nonstate actors that actually violate norms of gender equality and women's rights (Hunt 2002; Shepherd 2006). This is a not a new phenomenon. What is new, however, is that gender inclusion increasingly contests other values in international relations. In this way, state promotion of gender equality can be seen to facilitate the maintenance of power rather than representing a power shift in gendered states. It is certainly an advance on earlier assumptions that the rise of women leaders would destabilize the international order because they make feeble foreign policy chiefs (Fukuyama 1998). Though increasing the numbers of women in the public sphere may advance the cause of one state over another, it does not alter the relational aspect of power wherein masculine attributes, ways of governing, and values are ascendant.

At the same time as states promote gender equality policies domestically, they may be motivated to respond to claims for gender justice internationally. Gender equality and justice is an area for win-win cooperation among states—where international norms and policy borrowing can advance relative and absolute gains. Global trends in gender and class inequality are ultimately redressed at the national level through regulations, policies, and laws that remove discrimination and provide incentives for equality. However, the political and economic gains from addressing these inequalities will be shared among states—albeit some gain more than others. An example of cooperation in international relations on this goal is the creation of the W20 (Women in the G20), aimed at closing economic gender gaps (Harris-Rimmer 2015). Turkey founded the W20 in 2014 during the year it hosted the G20, showing its credibility as a state power willing to address a point of weakness in its own economy and society relative to European states.[1] The following year Australia hosted the G20 and established a target for members to close the economic participation gap by 25%, thereby demonstrating its diplomatic capacity as a "middle power" to provide an international good. In 2016, China, which was hosting the G20 and W20, used the opportunity to showcase its leadership and state strength in this area. This example illustrates how gendered states can pursue, and even share, interests and values regarding global equality, although the outcomes of their cooperation typically address the struggles for gender justice only in a limited way.

International politics redistributes the sources of power—enabling greater access for women to education, employment, business, and so on—while not shifting gendered power per se (see Arat 2015). For example, gender parity in secondary education enrolment has been virtually achieved in almost all parts of the world as a result of the Millennium Development Goals, but that has not changed the realities for many minority girls and women in accessing education (they may enroll but are prevented from going to school due to threats of harassment, violence, and conflict) nor the lesser returns to investment in education for women and girls globally due to the discriminatory attitudes, barriers, and hierarchies within the global economy and across societies. Addressing that discrimination would require unraveling all, not just some, gendered power relations.

Many states are driving the push for integration of women in militaries, diplomacy, and international policymaking, moreover. Evidence made in one realm of international politics—for instance, the global investment returns from women's participation on corporate boards (Credit Suisse 2012; McKinsey and Company 2007)—quickly travel to influence other realms—such as the greater sustainability of peace when women are present at peace negotiations (O'Reilly et al. 2015; Paffenholz et al. 2016). The universalization of rights, while often initiated by nonstate actors, may also be internalized by states, which increasingly advocate for human rights and gender justice as integral parts of their domestic and foreign policies. This normative change thus affects the quality of global politics. An example of this is the international diffusion of norms promoting women's human rights and prohibiting various forms of violence against women. That diffusion has set in motion a dynamics of universalization. However, the process also prompts localization responses, which may involve rejection, denial, or noncompliance with the intended gender equality norms, potentially undermining international consensus.

India provides an example of how gendered states resist international gender equality norms that challenge traditional patriarchal structures. Despite being listed as a country of concern where sexual and gender-based violence has been documented in urban, rural, and conflict-affected areas (Davies and True 2015), the Indian government has continually failed to adequately respond to egregious sexual and gender-based violence. Up until 2013, India denied there was systematic violence against women in the country, especially by the armed forces in conflict-affected areas, in periodical reports to the UN Convention on the Elimination of All Forms of Discrimination Against Women Committee, and India resisted the incursion of international actors. Civil society advocates of anti-VAW norms have used the shadow Convention on the Elimination of Discrimination against Women reporting mechanism to hold the Indian government accountable to a far greater degree than other governments in the region. Only after massive civil society protests, following the December 16, 2012, brutal gang rape and subsequent death of the twenty-three-year-old female tertiary student on a Delhi bus, however, did the government begin to fully respond to this violence. That fatal gang rape garnered a mass social movement in the streets of Delhi and great attention around the world through the global social and mainstream media (Gopinath 2015; Sharma and Bazilli 2014). The Indian government established a commission of inquiry to investigate the "Delhi rape" and laws and policies to prevent such violence against women and girls. The Justice Verma Commission was thus created. It invited civil society to make recommendations on the issue of legal reform, receiving more than seventy thousand submissions, and it organized public consultations called for by many civil society organizations (Women Against Sexual Violence and State Repression 2013; Chigateri et al. 2016). The commission made several progressive recommendations to the Indian parliament, some of which were passed, while others were rejected in the end. Five months after the Delhi rape, the Indian government also consented to a visit by the UN special rapporteur on violence against women (SRVAW), its causes and consequences in April 2013, having previously rejected requests for a mission visit to investigate VAW. Still following the SRVAW mission to India from April 22 to May 1, 2013, the Indian government dismissed the SRVAW's "labelling of violence against women as systematic."[2] The government stated that the report failed "to recognise that India, the world's largest democracy, values and respects the rule of law as one of its major strengths" (para. 3). The government disagreed that "physical, sexual and psychological abuse of women in the private sphere is widely tolerated by the state and community," citing immediate legislative and policy responses to the December 2012 Delhi gang rape.

A genuinely universal, global approach to gender inequality and injustice by states would need to go beyond addressing gender domination or patriarchal relations as a binary system that is reflected in the male/female international indicators of equality. It would need to assess the empowerment of women based on an understanding of how gender inequalities intersect with other social hierarchies and forms of oppression (such as race, ethnicity, sexuality, caste, class, age, nationality and immigrant status), and it would regard global migration and multiculturalism as salient in both Western and non-Western states.

How could such a universal approach address the persistent and egregious violence against women and girls, which is in seeming contradiction to the unraveling of patriarchal structures? The causes of this gendered violence are rooted in the political economy of power (True 2012). Importantly, states have diminished their own sovereign power in some respects by expanding capitalist markets and strengthening the freedoms of the "haves" over the "have-nots," the latter group including women in disproportionate ratio. As they compete for resources and investment, states have opened themselves to the productive as well as the destructive forces of capital, just as Marx had foretold. These forces undermine existing social contracts and deepen inequalities and tensions within and across societies. When social contracts break down between the state and civil society, so too does the prior "fraternal sexual contract"—the normative prohibition on perpetrating violence against another man's wife or daughter. That prohibition, of course, did not apply to violence in marriage or the family and has only been institutionalized in some, and not all, parts of the world.[3] Attention to violence in the family became a political issue in Western societies only in the 1970s, when women began exercising their political and economic rights to higher education, to vote, to be employed outside the home, and to control their own bodies. As Chris Reus-Smit argues, the notion that all biological humans have human rights is very recent, even more so the notion that women are humans and therefore have equal human rights (2013a). The underlying politics of human rights are still at work in today's gendered states.

When patriarchal social contracts break down as states facilitate economic globalization, men and masculinities are affected as much as women and girls. Some men's capacity to achieve recognition *as men*, an identity historically linked to dominant breadwinner or head-of-household status, is challenged and/or weakened by the global restructuring of production. Violence is one response when you cannot achieve the desired status or provide for your needs in a legitimate way. Men's loss of economic status, combined with residual patriarchal ideologies that support their rightful dominance and aggressive behavior, fuels a backlash of gendered violence and/or male suicide in some contexts, especially those affected by rising unemployment, poverty, inequality, displacement, conflict, and disaster (Hozic and True eds. 2016).

Traditional patriarchal structures extended protection to some women concomitant with their nonparticipation as equal citizens. But that protection came with a major risk; to the extent that women stepped outside of the gendered order (the social boundaries of their family and household), they could expect no protection from men; and historically gendered states have provided limited protection for noncitizens. This is indeed the case for many women and girls worldwide, one-third of whom are likely to experience some form of violent injury in their lifetime because they are women (Carter 2014; Ellsberg 2014). Today, though women have the protection of "national" and "international law" extending beyond the family and the state to which they belong, that law does not prevent the gender-based violence they experience. Laws may be poorly implemented by justice and public administration systems governed by masculine hegemonies and bureaucratic hierarchies that position women's safety as a low priority. Prevention responses to violence against women and girls are also often rooted in gendered protection narratives that assume women and girls are inherently victims and that men must be the ones to protect females, though many of them are also perpetrators. Moreover, improvements in women's status and the rise of political women (including women's human rights defenders) frequently provoke explicit targeting of women and girls for harassment and abuse. This violence is often the product of unresolved class, religious, and race/ethnic grievances, as well as gender ideologies and aggressive masculinities that are directly and indirectly supported by states.

We can see this process at work across the world but particularly clearly in those states recently subject to war and Western intervention such as Afghanistan and Iraq. The causes of violence or of economic and social injustice are deeper than the existence of the states system; they lie also in the complex overlaying of patriarchal domination across social relations. But that is not to let gendered states off the hook when they are complicit in creating the very material and ideological conditions that fuel gendered and other types of pervasive, global violence.

RESOLVING THE CONTRADICTIONS OF PATRIARCHY WITHIN GLOBAL POLITICS

If patriarchal gender relations once consolidated modern and postcolonial states, they now also challenge those states from within and without. The implications of the unraveling of patriarchal relations for the transformation and/or preservation of states in international relations are threefold. First, because patriarchal relations have shaped the formation of gendered states, their undoing also undoes a significant cultural foundation of international relations. However, the unraveling of patriarchal relations may mean the adoption of a less hierarchical order of nation states based on gendered distinctions and masculine domination. Second, the unraveling of patriarchal relations in the West has led to challenges to non-Western patriarchies, and contemporary responses to those challenges are taking reactionary forms, threatening the stability of international politics. Thus, to the extent that states have played a positive role in the unraveling of patriarchal relations, it is incumbent upon them to address these negative effects of that unraveling. Third, the diminishing of Western forms of patriarchal relations and contemporary challenges to non-Western forms of patriarchy through new global networks suggest the potential for the evolution of international society in the present and future.

With respect to the first implication of patriarchal unraveling, new or hybrid cultural norms and practices will have to replace patriarchal relations, and they will need to be broadly shared across postcolonial societies but also be diverse in their expression (see Narayan 1997; Narayan and Harding 2000). With the lesser influence of patriarchal norms in domestic societies, it should follow that, internationally, states are less likely to be perceived or ranked based on hierarchical gender distinctions. To take one example from recent research in West Java, Indonesia, gender equality and women's empowerment may be locally articulated within the Koran and Islamic teachings by male as well as female religious leaders with meaningful impacts on community understanding and support of social change (Muhummad et al. 2007; Rinaldo et al. 2011). If international relations are to be relatively peaceful, they will require cultural consensus across societies about values like gender equality, and not merely consensus among diplomatic and policy elites.

Historically, women's movements have been struggling to articulate new forms of intercultural dialogue and peaceful coexistence. After World War I, women's struggles for political rights in Europe began to pay off with the extension of suffrage. In 1915, twelve hundred women leaders from twelve countries across Europe and America, some of them suffragists, met in The Hague at a Congress for Peace to put forward their own detailed plan based on twenty resolutions to end the war (see Tickner and True, forthcoming). Some of the resolutions looked very similar to Woodrow Wilson's Fourteen Points. Woodrow Wilson himself did raise women's suffrage with fellow political leaders, but they rejected the inclusion of women's rights in an "international" agreement. Though the women peace activists achieved no recognition from state leaders, they formed the now century-old Women's International League for Peace and Freedom, with two members receiving the Nobel Peace Prize in 1919 for their efforts at The Hague (Confortini 2012).

While states did not recognize these early efforts by women activists to create a new cultural underpinning for international relations, one could hardly ignore them today. Women leaders are proving that they play crucial roles in bringing consensus in major areas of international cooperation, notably in this decade in nuclear disarmament talks and climate change negotiations among states (Ivanova 2015; Robinson 2016), and in sustainable international peace agreements (Paffenholz et al. 2016). They are pushing gendered states to engage more widely with society and nonstate actors and in building coalitions of unlikely allies around shared global challenges. William Hague's efforts to establish an international norm prohibiting the use of sexual violence in conflict at the core of UK foreign policy illustrates what is possible when a foreign policy leader within a powerful state joins together with nonstate actors, including women's organizations, to promote such a transformation of diplomacy and national interests to accord with human rights values (Davies and True 2017). As Hague has argued, "The networked world requires us to inspire other people with how we live up to our own values rather than try to impose them" (2010). Swedish foreign minister Margot Wallström took this movement for transformation in the culture of diplomacy even further when she announced in 2015 that her government would pursue a "feminist foreign policy" (2016; see the chapter by Chris Agius in this volume).[4]Among powerful state and nonstate actors, that statement of foreign policy has provoked skepticism comparable to men's dismissals of suffragettes campaigning for the right to vote over a century ago (see, for an example, Dangerfield 1996).

Albeit incipient and uneven in its progress, the empowerment of women around the world is gradually having an impact on global politics. Wallström, like Hague, is determined that the exclusion of the views and perspectives of women in foreign policy will gradually become more unacceptable in this century due to its morality and pragmatism.

With respect to the second implication for international relations, the unraveling of patriarchal relations in the West has increased the challenges to non-Western patriarchies, as well as prompting a backlash against the West and against norms of gender equality. Contemporary responses to this gender transformation are taking especially reactionary forms in some parts of the world, provoking conflict and threatening the values upon which international order rests. A visible contemporary illustration of this is the assault mounted by the so-called Islamic State, the armed nonstate group that is currently fighting for territory in Syria and Iraq, and for hearts and minds worldwide, to constitute itself as an alternative to the current state system (in so doing, though, replicating many aspects of historically gendered, sovereign states—as discussed in the chapter by Katherine Brown in this volume). ISIS addresses its message of "the caliphate" world society to men and women from Western and non-Western, Islamic majority and multicultural states. In particular, it provides a gender-specific, if not gender-inclusive, vision of a society where no one wants for anything. In the caliphate, women's roles in the family and home will be fully recognized and appreciated and no woman will have to work a double shift to provide for the needs of her children. Men can be warriors and heroes and are guaranteed a wife and sexual partner as well as privileged status as head of household. Moreover, both women and men have a moral purpose and a place in heaven according to ISIS (Quilliam 2015). International relations commentators have mostly missed the gender dimensions of ISIS, likely because the ISIS death cult trumps and obscures the ISIS rape cult in global media depictions, but importantly because they have failed to appreciate the historically gendered nature of state formations.

It is clear, however, that ISIS's recruitment strategy has deliberately targeted the weaknesses and contradictions of contemporary gendered states. The targeting of women and girls for sexual violence and slavery that has accompanied the transnational rise of extremism is not incidental, but premeditated, systematic, and strategic. Importantly, sexual and gender-based violence is both a *push* and *pull* factor for violent extremism. In the case of ISIS, it is being used to recruit men as (foreign) fighters with the promise of sex slaves and wives—and all their sexual needs being met. This political strategy is also being used to take over territory and resources by displacing populations who flee for fear of rape and the shame that accompanies it within traditional societies, and by expelling religious and sexual minorities and nonconformists. In this way, ISIS aims to recreate society as a caliphate, with parents from various nationalities and cultures, but all faithful to a global umma. ISIS is thus not merely an insurgency; it is a countercultural movement *for* patriarchy and *against* cosmopolitan society. It is also a countermaterial movement against neoliberal capitalism, which subordinates many women and men, especially in non-Western states. There are numerous other localized examples of such countercultural movements: Boko Haram in Nigeria, US alt-right, and European neo-Nazi movements among them.

To the extent that states have played a positive role in unraveling the gendered relations at their core, it is incumbent upon them to address the contradictory effects, such as violent extremist backlash, and the residue, such as ongoing discrimination in practice, of that unraveling. This will require much more concerted international cooperation to create the structural conditions of gender justice and equality that enable the exercise of freedoms, not merely access to them, for the groups of women and men most at risk of sexual and gender-based violence. Women's rights, including demands for the elimination of systemic discrimination and violence, may be marginalized in the interstate consensus and may even be traded off for seemingly more pressing priorities—as we have seen with the withdrawal of International Security Assistance Force troops and negotiations with the Taliban during the transition in Afghanistan in 2014–2015. However, if women's human rights are not addressed, this will be a lost opportunity for strengthening international cooperation and thus for the realization of the basic human goals of well-being and peace.

The third implication of changes in gender relations underpinning states is that immanent within this change (and the reactions to it) is the potential for the evolution of global politics in the present and future. The unraveling of Western forms of patriarchal relations and the potential to challenge non-Western forms of patriarchy through emerging transnational feminist networks could redefine the normative and cultural consensus required to sustain international cooperation.

The current international system does not reflect the diversity of political identities and as such lacks legitimacy among some groups. Achieving economic and social justice for marginalized groups would not only provide greater legitimacy for international order, it would generate the constituency to activate and reinforce shared international values and norms. In that respect, the realization of justice for half the world's population—as part of global movements for women's rights to bodily integrity, to equal participation in decision-making, to equal economic opportunity, and to recognition of domestic and care labor—is essential to the prospects for international peace and security. However, this would require a rethinking of the conception of justice within and by gendered states—as feminist scholars and women's rights activists have demonstrated in their efforts to address the intersections of gender and racial oppression (see Ackerly 2017). Gender justice, as Nancy Fraser (1997) has argued, involves not merely *redistribution* or redress for past wrongs but *recognition* of difference, and substantive political *representation* for diverse groups in situations where patriarchies are simultaneously becoming weaker and more resurgent (Fraser 2005).

CONCLUSION

At a time when international institutions like the United Nations are barely able to mitigate problems of war and conflict, let alone stem them, the idea that the state is the best means to secure the control of violence, economic and social justice, and protection of the environment is one that should be subjected to rigorous, critical scrutiny. I have argued in this chapter that gender hierarchy and patriarchal values privileging masculinity over femininity, reason over emotion, men over women are constitutive (albeit hidden) foundations of states and international relations. These relations are undergoing significant change, from social forces both within and without, which include capitalist institutions, social movements for the universalization of individual rights, and the agency and resistance of diverse groups of women to masculine institutions and norms, the reach of which extends across all boundaries of nation states, race, class, geography, caste, and culture. However, periods of change and transition are frequently also periods of violence and upheaval. Thus we can see connections between the breakdown of patriarchal social contracts and the heightening of gendered violence, which cut across various sites of conflict and change. Observing the resurgence of patriarchal, extremist movements and challenges to the current international system must lead us to rethink the gendered foundations of states rather than to incorporate the contested, patriarchal aspects of societies in efforts to accommodate broader interests and values in international relations. Today's gendered states have a responsibility in their domestic and foreign policies to counter the violent backlash against women's human rights by recognizing gender differences within a framework of equality that empowers women as well as men of different races, ethnicities, sexualities, nationalities, and so on to participate in decision-making, and to realize their full social and economic potential.

Toward this end, feminists in the academy, in social movements, and now in positions of state power argue, for both pragmatic and moral reasons, that foreign policy and international society should be more centrally guided by values of human rights and social justice. Indeed, globally connected women's movements seek to transform international values and to hold states accountable for institutionalizing and enforcing these new norms locally and globally (see Htun and Weldon 2012; Naples and Desai 2002; de Jong 2017). Women's movements from the global North and the global South are relatively united in this purpose. This is even more the case in the wake of economic globalization and of the rise of populist, nationalist revolts against it, which commonly seek to restore patriarchal relations and to relegate women to limited, feminine roles (see Tanyag 2017; Hozic and True eds. 2017). In this way, bringing women into the foreign and international policymaking does not just add new voices to existing, and historically gendered, states. Bringing diverse women *as women* engaged in struggles against local and global patriarchies into the debate about common values is crucial to averting the rise in global discord, violence, and conflict as well as to redressing globalized, gendered injustices.

NOTES

1. For an account of the militarized masculinity of the Turkish state and current leadership under President Erdogan, (see Bilgic 2016). The promotion of gender equality and women's participation in the labor market may be quite consistent with an overall authoritarian neoliberal approach to state governance (see Tansel 2017).

2. See http://daccess-dds ny.un.org/doc/UNDOC/GEN/G14/043/76/PDF/ G1404376.pdf?OpenElement (accessed on December 26, 2016).
3. According to UN Women (2011), there are 127 countries that do not explicitly criminalize rape within marriage.
4. The official Swedish government statement of feminist foreign policy considers "equality between women and men" to be "a fundamental aim of Swedish foreign policy" in itself, as well as a prerequisite for reaching Sweden's broader foreign policy goals on peace, , security, and sustainable development. It seeks to "strengthen women's rights, representation and access to resources" by implementing systematic gender mainstreaming, based on knowledge and analysis, throughout the foreign policy agenda. In 2016, the focus areas toward these long-term objectives are strengthening the human rights of women and girls in humanitarian settings, combating gender-based and sexual violence in conflict and postconflict situations, and highlighting the potential of women and girls as actors within the framework of peace processes, peace support operations, and sustainable development efforts (Wallström 2016).

PART II

The Making of the Gendered State

CHAPTER 4

Manly States and Feminist Foreign Policy

Revisiting the Liberal State as an Agent of Change

DAVID DURIESMITH

International feminist engagement with the liberal state has been fraught with contradiction.[1] Feminist activist groups and scholars have continued to demand that states take women's equality seriously by substantively addressing economic inequality, discriminatory laws, inequitable access to state services, and the prevalence of men's violence against women. At the same time, fundamental challenges to the state have been mounted by those who argue that it is a patriarchal institution forged through a gendered history of men's domination in the public sphere and the use of the public/private divide to subjugate the needs of women.[2] After more than one hundred years of activism from the women's movement, some states have begun to adopt aspects of feminist thought in their international policy and practice. By the late 2000s, key state leaders showed support for feminist campaigns against gender-based violence and the women-friendly United Nations conventions, such as the Convention on the Elimination of All Forms of Discrimination Against Women (CEDAW), and the Declaration on the Elimination of Violence against Women (DEVA), have motivated direct policy initiatives drawing on feminist ideas. Key state leaders' support for antiviolence campaigns represents a significant step forward in mobilizing the state in achieving feminist goals, while at the same time these actions uncover underlying tensions in drawing on institutions that are defined by masculine modes of action to challenge gender inequality.

The tension between desires to utilize the state to implement feminist changes and discomfort with the exercise of state power is not new, and the capacity for the liberal state to contribute to feminist international politics has been actively considered within the discipline since the 1980s. In *Gendered States*, when Mona Harrington (1992) asked, "What exactly is wrong with the liberal state as an agent of change?" she was connecting with this deeply divisive question of how feminists should engage states while remaining critical of their inequitable policy orientations and formal structures.

This chapter does not attempt to address all aspects of the complex intersection between state action and feminist politics, or to fully reconcile the tensions surrounding patriarchal states' contributions to feminist political goals. Instead it looks to respond to the account of liberal state action set out by Harrington through the examples of international profeminist activism from states.[3] It will focus directly on Harrington's defense of securely bounded, sovereign states within the liberal tradition's capacity to protect their populations from oppression. By introducing the lens of critical studies of men and masculinities, I will argue that even when liberal state actors attempt to adopt the mantle of a feminist actor, they risk reifying the role of the masculine protector. The chapter will make the case that this approach is inescapably masculine, and therefore ask, can the *manly* state become feminist?

Most existing scholarship on states as feminist actors in the international sphere has focused either on the cynical use of feminist language to justify states adopting the role of masculine protector without any real commitment to feminist goals, or on the provision of a social safety net as a justification not to address basic gender inequality (Young 2003; Pateman 1988; Basham 2013; Kronsell and Svedberg 2001). I look to extend the work on the liberal state as a masculine protector by focusing specifically on attempts by masculine actors to become feminist agents of change, rather than broader attempts to protect "women and children." I do not argue that states are incapable of contributing to contained feminist goals. Rather, by exploring the example of the HeForShe campaign, I suggest that for state institutions to aid feminist politics, they need to adopt the position of reflective allies to feminist causes, rather than independent agents of change.

LIBERAL STATES AND MANLY PROTECTORS

The defense of the liberal state as an agent of change that Harrington sets out in her 1992 chapter directly responds to what she sees as the Marxist-inspired antistate tendencies of feminist theory at the time, which identifies the liberal state as a manifestation of patriarchal and class oppression. In contrast to her peers, who viewed the liberal state with mistrust, Harrington (1992, 78) argues that the sovereign state can serve the vulnerable, acting as the most promising agent of feminist change. The "antistate" approach identified by Harrington can be charted directly back to the work of global North feminists within radical, socialist, and ecofeminist traditions who connected the state with broader structures of oppression. A rich body of critical scholarship engaging the state has also originated from the global South, drawing on postcolonial experiences of the liberal state as a "civilizing" imposition on racialized peoples (Oyěwùmí 2003; Parpart and Staudt 1988; Lovett 1988). Although Harrington does mention the idea of some global South women opting out of the state, her attention is solidly on challenges to the state from the global North.

The germinal critique of the liberal state as a patriarchal institution within the Western tradition comes from radical feminist Kate Millett (1969, 25) who characterized state patriarchy as "the institution whereby that half of the populace which is female is controlled by that half which is male." This approach has understood the state as a direct extension of the oppressive practices of men into a formalized structure, leading eco-feminist Maria Mies (1986, 26) to characterize the state as the "general patriarch." Mies's approach adopted Millett's treatment of the state as an embodiment of men's domination, but aimed to interject a more nuanced view that accounted more directly for questions of capitalism and the environment. This framework mirrored the distrust of the state present in earlier radical feminist work but sought to provide a model of historical development and specificity, particularly with regard to the development of capitalism and its imposition on the global South. These scholars, and many others like them who have challenged the state, are unified by a suspicion of the state's foundations and actions as potentially complicit, or culpable, in the oppression of women by men.[4]

Harrington rejects these lines of theorization (with particular reference to Spike Peterson and Carole Pateman) on the basis that they fail to recognize the utility of the state as a powerful protective actor. If states remain sovereign, Harrington (1992, 78) suggests, it is possible for them to become "protectors of subordinated groups." Although Harrington (1992, 80) does not deny that states remain male-dominated institutions, she argues that by rejecting overly militant or economically predatory modes of state behavior and by placing liberal values at the heart of liberal institutions they may be reformed. Domestically, Harrington (1992, 76) argues that the nation state can give voice to subordinate groups, by protecting them from the predations of would-be oppressors. Internationally, for this to be achieved, she suggests that states join together to protect their national borders, allowing them to defend their own population without worrying about potential encroachments.

Where liberal states have sought to adopt the role of protector, this has not necessarily resulted in the emancipatory outcomes that Harrington envisioned. Young's analysis of the United States' appeal to protecting vulnerable women as a justification for the invasion of Afghanistan has shown a pattern of protection that follows a masculine logic (Young 2003, 4–5). In justifying the war in Afghanistan, Young suggests, US politicians callously employed the justification of protecting women as a way to pursue militarist national interests. Young argues that states' attempts to adopt the role of a protector mirror the existing trope of the man as a head of the household and defender of his family (Young 2003, 4–5).

In this mode, the role of the protector is not just about the security of those who are vulnerable from attack, but also about stratifying the rightful authority of the male figurehead, whose dominance is protected by his capacity to protect those under him from the attentions of other men (Young 2003, 6). With this understanding, the positioning of the state as a protector of its citizens reproduces the dichotomies between male protector and female subordinate, as well as creating hierarchies between good men and bad on the basis of who protects and who needs to be protected against (Young 2003, 14). By mirroring and reproducing masculine modes of action, the state's capacity to act comes from that broader, gendered mode of action. While Harrington's focus is on defending the state's capacity to defend people *within* its border, this distinction does not escape the problem of the masculine protector that Young identifies in the US invasion of Afghanistan.

Despite a focus different from Harrington's, Young's analysis of the protective liberal security state shows the potential dangers of a state's adoption of states' self-identification as a protector of the weak to valorize their authority (Young 2003, 16). As Raewyn Connell has warned, the gendered composition of the state means that attempts to transform it into a feminist agent (even internally) risk asking the institutionalization of dominant masculinity to redress the excess of masculinity, or, as framed by Connell (1990, 508), "appealing from Caesar unto Caesar." The difficulty of having the state escape masculine modes of engagement is "substantively, not just metaphorically, gendered" (Connell 1987, 73). This means that the state is a collection of formally structured practices and social relations that are ordered by "a gender configuration of recruitment and promotion . . . of the internal division of labour and systems of control . . . of policymaking, practical routines, and ways of mobilising pleasure and consent" (Connell 1987, 73). The state in this understanding is the institutionalization of gender by formalizing the legal system through the public/private divide, delineating the sexual division of labor, and structuring state violence along gender lines (Connell 1987, 125–134). The state is historically constructed as the bearer of gender, organizing labor, structures of formal power, and structures of attachment (cathexis) along gendered lines (Connell 1990, 523–526). The institutionalization of gender can be seen in those Western democracies that give special status to formal, monogamous couplings in taxation, family benefits, legislative protections, and other formal legal apparatuses (Connell 1987, 105). In this instance the state represents the formalization of gender configurations both in the formal structures it enacts and in the informal practices it encourages.

States do not entail a single gender construct (such as a dominant masculinity), but represent the formalization of relationships between differing gendered configurations and the practices that these configurations produce (Connell 1990, 527–529). For example, the state's ordering of gender may simultaneously draw on the academic masculinity of the expert, the perfunctory rationalism of bureaucratic masculinities, and the heroics of soldiering masculinities.[5] Each sanctioned configuration of gender is defined in relationship to another (among many others) against delegitimized gender configurations outside the state. Because of the state's reliance on these gender categories as the basis of its action, it has a major stake in their maintenance (Connell 1990, 530–532).

The configurations of gender that constitute the state are also organized hierarchically to reflect the prevailing "gender order," a term used by Connell (1987, 125) to describe these sedimented and hierarchical arrangement of gender in society. Within a given society there will be multiple configurations of what it means to be a man or a woman (not to mention other gender positions that are not constrained by this dichotomy). Some configurations of gender will be materially privileged, such as corporate masculinities in Australia; others are complicit without being most privileged, such as policing masculinities; and others still are structurally oppressed, such as indigenous femininities in Australia (Connell 2005a, 71–76; Doucet 2004).

These hierarchical arrangements are also situated internationally, as the gender configurations that the state privileges are situated within global hierarchies of power. Hooper (2001, 55) has extended Connell's work on masculinities by further situating the internal struggles over masculine dominance within the international and exploring the international as an important site where masculinities are forged.[6] For one gendered mode of engagement to exist, it needs to be defined against others; in the case of states, the relationship between hegemonic and subordinate masculinities is essential to the construction of the international gender order (Hooper 2001, 69, 219–220). As Hooper stresses, the configurations of meaning that construct particular masculinities (heterosexual, white, rational, militarist, etc.) are necessarily defined against stigmatized others (real or imagined) that fail to satisfy this criterion. These oppositional relations are not contained within states; the histories of broad tropes that are employed to produce masculinities (heterosexuality, rationalism, etc.) have international as well as local histories that need to be understood in a global context (Hooper 2001, 55).

Within the international sphere this means that state behavior is built on gendered histories of the subordination of racialized groups, religious minorities, economically marginalized peoples, sexual minorities, indigenous peoples, and others. These histories affect the way in which the performance of state power may be utilized to engage in profeminist politics. For the state to exercise power, it is necessary for certain groups to be legitimized as powerholders, in the role of protector, of administrator, lawgiver, or other formalized position of gender power. Hooper reminds us that the particular configurations of masculinity that exist are utilized in international politics build on well-established genealogies that inform their meaning. When state leaders draw on their position of authority to produce change on an issue that is important to them, they do so in relation to a "complex, global set of racialized gender identities" (Hooper 2001, 80). This means that the impact, significance, or substance of these gendered actions is defined both by masculine configurations of those that act, and by their relation to other configurations through which they are given meaning.

Demands for the state to mobilize on behalf of women's rights in the international arena are fraught not only because they draw on problematic gender hierarchies, but because they risk highlighting some forms of masculinity as "good" or valorous examples of masculine action. Demands for the state to mobilize on behalf of women's rights looks to reformulate the hierarchy with a more tolerable, less violent patriarch at its helm. If "good" masculinities (and "good" men) in the international sphere are promoted, subordinate gender positions among states may disappear from analysis, rendering the hierarchical nature of gender invisible. This multiplicity of gender positions is absent in Harrington's (1992) defense of the liberal state as an agent of change, as is a recognition of the gendered quality of liberal state action, because her chapter explores gender as an individual social relation, rather than a structure present in institutions. By focusing on the liberal state as the best possible agent of change, Harrington's defense did not address the role of liberal rationalist masculinity in supporting the state, and the role of the state in supporting liberal rationalist masculinity.

Defenders of liberal rationalist masculinity have tended to choose favorable ground, contrasting the liberal "good" men with more bellicose articulations of manhood. While liberal rationalist masculinities are defined against more militant nationalist forms, they are also positioned against a range of subaltern gender positions. Liberal/rationalist masculinity within the global North has historically been defined against masculinities from the global South, queer articulations of gender, and a range of femininities. The positive qualities attached to liberal/rationalist masculinities are informed by a colonial legacy that placed wealthy European men as rightful rulers over men of color, who were seen as brutish or effeminate (Hooper 2001, 72–73). This understanding is explicit within the writing of early liberals, such as J. S. Mill (1971, 73), whose arguments for liberty and freedom did not apply to "those who are still in a . . . backward state of society in which the race itself may be considered as in its nonage."

The colonial quality of liberal rationalist masculinity has historically developed through the experience of empire (Uchendu 2008). Both in the British public school system and in colonial dominions, the rightful rule of liberal/rationalist masculinity was defined against colonial others who were either defined as dangerously hypermasculine brutes or effeminate and morally corrupt savages (Sinha 1995). Historically, liberal/rationalist masculinities justified their authority on the basis that subordinate groups needed their guidance and protection from savage "others." The strength of liberal/rationalist masculinity was framed against feminine/effeminate groups who needed their protection and dangerous savages who needed to have their violent urges controlled by "good" men.

While the most overt aspects of colonialism within liberal/rationalist masculinity have retreated to the background, reliance on a savage "other" to define its position of dominance remains in place. Julia Welland's (2015) exploration of contemporary British soldiering through memoirs of the Afghan war exemplifies the continuing importance of colonial logics within liberal/rationalist masculinity. The soldiers Welland studied identified with key aspects of a benevolent liberal/rationalist archetype, attempting to embody the role of peacekeeper and emphasizing their role as enlightened protector. These soldiers often employed discourses of liberation and anti-conquest, framing themselves as valorous protectors (Welland 2015, 294). Despite this rhetoric of liberal/rationalist warriors, Welland's work suggests that the men of the British armed forces defined their identity through the neocolonial encounter with the Afghan National Army. She suggests (Welland 2015, 295, 299) that the Afghan soldiers were constructed both as effeminate (cowardly, flower adorned, with kohl-rimmed eyes) and as hypermasculine (excessively violent, brutal, and chaotic). For the British soldiers, their masculine position was defined against the Afghan soldiers' masculinity, and their authority was justified by the presence of a dangerous subaltern "other."

This example is instructive because it demonstrates the relational nature of liberal masculinity. The soldiers' masculinity was given form through reference to those who had failed, the effeminate or hypermasculine man; the scholar-gentlemen needs a savage brute to be defined against. The articulation of this "softer" form of liberal warrior masculinity is still defined relationally in opposition with the colonized other. While Harrington (1992) defended the neutrality of the potential liberal state, this position relies on asking subordinate groups to be protected by the liberal state, rather than achieving liberation on their own terms. However, it is worth remaining skeptical of this move, whose universality follows the colonial mode of managing "to appear logical in its own eyes by inviting the sub-men to become human" (Fanon 1967b, 131). Internationally the manly liberal state cannot easily escape its position within the international gender order without deconstructing it. By valorizing masculine liberal state leaders as valuable agents of change, this risks in turn valorizing white rationalist liberal masculinity more broadly, while retrenching the subornation of other gender configurations.

The relationship between masculinities and international relations here is also two-way; the history of these masculinities has produced the practice of international politics (through the promotion of white rationalism, militarism, etc.), and at the same time the configuration of international relations produces certain kinds of masculinities as individuals look to conform to the configurations that are sanctioned within the world of "high" politics (Hooper 2001, 80–89). This means that attempts to utilize the state must tread carefully, precisely because they do not look to utilize a neutral unitary actor, but are instead drawing on a hierarchical arrangement of gender that privileges certain gender configurations (Hooper 2001, 229).

MASCULINE ALLIES AND FEMINIST CHANGE

Although states are not able to escape the gendered qualities of their actions, this does not mean that they can play no role in producing change. Although state institutions have a unique capacity to enact change, the problems surrounding the use of masculine actors as feminist agents of change is not unique to the state. The role of men in the feminist movement has garnered considerable debate and disagreement, with some arguing that an inclusive approach, which invites men to become feminists, will create the most significant changes in their attitudes, while others have argued that their role should be as profeminist allies due to the continued privileges they receive as masculine actors (Casey and Smith 2010). As privileged actors who continue to benefit from oppressive gender hierarchies, men are involved with feminist politics both as agents and as subjects of change. States are similar to men, in that they are direct beneficiaries of patriarchal gender orders that grants them material advantages, gendered social status, and legitimacy (Jabri 2004). Adopting this position of ally to the feminist cause, rather than independent agent of change, would assuage the potential risks of states reinforcing their hegemonic position, while maintaining the centrality of women's autonomous organization in implementing feminist politics.

Men's involvement in feminist politics has become more visible over the past two decades as domestic violence-prevention efforts, such as the White Ribbon Campaign, have invited men to take up a model of "chivalrous masculinity," rejecting violence against women and fighting against predatory men (Seymour 2012). In Australia men have been encouraged to take the White Ribbon Oath, publicly committing to supporting women's equality and opposing their peers' use of violence. Within this context men often do not take proactive steps to abandon the patriarchal privileges they receive; instead, through their participation in violence prevention programs they are promoted as "real men" who are capable of treating women respectfully (Pease 2015, 59). Unfortunately, these programs often construct a harmful false dichotomy, with violent, patriarchal men on one hand and chivalrous, "good" men on the other.

As men have become more involved in domestic violence-prevention campaigns over the past twenty years, discourse on the causes of gender-based violence has subtly shifted. Originally feminist discourse within violence-prevention programs focused on changing the behavior of men collectively' this has changed as more men have become involved to focus on challenging traditional/toxic masculinity and the "bad" men who perpetrate it (Flood 2015; Baker 2013). There has been a concerted effort to avoid accusatory language within programs looking to engage men, out of a fear that accusations may alienate potential allies by implicating them in patriarchal violence (Katz 2006). Where possible these campaigns have attempted to temper radical language by "reassuring non-violent men that they are not part of the problem" (Pease 2015, 63).

Domestic male violence-prevention efforts, such as the 2001–2011 American campaign My Strength Is Not for Hurting, the 2013 Australian campaign reminding us that "Real Men Don't Abuse Women," and the international "Man Up" campaign have all used the social status and authority of men to shame others into ceasing violent practices by threatening them with failed masculinity (Flood 2014; Salter 2015, 11). These domestic campaigns have also drawn on male ambassadors for nonviolence, hoping that their social cachet will make them effective agents of profeminist change (Murphy 2010). Male-led campaigns such as White Ribbon have been able to effectively utilize sporting figures as ambassadors to gain media attention (Caneva 2015). However, this tactic has also caused considerable disquiet over the ways in which masculine actors engage with feminist politics, as sporting men are exhibited as exemplars of hegemonic masculinity, or held up as "'bell cows,' able to lead other men into this work because of their conformity to gender norms" (Flood 2015, 11). This approach does not leave space to substantially question masculinity itself; instead it remains focused on "deviant" men, at whose feet blame for violence is placed.

These campaigns frame violence as aberrant behavior, emphasizing that not all men are violent. Men often respond with hostility to feminist activism that recognizes collective culpability in the performance of violence. In 2014, after Elliot Rodgers brutally attacked women in Isla Vista, California, on the basis that they (as a group) had rebuffed him, undermining his masculinity, feminist commentators were quick to point out the role of misogyny in his attack. After much of this commentary emphasized Rodgers's relationship with men's rights activist websites, the Twitter hashtag #notallmen exploded, arguing that feminists were unfairly tarring all men with the patriarchal brush without recognizing that *not all men* are violent (Plait 2014). While it is true that not all men engage in aggressive sexual violence or gender-based brutality, it does not follow that violence is inconsistent with masculinity, or that most men are not culpable for violence (Pease 2015, 64). Despite the differences how men relate to violence, it is unhelpful to try to identify particular deviant men as the cause of this violence (Hearn 1998). Men who themselves do not participate in the most visible excesses of patriarchy often remain complicit in it by minimizing its significance, accepting the benefits they receive from male dominance and individualizing its causes (DeKeseredy and Schwartz 2005).

Both men and the state benefit immensely from the gender hierarchies that underpin patriarchal violence, as these hierarchies affirm their positions of authority while reinforcing the subordinate status of those oppressed along gender lines. When framing change around particular issues (such as ameliorating domestic violence in the case of the White

Ribbon Campaign), it is easy to valorize powerful actors as feminist agents due to the potent contributions they can make in achieving these specific goals (Robinson 2003). Masculine actors are framed as valorous precisely because their position of dominance provides them with a privileged ability to act. Michael Flood's (2014) research on domestic antiviolence campaigns has suggested that men often frame their involvement in ways that reinforce male supremacy. While opposing violence against women, Flood found (2015, 4), these men often held stereotypical views of masculinity that maintained the position of protector, devalued women's contributions, and responded in homophobic ways when others questioned their masculinity. Although some of these men succeeded in advancing the specific causes they worked on, in doing so they often sought to reinforce their own hegemony as enlightened protectors. While states are not directly analogous to individual men, states' pattern of engagement with gender politics is not dissimilar to that of men.

International state action on gender-based violence has overwhelmingly taken the form of the signing of UN resolutions or treaties and expressions of support for international campaigns that focus on violence against women. When state leaders from the global North express support for antiviolence resolutions, such as CEDAW, the response to these is almost exclusively focused on other states from the global South, which are singled out as particularly problematic (Jeffreys 2005). Although states that are commonly highlighted as having problematic records, such as Sudan, are singled out on the basis of their profoundly problematic records, these states are far from alone in their imperfect practices. Despite this, little attention is paid to harmful cultural practices from the global North, and those states that advocate for change in the practices of states in the global South rarely demonstrate reflectivity in their involvement (Jeffreys 2005). Instead, the problem of harmful practices is always some *other* state's problem.

By framing international gender action as striving for a change in the behavior of *other* states, international state leaders have failed to adequately recognize the benefits they receive from the patriarchal international system. Similarly, when states adopt conventions that demand internal action, the response commonly entails substantially more rhetoric than meaningful action (Shepherd and True 2014). This mode of action appears to mirror that of individual masculine actors, both in failing to recognize states' complicity in systems that create violence, and in the targeting of "deviant" states. Considering the state as the formalization of the dominant gender configurations, it is unsurprising, then, that when its representatives engage in gender politics, they mirror the patterns of adherence to the dominant scripts of masculinity. Because the actions of the state are produced through these gender arrangements, it is fruitful to look at the idea of reflective male allies as a model through which states might pursue feminist political objectives.

The position of ally does not entail full adoption of the identity of feminist or command leadership in the fight against oppression (Atherton-Zeman 2009). For supporters of movements against oppression who are part of the dominant group, the status of ally provides a space for them to contribute to change, without trying to escape their culpability for structures of oppression or co-opting emancipator movements (Goldstein and Davis 2010). Within other emancipatory movements, such as black liberation or LGBT rights groups, the idea of admission to implication has been central to becoming a good ally (Pease 2015, 61). Rather than trying to put themselves forward as exemplars of "good" whiteness or heterosexuality, allies have been encouraged to be forthright about their own implication in these systems and the benefits that they receive on this basis (Kutz 2000, 122).

For this reason I propose thinking of states as potential allies for feminist action, because although they can contribute to feminist goals, their contributions are fundamentally limited by their own positioning within hierarchies of oppression. By repositioning men from being feminist agents of change to profeminist allies, their capacity for dismantling, and culpability in, oppressive gender hierarchies can be recognized. Within the LGBT communities the model of "straight allies" has been particularly powerful in providing a space for supporters to contribute to queer politics, while emphasizing the need for allies to become more conscious of oppression, to reflect on how their own behavior contributes to heteronormative social structures, to support queer efforts without monopolizing them, and to disrupt hostile spaces that are inaccessible to queer communities.[7] For men who wish to be good allies of the feminist movement, this means that critical reflection needs to be directed inward, as well as to their peers (Hearn and Morgan 1990, 204).

If activism focuses only on opposing bad men or bad states, there is a risk of "phallocentrism" (Macleod 2007), where the common benefits that men receive on the basis of their male status are hidden by those focusing on the contributions of "new men" to feminist politics. This has meant that, within masculinities activism, "masculinities are pitched against each other. Resistance to 'hegemonic' masculinity is cast within the same signifying boundaries—masculinity. There is no escape . . . masculinity is never undone, but rather mutates into new kinds of masculinities" (Robinson 2003, 10). For allies of the feminist movement, this requires that they remain open to critique, not only on limited single-issue terms, but also regarding the fundamental structures that underpin their capacity to act.

"GOOD" MEN AND "GOOD" STATES

The difficulties of enlisting state action on behalf of feminist goals can be seen in the example of the HeForShe campaign. When HeForShe was launched in 2014, one of its strategies was to "create a platform to highlight as role models, men and boys who are taking a stand against gender-based discrimination and violence against women and girls globally" (UN Women 2014). The main focus of the campaign was encouraging state leaders (along with business figures and other men in positions of power) to publicly express their support for women's rights. This central strategy looked to transform state leaders into meaningful agents of change by spotlighting them as role models who could be emulated. This effort has succeeded in mobilizing international political leaders such as president of Indonesia Joko Widodo, US president Barak Obama, Canadian prime minister Justin Trudeau, President Ernest Bai Koroma of Sierra Leone, UN secretary-general Ban Ki-moon, and Prime Minister Stefan Löfvén of Sweden to become advocates for women's equality. These ambassadors were encouraged to make statements in favor of gender equality and against violence, which were then used in ad campaigns that aimed to recruit men into committing to oppose gender-based discrimination or violence.

In making commitments to gender equality both states, through their representatives, and individual men were encouraged to participate in the campaign. The HeForShe campaign represents an interesting interface between international state action, such as signing or supporting international conventions against gender-based violence, and individual men's actions in support of women's equality. Not only are state leaders held up as exemplary individuals, but states are encouraged through HeForShe to develop policies for recruiting as many of their men to the campaign as possible, including holding public events and developing programs that can encourage men to "become HeForShe."

Similar to domestic campaigns, international efforts such as HeForShe are careful not to implicate all states in gender inequality, targeting instead the problematic behavior of "deviant" states and men. The campaign has been successful in encouraging state figures such as US ambassador to Georgia Richard Norland to come out against gender-based violence under the slogan "Real men don't hit women," which was previously employed by actor Antonio Banderas in supporting the campaign (Salter 2015; Agenda

2014). Unfortunately, this framing has been common in state-oriented responses to HeForShe. While some aspects of the campaign have emphasized men's personal role, such as the antiviolence campaign that encourages men to become active bystanders when they see men victimizing women, even these efforts frame the problem of gender violence externally, asking men to stop other men rather than reforming themselves (HeForShe 2016).

This individualises and depoliticizes the problem, focusing on "failed" masculine behavior rather than highlighting the need to deconstruct patriarchal gender orders. Representatives of liberal states are asked to change a small aspect of their gendered performance by positioning themselves against the "bad" men and "bad" states that are painted as responsible for women's oppression. In exchange they are held up as ambassadors for change, exemplars of valorous manhood, or good international citizens. One of the key moves HeForShe took to target state behavior has been the IMPACT 10x10x10 Initiative, which brought together the leaders of ten states to become "champions" who could "pave the way for others to join in" (UN Women 2015).[8] This effort, like others in HeForShe, emphasized the importance of women's empowerment in society (framed in terms of access to education, health, work, politics, expression of identity, and freedom from violence), and the need for powerful state leaders to become examples of ideal behavior. However, in constructing the narrative of men and boys as "agents of change," the framing of the IMPACT 10x10x10 stays safely clear of indicating that the men who become "champions," or the states they represent, need to meaningfully change their own behavior or the structure of the institutions through which they are privileged. Instead, they are put forward as already formed feminist agents by supporting women's rights.

IMPACT 10x10x10 avoids mentioning that the leaders themselves need to change their own behavior. Similarly there is no mention of the structural factors that prohibit women from gaining full access to the positions of power and authority on which the campaign is focused. Masculine actors who adopt the mantle of feminist agents also risk dominating existing movements that look to fight the oppression, further marginalizing subordinate groups. The IMPACT 10x10x10 campaign recruitment emphasizes men's commitment to the politics of women's equality but does not address the relationship of such an effort to the existing feminist attempts to achieve women's equality in dominant institutions, which have been continuing for more than a century.

So far it has been argued that most attempts to transform manly states into agents of change do not also look to dismantle the gender hierarchies that privilege the bearers of hegemonic masculinity in the state. Considering the difficulty of utilizing masculine actors as agents of feminist change, it is worth investigating what role the liberal state might play in forging feminist change. It may be unhelpful and unrealistic to eschew the state completely in trying to achieve international change. Not only do states have the greatest capacity to enact international change, but much of the change required for feminist objectives to be achieved needs to come from states as the current bearers of power. This means that although it is problematic to think of liberal states as feminist agents of change, manly states can still be conceptualised as feminist allies rather than actors. The position of ally (rather than actor) refers to those who support feminist objectives while recognizing the ways in which they continue to be privileged as part of a dominant group. This reframing also provides space for actors to contribute to incremental change without claiming to be the core subject of the feminist movement or to have a place at its table.

For states to become meaningful feminist allies, it is necessary that those who benefit from states' enshrinement of oppressive gender configurations recognize their complicity in supporting the masculinist state system that marginalizes other actors. States, even liberal states such as Iceland, are constituted by the gender orders that underpin them and define their capacity to act; this places them in a similar position to men who look to support feminist politics. What is needed for liberal states to fully support feminist politics is not a process of reformation into "good" manly states, but a process of dismantling and unmaking of the structures that privilege masculine actors to act on behalf of states. By recognizing that masculinities and gender structures are relational and hierarchical, it is necessary for manly states to be fundamentally changed so as to no longer rely on patriarchal configurations of gender in the performance of their actions. This would involve contesting the hegemony of men within liberal institutions and unmanning state structures, by challenging masculine modes of engaging in politics so as to no longer draw on male privilege to enact change, and by refusing to valorize political institutions simply for not supporting gender-based violence or oppression. This process requires that when state representatives express support for feminist goals as part of their commitment to liberal values, they do so in a way that mirrors feminist goals. This would mean maintaining an active role for women's autonomous organization, refusing to draw on patriarchal patterns of behavior, and maintaining accountability to those whom feminist politics looks to empower. Although this is by no means an easy or straightforward project, it is a necessary one if feminist activism is to account for the relationship between the state and the perpetration of gender oppression.

In the effort to mobilize liberal states on behalf of the most marginalized, there is a risk that the approach taken will reinforce the existing hierarchies of legitimacy, and further marginalize those groups who have limited access to state authority. To move beyond such limited discourse, it is necessary for international actors to adopt a position of reflective allies, rather than valorous protectors of the weak. This requires the development of a set of strategies that can keep liberal states and their elected representatives accountable to oppressed groups, and to remain actively aware of the ways in which the privileges they receive exist in relation to the subornation of other groups and modes of doing politics. In doing this, liberal states would need to begin by recognizing the culpability of formal liberal modes of politics in the perpetration of gender oppression and to begin the process of rejecting the privileges that come with a position of dominance. Adoption of the position of reflective allies would also avoid some of the risks around liberal states being positioned as the "good" saviors of women in the global South, and the patriarchal gender logics that such a protective framing entails. As with men who have been involved in gender politics, this cannot take the form of demanding a seat at the feminist table. Instead liberal states need to first make space in the halls of power by relinquishing some of their institutional authority, so oppressed groups can become agents of change on their own accord.

CONCLUSION

Although liberal states remain shackled to the masculinist structures, norms, and identities that define them, they retain the unique capacity to act. Although Harrington argued for the value in the liberal state of an agent of change, recent examples suggest that when state representatives do this without first reflecting seriously on their positions as dominant actors within a male-dominated space, they do so in ways that reinforce the authority of white, liberal, rationalist men and the masculine modes of authority that this entails. Particularly in the case of HeForShe, it has been argued that international attempts to draw on the liberal state as an agent of feminist change risk reproducing hegemonic scripts of the state as a liberal, rationalist protector, and that this in turn relegitimizes dominant masculinities internationally. Instead of adopting the mode of exemplified masculine actors, the model of reflective allies has been suggested as a way for those who occupy positions of masculine power to meaningfully contribute to feminist goals without dominating women's efforts, or reinforcing the authority of manly states as the only legitimate agents of change.

By accepting liberal states' culpability for perpetuating structures of oppression, by actively disengaging from patriarchy, and by working to dismantle the hierarchies of male supremacy, powerful masculine actors can become meaningful allies of feminist politics without demanding further privileges for their participation or losing sight of their privileged capacity to act. If arms of liberal states choose instead to continue to adopt the trappings of feminist politics when responding to particular "gendered" issues without undergoing more foundational change, their contributions will reinforce the dominance of masculine institutions, thereby hiding their pervasive impact.

NOTES

1. This chapter employs the concept of the "liberal state" in response to Harrington's defense of state sovereignty as the best agent for creating social change. The use of the term "liberal state" follows from Harrington's account of Western-style states defined by robust external state sovereignty, provision of internal welfare, and support for the protective tradition of social liberalism. As the core focus here is on the potential of the state to become an agent of change, it doesn't explore the more expansive understandings of the "liberal" state, which could encompass "low-intensity democracies" such as Singapore or Russia. The focus here is on the most straightforward examples of liberal states' attempts to become international agents of feminist change, rather than looking at the many instances where they clearly do not fulfill these criteria. Instead, examples where state attempts to enact feminist change have consciously been chosen as the basis for revisiting the state as an agent of feminist change.

2. Note that in this chapter I use the concept of patriarchy to refer to the multiplicity of forms of male domination that exist internationally. See Bryson (1999) and Macleod (2007) for a fuller account of the concept as it is used here and Hooper (2001) for a critique of this framework.

3. "Profeminist" is used to refer to actors and enterprises that look to contribute to feminist goals without necessarily adopting the mantle of feminism in full.

4. The three authors identified here exemplify Western feminist scholarship that is antistate. There are many other contributions, including those by Catherine MacKinnon (1989), Carole Pateman (1988), Sylvia Walby (1990), and Zillah Eisenstein (1979), that could also be named.

5. The mobilization of different forms of masculinity can be seen in the marketing of military masculinities to economically vulnerable young men of color in the United States in the early 2000s. Although the politicians who promoted this recruitment policy were not men who embodied military masculinity, the promotion of this model of manhood made war-making possible. For more detail on this process see Barry 2010).

6. Connell's account of gender orders and the state is also critiqued by Hooper (2001, 56–57), who argues that it suffers from "residual structuralism." Hooper suggests that Connell's account of hegemony is not clear enough about whether it is consciously produced by ruling elites, is the unconscious practices of a ruling

majority, or is somewhere between these accounts (Hooper, 2001, 57). To skirt around the "residual structuralism" and lack of clarity around hegemony, Hooper (2001, 57–58) encourages authors to focus on a Foucauldian interpretation of hegemony, as the combination of micro-level power acts that produce hegemonic effects. This critique, which has been leveled by feminists elsewhere (Beasley, 2015), is not one I have adopted in this chapter on the grounds that materialist masculinities scholarship has the capacity to overcome the question of discourse without rejecting its structural underpinnings. For defenses of the approach taken toward gender in this see Connell (2004) and Hearn (2014).

7. There is an expansive body of literature on allyship within queer communities, particularly within education literature. For examples of this work see Evans and Jamie (1991); Wells (2006); Lapointe (2015); Herek and Capitanio (1996).

8. Leaders of Malawi, Indonesia, Romania, Rwanda, Finland, Japan, Iceland, Sweden, the Philippines, and Uruguay signed up to be "Impact Champions" alongside leaders from business and higher education. Impact champions agreed to publicly report on their institutions progress on gender equality as well as to advocate for gender equality (HeForShe 2014). The activities prescribed for state leaders included running public events to raise awareness, recruiting a certain number of men within their state to take the HeForShe commitment online, including gender-sensitivity training, and promoting the campaign through state media channels. Although they were asked to commit to "explore obstacles to gender equality at the country level and encourage men to find innovative solutions," becoming an 10x10x10 Impact Champion did not include hard substantive commitments to change behavior or fundamentally restructure problematic institutional arrangements.

CHAPTER 5

Rescuing the State?

Sovereignty, Identity, and the Gendered Re-articulation of the State

CHRISTINE AGIUS

The state has occupied a complex and troubled position within feminist international relations and security studies scholarship. Feminists have long critiqued the role of the state as a provider of security, facilitator of equality, and protector (Brown 1992; Peterson 1992c; see also Duriesmith in this volume). Likewise, in an era of globalization, transnational forces, and the perceived decline of the state and sovereignty, feminists have questioned whether the state can be "explicitly protectionist" (Harrington 1992, 66–68). For some, the loosening of sovereignty, the diffusion of power, and the range of nonstate actors offer possibilities for advancing feminist concerns, such as the lack of representation of women in politics and positions of power, unequal distribution of resources, labor inequalities, health and reproductive rights, and the role of women in conflict resolution. Internationalizing gender equality and promoting global norms in this regard are widely hailed by feminists as positive developments, notably in efforts by international organizations such as the United Nations to take seriously the impact of conflict and war on women through Security Council Resolution 1325. Conversely, globalization can increase inequality and undermine the achievements feminists seek; thus Harrington's suggestion of reforming the liberal state in order to make it more attentive to the most vulnerable in society is to be taken seriously (1992). Peterson's efforts to think through gendered states and decenter IR theorizing is instructive here: asking the question "What difference does gender make?" prompts consideration of how the state and theories about it have been constituted in gendered terms. This reproduction also highlights the fact that the state is not a completed "thing" but rather an ongoing process—one that is marked and embodied by gender (Peterson 1992c, 4). For Peterson, gender thus remains a structural feature of world politics.

This chapter explores efforts to reimagine the state in the case of Sweden and Australia. As middle powers, both offer a novel lens through which to illustrate the contrasting intricacies of gendered states. Middle powers are those that possess limitations in their material capabilities yet can "negotiate and defend their interests and not just follow great powers" (Beeson 2011, 564). Categories of middle power behavior range from rationalist to internationalist and normative. Gareth Evans, Australian Labor minister for foreign affairs (1988–1996), defined it as "the pursuit of enlightened self interest" (1990). Associated self-conceptions, such as the promotion of "good international citizenship," often accompany the profile of middle powers, such as Sweden's postwar active internationalism. Falling outside the binary of great powers / weak states, middle powers offer an additional way to theorize gendered binaries in the international system. But the concept nonetheless relies on a mainstream discourse of what power means and how to exact it to "be" a state.[1] Middle powers still engage in masculinist forms of protection, to differing degrees.

In the case of Sweden, efforts to disengage from the legacy of neutrality through more robust military engagements entails a (re)*making* of the state. Sweden's postneutral status conditions debates about national identity that have been structured along gendered lines in response to external threats, its role as a "humanitarian superpower," and now its stated "feminist foreign policy." Australia's efforts to secure its border against asylum seekers and boat arrivals under Operation Sovereign Borders (OSB) entails a masculinist discourse and practice that seeks to reclaim a traditional bounded concept of the state. Militarized border security ostensibly claims to "protect" vulnerable others but is geared toward protecting the territorial state. Both case studies explore the inherently gendered and securitized revisioning of the state through the politics of masculinist protection (Young 2003) and gendered concepts of security that propose in one case (Sweden) to protect external others and in the other (Australia) to protect the state itself from external threats. In the cases examined, gendering functions through identity and discourse, making logical the enactment of specific bordering practices.

The chapter proceeds with a consideration of the concept of gendered states, foregrounding aspects of identity and security in the politics of protection. It then examines the cases of Sweden and Australia and how a masculinized protection informs their imagining of the state and sovereignty in complex and divergent ways, illustrating tensions in discourse and policy practice. Simultaneously, the contrasts between the two states are not necessarily fixed. Sweden has recently tightened its borders in the wake of the so-called migrant crisis in Europe, and Australia has faced widespread domestic and international criticism for its offshore detention practices, demonstrating that efforts to reimagine or reclaim the state can be resisted. Viewing such machinations through a gendered lens also invites further thinking about how it may be possible to achieve a "postsovereign" politics where an "ethics of responsibility" (Elshtain 1992) might challenge a politics of protection.

GENDERED STATES AND DISCOURSES
OF PROTECTION: CONSTRUCTING IDENTITY AND SECURITY

The politics of protection is built into the very discipline of international relations theory. Realist theorizing sees the protection of sovereignty and territorial integrity as the primary function of states, necessary for survival in the anarchic international order. Accordingly, the state has been the prime site and referent object of security in the discipline. Yet the relationship between the state, sovereignty, and security is dependent on discourses of self and practices of protection. Not all states read sovereignty and security in the same way. Such readings are informed by history, interactions with others, self-narratives, and identity, which have significance for how the state defends its material being and identity.

However, the protection of sovereignty and identity is more layered than first appearances suggest. Feminist scholars have critiqued the overt and subtle gendered logics of protection. For Iris Marion Young, the masculinist role of the state as protector is one of domination: the security state waging war externally while demanding obedience and loyalty domestically. Yet it also contains another image, that of self-sacrifice and chivalry, which constitutes the image of the protector (Young 2003, 4). In the same way as the idea of protection contains duality, the dynamics of masculinities that underscore it are also complex and multiple (O'Reilly 2012; Hooper 2001; Tickner 1992). For instance, the post-9/11 context has seen a resurgence of masculinism where discourses of danger masculinize the state while feminizing the population (Wadley 2010, 48). Masculinist forms of protection have implications for gender equality and violence in the international system (Eichler 2014; Tickner 1992; Stachowitsch 2013). The politics and discourses of protection legitimize a range of power relations at the domestic and international level and in the context of security, (neo)colonialism, imperialism, silencing, and exclusion (Rai 1996; Shepherd 2006). Protection has thus been widely critiqued as a "racket." In exchange for security, the "protected" become subordinate and dependent, raising substantive questions such as "Through which gendered identities do we seek security?" (Peterson 1992c, 53). Protection reaffirms forms of structural dependency as well as the identities of "protector" and "protected"; one constitutes the other, or as Stiehm claims, "The protected are essential to the protector" (1982, 370; Peterson 1992c, 50). It is this juncture that speaks to the relationship between identity and the politics of protection that the following case studies explore. States offer protection yet, in doing so, reaffirm or remake their identity. To understand how states claim to protect, it is important to observe the gendered discourses of identity that underpin and make permissible certain articulations of self and resultant policy moves. How do discourses of protection work with ideas of identity to (re)produce the state? The following section explores how middle powers engage in gendered articulations of statehood and security, and enact different notions of masculinity, power, security, and protection specific to ideas about self.

REMAKING THE SWEDISH STATE: NEUTRALITY AND SOFT/HARD SECURITY

For over two centuries, Sweden has been a neutral state. In the postwar period, Sweden developed a reputation for active internationalism, aiming to address structural violence through overseas development assistance and nonmilitary approaches to security through mediation and peacekeeping. Its neutrality policy was also deeply connected to social democratic norms and values, defined by consensus, welfarism, and solidarity, embedded in Sweden's national identity (Agius 2006). Sweden's self-narrative is that of an internationalist state that is other-regarding (Bergman Rosamond 2013, 327), a "humanitarian superpower," as described by former foreign minister Carl Bildt regarding Sweden's generosity in humanitarian aid and intake of refugees (Bildt 2013).

Starting in the 1990s, however, the discourse surrounding neutrality began to shift. Sweden joined the European Union (EU) in 1995, as it transitioned from a "civilian" power to one that included a security and defense dimension. As the EU discourse moved from "soft" to "hard" security, Sweden became closer to NATO, part of the EU Battle Groups, and has taken part in combat-intensive peace missions in Afghanistan. In most policy circles and academic literature, this change was logical and rational. Post–Cold War, neutrality lost much of its rationale, and Sweden's peace-keeping strength suited EU security. The discourses that accompanied this shift had to be coherent with a broader set of narratives about neutrality and national identity. Here, what I label "hegemonic discourses" of neu-trality (Agius 2011) come into play, and do so in a strongly gendered way, engaging rationalist and moral narratives.

Historically, neutrality has been a troubling category in the interna-tional imaginary, and is inextricably linked with foundational lessons of power politics; the narrative of neutrality in the Melian Dialogue[2] portrays it as the unwise policy of weak and small states, who reject the protection of a stronger power. Neutrality defied the Schmittian friend/enemy distinc-tion, and was regarded as a position of indecision. Neutral states were also equated with immoral and indifferent bystanders who benefited from war, refusing to protect others or fight for a just cause. Furthermore, neutrality was often assumed to be exogenously given or imposed by larger powers; postwar "Finlandization" and Austria's "neutralization" invoked associations of submissiveness (Agius 2011, 372–375). Accordingly, neutrals were seen to be passive, marginal players in the international system, lacking agency, the pawns of stronger states (Joenniemi 1988) that readily violated neutrality to further their war efforts. The overtly gendered language to describe neutral states conjured images of inexperienced, immature, and unrealized states; neutrality is equated with "virginity" (Ogley 1970, 1) and duplicity: Friedrich Dürrenmatt said Swiss neutrality "makes me think of a virgin who earns her living in a bordello but wants to remain chaste" (cited in Agius 2006, 4). During the Cold War, the role of neutrals as balancers through mediation fulfilled a role in the bipolar environment, but their real potential lay in this space inbetween, offering a possible third way that rejected the use of force. This interpretation of sovereignty was one that nonetheless never fully gained traction in an era when power politics dominated.

Swedish neutrality was both an idealistic and a rational policy. Neutrality was part of the social democratic project of the Swedish Model, consensus, and active internationalism. Yet Sweden's postwar "credible" neutrality relied on a strong military defense, and was support by its arms indus-try. Kronsell also argues that neutrality was inherently gendered, with the home front militarized and a specific type of masculinity enacted: the con-scripted "just warrior," in the Swedish context, became the "neutral soldier," protecting the state and exemplifying the values of neutrality internation-ally via peacekeeping (2012, 29). Elements of a protectionist relationship externally can also be observed with the "secret" NATO arrangements with the United States for military assistance during the Cold War. This not only laid claim to the "myth" of Swedish neutrality but also feminized the label in a curious way; despite rejecting *realpolitik* through active internationalism, Swedish security and sovereignty relied on its very framework for its own sovereign security, while maintaining distinctions between the domestic and external realms. Even reading neutrality in its most idealized formulation, securing sovereignty bought into the dominant masculinist rationale underwriting global politics. More so than the exclusion of neutrals in the international system, neutral states themselves are caught up in the logic of a masculinist imagery of the international through a reliance on militarism and internal contradictions at the domestic level.

Beyond Sweden's borders, peacekeeping was giving way to more robust forms of humanitarian intervention that promoted "cosmopolitan values," including protecting women beyond its borders (Bergman Rosamond 2013, 334) and deploying women to conflict zones.[3] Yet Sweden's tradition of participating in UN-mandated missions was under Chapter VI of the UN Charter, which concern peace settlement via monitoring buffer zones and demilitarized areas. More recent operations have invoked Chapter VII powers and responsibilities, which can permit the use of force beyond self-defense to restore peace and security (Matz 2013, 187). O'Reilly notes the increasingly masculinist activities of peacekeeping and peacebuilding are more about bringing order to unruly, dangerous regions (2012, 535). The discourses of cosmopolitan militaries also fall back on masculinist foundations about legitimizing interventions to protect (Kronsell 2012, 84–92).

Part of Sweden's willingness to move toward this interpretation of security and internationalism is explained as an extension of its traditional security-making practices. It is also an effort to carve out a different identity. Sweden's engagement in Afghanistan (2002–2014) and Libya (2011) was framed as "other regarding" in terms of civilian protection, particularly the protection of women. Yet such participation is also about demonstrating Sweden's value as a partner in NATO and loosening the "free-rider" label that is associated with neutrality (Doeser 2014, 198). Debates about intervention and NATO membership are constructed along binaries of being *engaged*, *proactive*, and *protectionist* rather than *isolationist*, *reactive*, and facilitating human rights abuses through *inaction* or *passivity*. Within these discourses is a particularly gendered idea of revising state sovereignty and identity, which plays to gender binaries of weak/strong, public/private, moral/immoral, even in areas of "soft security" such as peacekeeping. These binaries have been part of the constituting discourses of neutrality for centuries and are reworked in a way that maintains a line to the past while plotting the future self. The state still protects, but protection is guided by different logics that are intended to remake the state into a new security actor.

At the same time, different gendered ideas of protection are at work regarding traditional security debates, which invoke a masculinist framing, particularly concerning Russia (see Wilkinson in this volume). Since the 1960s, and particularly in the 1980s, Russian submarines, some considered nuclear-capable, have violated Swedish sovereignty. Media and official portrayal of the incidents contained a highly gendered dimension, pointing to the weaknesses of Swedish defense capabilities (Åse 2016). Recent incursions by Russia in Swedish territorial waters, airspace, and the Baltic Sea, as well as the Ukraine conflict, have revived Cold War insecurity. Sverker Göranson, the supreme commander of the Swedish Armed Forces, claimed that because of post–Cold War underfunding, Swedish defense would not last beyond a week (Forsberg 2013). Prior to 2012, public opinion consistently rejected NATO membership (Dagens Nyheter 2015a). Data from the Society, Opinion and Media (SOM) Institute at Gothenburg University in Sweden found more support for NATO than opposition in 2015 (38 percent, compared to 31 percent in 2014) for the first time since it began polling in 1994. SOM poll results also show that women have consistently viewed NATO membership negatively; the highest gap recorded was in 2012, when only 19 percent of women supported NATO membership, compared to 38 percent of men (Bjereld 2014, 489).

Amid more robust interventions and responses to sovereign incursions, Sweden is also promoting an overtly "feminist foreign policy."[4] Articulated by the current Social Democratic foreign minister, Margot Wallström, it seeks to promote gender equality and women's issues at the international level, with a focus on "rights, representation and resources" (Ministry of Foreign Affairs, Sweden 2015; see also True, in this volume). Gender is emphasized across all policy areas, from taxation and housing to trade, development, and conflict resolution, and is backed by the current "feminist government" led by Social Democrat Stefan Löfven. Sweden's "gender cosmopolitanism" denotes a commitment to women's rights and protection both within the state and beyond, "informed by an understanding of national borders as porous social constructs, the juridical significance of which can be set aside in consideration of the needs of distant other women" (Bergman Rosamond 2013, 320). The transformative potential of a feminist foreign policy is not only in its promotion of gender equality but in its challenge to structural violence and the masculinist hegemonies that fuel global conflicts through the arms trade and the military-industrial complex (True 2015b).

There are suggestions that aspects of a feminist foreign policy approach are embedding into current practices. The recognition of Palestine as a state has been defined as part of efforts to reach a peace deal based on a two-state solution and end the deadlock of the crisis. It also reflects the government's goal of a more active foreign policy, or more accurately, a *return* to activism in response to what Löfven describes as Sweden's "too passive" foreign policy of late (Scrutton and Sennero 2014). This way of thinking through foreign policy as active or passive is an interesting inversion of recent developments. Neutral states are assumed to be passive in global politics, but Sweden interpreted its role as an active internationalist state. In the last decade, several critics have suggested that Sweden has lost its edge in this regard, preferring integration with Europe and the turn toward NATO (Kronsell 2012, 121; Agius 2006, 2011).

Under a feminist foreign policy, efforts to reclaim a principled position still face obstacles. Wallström's diplomatic row with Saudi Arabia over human rights in 2015 and the cancellation of an arms deal[5] elicited a strong response from Sweden's business and political community, who criticized the move as naive, harming Swedish jobs and trade. Carl Bildt tweeted that the decision damaged Sweden's reputation and credibility as a contract partner (Dagens Nyheter 2015b). King Carl XVI Gustaf requested Wallström compromise, and a delegation of Swedish officials was soon dispatched to Riyadh, with letters from the king and the PM to smooth over relations (Nordberg 2015). A feminist foreign policy has quickly been evaluated in binary terms, as an idealistic position in contrast to the so-called real world of international politics, where states are required to behave rationally to secure their national interests. Wallström's advocacy of a somewhat more liberal feminist rationale and the openness to "hard" as well as "soft" power (Aggestam and Bergman Rosamond 2016) may also provoke debate,[6] particularly in the context of Russia and increasing the defense budget (Rupert 2015). The contradictions at work here point to the importance in grasping how gendered ideas of security and protection function in the way a state imagines itself and the discourses it relies on to make legible its identity and policy choices. In this vein, Australia provides a contrasting case on questions of sovereignty, identity, and the state. As the following section covers, the gendered underpinnings of middle power politics take on a more overtly masculinist form.

RECLAIMING THE STATE: AUSTRALIA'S MUSCULAR FOREIGN POLICY DISCOURSE

Australia's international profile has veered between that of a "middle power" and "good international citizen" in recent decades. Its active internationalism has been a part of its self-narrative, notably in its early contributions to establishing the United Nations and support for the Universal Declaration of Human Rights under Dr. Herbert Vere Evatt, the head of Australia's delegation to the UN. Australia was also a central player in the promotion of the principle of Responsibility to Protect, which was adopted by the UN in 2005. At the same time, warfare has also played a central defining role in the Australian self-narrative. "Mateship" and the ANZAC (Australian and New Zealand Army Corps) myth underwrite the story of the nation and routinely perform and celebrate the mainstream narrative of national identity. Gallipoli remains a moment of "national awakening," littered with metaphors of maturity, adulthood, and birth of the nation (Garton 1998, 86). This has implications for the national narrative, as Marilyn Lake explains: "When participation in foreign wars becomes the basis of national identity, it requires the forgetting or marginalising of other narratives, experiences and values" (2009).

Australia's sense of security, as Burke writes, rests on the paradox of its "isolated strategic location" and "physical and existential insecurity" (2007, 126). Its national story and development has been constituted by "discourses of danger" evolving from fears of Asia (Cheeseman 2004, 219). As such, protection forms an important part of the Australian narrative, seen in the dependence on greater powers for its security, first the UK, and, in the postwar period, the United States. Beyond its own borders, Australia has regarded itself as a "humanitarian warrior" in the region, leading missions in East Timor and the Solomon Islands (Cheeseman 2004, 224). Beyond its region, Australia was the largest non-NATO contributor to the International Security Assistance Force (ISAF), and its strategic narrative on Afghanistan has been "derivative and uncritical," with the major political parties supporting Australia's Afghanistan deployment, which is unusual compared to many European states, where more divergent views existed among political parties (Maley 2015, 81–82).

Burke (2007, 123) contends that identity is deeply tied to Australian security, whereby a legacy of exclusion can be traced in the White Australia policy of the early twentieth century, multiculturalism, and the securing of values, which have become a crucial part of its construction of the war on terror. Most pronounced under the Liberal-National coalition governments of John Howard (1996–2007) and Tony Abbott (2013–2015), Australian identity and security require protection from internal and external others. Furthermore, this idea of identity and how to secure it takes on a particularly masculinized form, with clear boundaries marked between the internal and external realm. Internally, misogyny and domestic violence remain constant markers of gender (in)equality, reflected most prominently during Labor prime minister Julia Gillard's (2010–2013) leadership and her treatment by the media and public commentators (Johnson 2015). While many observe that "aggressive masculinity" is not unique in contemporary Australian politics, under the Abbott government, there appeared to be an overt turn toward masculinist policy discourses and practices. Abbott embodied the notion of the "unitary masculine actor" (Cohn 1993, 240–241), both physically in terms of his "hypermasculine" image (Johnson 2015, 297) and in domestic and international security discourse (notably in his promise to "shirtfront" Putin at the G20 Summit in Brisbane in 2014). He appointed himself minister for women while Foreign Minister Julie Bishop—the only female minister in his cabinet—overtly rejected the label of feminism as "not part of my lexicon" (Sydney Morning Herald 2014). Malcolm Turnbull, who succeeded Abbott as prime minister in 2015, embodied a rejection of this type of masculinity, describing himself as a "feminist." Although he increased the presence of women in his cabinet, his masculinity is still celebrated in terms of his business acumen, decisiveness, and power (GQ Australia 2015).

It was during Gillard's time as leader that the promotion of gender equality, presence, and participation was made central in foreign policy, evident in aid and economic diplomacy regionally and globally in the form of support for the UN Women, Peace and Security (WPS) agenda. True (2016, 229) contends that the promotion of women's human rights in conflict and their role in conflict prevention and peace "has been the most significant new inclusion of gender in Australia's international affairs" in the last five years. The WPS agenda was centralized in Australia's successful bid for a nonpermanent UN Security Council seat for 2013–2014, and extensively promoted across different policy areas. But when Kevin Rudd deposed Gillard as prime minister in 2013, WPS was demoted in favor of combating small-arms proliferation. Although the use of such weapons to perpetuate sexual and gender-based violence was a key clause in what would become the first UN Security Council resolution on small arms and light weapons, it was at the expense of demoting postconflict peacebuilding as a focus of the Council's work (True 2016).

Yet it is also at the border that we see the tensions around protection at play. Efforts to "stop the boats" (the much-repeated, and often-derided, slogan of the Abbott government) have a long legacy, dating back to efforts to curb migration since the late 1980s. Immigration has been a constant focus in election campaigns, and the major political parties have invoked "tough" stances on the issue in order not to be seen to be "soft." Offshore processing of asylum seekers was also framed in its initial guise in ways that sought to protect the borders of the nation when first enunciated in Howard's "Pacific Solution" of 2001, when he declared: "We will decide who comes to this country and the circumstances in which they come" (Howard 2001). This early signal asserted the Howard government's distancing from the "good international citizen" label and sought to reinscribe control over borders. Labor, the party more inclined toward good international citizenship, dismantled the Pacific Solution under the Rudd government in 2008. Even so, mandatory detention and offshore processing remained. As boat arrivals and deaths at sea increased, "Pacific Solution II" was established under Gillard in 2012, who justified the policy in an emotive speech in terms of "saving lives at sea" (Sydney Morning Herald 2012). Foreign aid—widely regarded as a marker of good international citizenship—was also cut. In 2012, $375 million of the aid budget was diverted to Australia's asylum regime, making Australia, according to then opposition leader Abbott, "the third biggest recipient of its own foreign aid budget" (Cullen 2012). As support for border protection rose ahead of the 2013 federal election, Rudd returned to a tougher stance, proposing that all those who arrived by boat would be processed offshore.

OSB formed part of the Liberal-National coalition's election campaign in the lead-up to the 2013 election. In describing the "illegal" boat arrivals as a "national emergency," the policy proposed a military-led response to the smuggling of people. Once the coalition was elected, OSB was instituted in September 2013. It placed a military commander, the deputy chief of army, Angus Campbell, as the head of the taskforce. The policy offered the "discipline and focus of a targeted military operation" to deal with boat arrivals (cited in Chambers 2015, 405), and in doing so articulated a tougher response than the Labor Party's position, which was increasingly viewed as weak and changeable. The threat was also articulated in militarized terms. Former immigration minister Scott Morrison has said that the effort to "turn back the boats" is a "battle" that is "being fought using the full arsenal of measures."

OSB was also an exercise in "silencing" opposition and dissent. The reporting of "on-water" operations was banned (ostensibly to avoid giving information to smugglers). Non-operationally sensitive information was provided in weekly briefings to the media, a policy later abandoned in January 2014, when information would only be released on an "as needs" basis. Abbott defended secrecy of this "battle" by stating: "If we were at war we wouldn't be giving out information that is of use to the enemy just because we might have an idle curiosity about it ourselves" (McLeod 2014). The government's "counter people smuggling communication," such as narrative graphic novels and advertisements, forms another part of this discourse, directed as much toward reassuring the Australian audience of governmental action and protection, as toward external deterrence. The mediation and control of images and discourses in the politics of protection render the performance of sovereignty an opaque activity. This silencing redirect notions of protection in important ways. Recent reports about the level of abuse—including sexual and physical abuse of minors and rape of women by "protectors" in offshore facilities—speak to what Hansen has called the "security of silence" and "subsumed security." The former refers to the insecure who lack a voice. The latter speaks to multiple inscriptions of "otherness," such as religion, race, or nationality, in addition to gendered identity, that render a subject insecure (2000). The domestic discourse that constructs asylum seekers as "not like us" further silences their (in)security. Despite the real insecurities experienced by these excised bodies, the body deemed in need of protection is that of the sovereign state in a globalized world.

Wendy Brown argues that borders do more than protect: "They produce the content of the nations they barricade," and at times when identity and sovereignty are deemed to be at risk, they require re-articulation (2010, 41, 118). This is exemplified by the former immigration minister Scott Morrison, who conceptualized the border as constitutive and protective:

> Our border is not just a line on a map. Our border is a national asset. It holds economic, social and strategic value for our nation. . . . Our border creates the space for us to be who we are and to become everything we can be as a nation. Border security is the platform upon which we enable the seamless flow of people and goods legitimately across our borders. . . . Maintaining our border as a secure platform for legitimate trade, travel and migration is what border protection is all about. (Morrison 2014)

Australia is an example of a state that reifies itself "through performances of security, particularly those which establish them as stable and masculine protectors" (Wadley 2010, 40). For Chambers, OSB is a case of a nation "seeking to secure a space for itself through enacting domination of space as border security" (2015, 412). Perera (2013, 66) refers to this "insularity" as a "logic that underwrites Australian assertions of nationhood . . . [that are] violently defended."

The relationship between globalization, insecurity, and borders has "brought the state back in." As Brown claims, in an era of declining sovereignty, we are witnessing the rise of borders and walls, which represent anxiety over "sovereign impotence" (2010, 26). McNevin foregrounds the inherent contradiction between globalization and the state in her focus on the performance of sovereignty that aims to reinforce a traditional idea of state sovereignty in the case of asylum and border protection, but desires the openness of the free, globalized market for its wealth and survival. The practice of outsourcing security to keep the idea of the state consistent and whole is also a feature of this practice; it is not simply drawing new lines in the sand—or sea in this case, with Australia's excision of its own territory from the migration zone—but also a separation of sovereign responsibility from the protection of others (2011). This dissociation is evident in the continuation of Australia's asylum policy under Turnbull, who has squarely laid the blame for the abuse of detainees on the governments that "manage the centres"—Nauru and Papua New Guinea (PNG)—not Australia. Outsourcing detention means "we [Australia] don't hold them there" (Taylor 2016). The enactment of state violence, when the state may not be present, demonstrates the mobility of sovereign power (Mountz 2011, 119). Offshore detention also engages a form of (neo)colonialism and silencing which can be read in gendered terms. The privatization of security is not simply a new market model of militarized masculinity, but "a process of remasculinization" (Stachowitsch 2013, 77) that also relies on non-Western labor, reinforcing a global hierarchy of masculinities (Eichler 2014, 86). Such structures of managing the border produce not simply an outsourced performance of security but also a confected protectionism of the sovereign state: the state distances itself from human rights abuses and gender-based violence within these zones while at the same time offering to keep borders secure.

REMAKING, RECLAIMING, AND GENDERING THE STATE: PROTECTING SOVEREIGNTY?

The Australian and Sweden discourses both perform an important role in shaping and changing ideas about national identity. But they do not do this alone through the power of slogans or words. Discourses are also gendered and positioned in relation to existing norms, values, and ideas of self. For Iris Marion Young, gender is not an element of explanation but one of interpretation. Viewing issues of war and security through a gender lens means "seeing how a certain logic of gendered meanings and images helps organize the way people interpret events and circumstances, along with the positions and possibilities for action within them, and sometimes provides some rationale for action" (2003, 2). Peterson delineates between gender as an *empirical* category (where gender is a variable) and gender as an *analytical* category, a "signifying system of masculine-feminine differentiations that constitutes a governing code" (2010, 18). The state can be masculinist without intentionally or overtly pursuing the "interests" of men. Socially constructed masculinity contains many dimensions, which have historically shaped the modes of power circulating through the state (Brown 1992, 14). For example, militarized masculinities re-articulate the state across multiple sites that include public militaries, culture, identity and security discourse, state policies, and ideology (Eichler 2014, 81–84). Necessary to resisting such modes is the ability to decipher the discourses and practices that permit such forms of masculinism to underwrite not only policy but also the very identities of the state.

Middle powers use protectionist discourses to replicate or reinvent forms of masculinist security in different ways. The middle powers examined in this chapter provoke the necessity for a more meaningful discussion about how self-narratives can work in intricate ways when states imagine themselves as protectors, and the tensions associated with how they enact that image. Both states negotiate contradictions within their own foreign and security policies in ways that speak to a gendered account of the state—mired either in making the state a "tougher" active internationalist or protecting the state through practices and discourses that rely on masculinist imaginings of what it means to be a state or to retain "state-ness" in a globalizing world. A gendered analysis of how middle powers enact sovereignty is also significant in terms of how gender circulates and responds to new phenomena. For instance, the ongoing outcry over offshore detention and the very real human rights abuses—long known and documented—have seen public pressure increase. Wilson Security, the private security firm contracted to run the camps, has withdrawn, and the Manus Island detention center on PNG is set to close. In Sweden, borders are retracting; in July 2016, restrictive laws came into force for those seeking asylum, with limitations on family reunification and residency.

Under a gendered analysis, the middle power concept becomes strained. Both states have claimed the label of good international citizenship in varying degrees across different policy areas. Yet claims to progressiveness become limited once traditional binaries are engaged, which are demonstrated in the ways in which protection is articulated and enacted. This prompts consideration of the silences produced when this gendering takes place. Identity may drive ideas of self, but the thread across both states is that of sovereignty—and more importantly, the need to rethink sovereignty to untangle the gendered associations that constitute it as a concept. Here Elshtain's earlier challenge, to think through a rejection of sovereign politics, serves as a useful starting point. For Elshtain, the pursuit of a postsovereign politics—one where sacrifice is removed from political loyalty and identity and is exchanged for responsibility (1992, 150), opens the possibility of becoming unbound from the border that constructs the idea of the state. Although speaking in the context of warfare and the demands for sacrifice for the "mother country," Elshtain's point also bears on the subtle and overt ways in which states aim to invoke or "harden" the boundaries that define them. A focus on responsibility would require interventionist moves to be other-regarding and question the sovereign state as a bounded, exclusionary unit. Middle powers could be well positioned to engage with this alternate reading of sovereignty, but doing so would first require an untangling of masculinized notions of power and protection. Part of the problem here lies in the concepts and language that characterize "middle powers"—the notion that such states can exercise some forms of traditional power and influence in ways different from those of great powers.

CONCLUSION

The importance of understanding the changing character and gendered nature of the state and security is perhaps more pressing now than at any time since the postwar period. In response to globalization, economic crisis, inequality, and ideological challenges that intend to reverse gains in gender equality, the rise of the masculinist state represents a cause for concern. Claims to strengthen and protect the state are increasingly interlinked with discourses and performances of masculinist protection. This is evident in Putin's Russia, Trump's United States, and in states across Europe and Asia where promises to return the state to "order" or "greatness" combine with masculinist and violent policies and practices.

By exploring the potential of middle powers to offer a "middle way" in global politics, this chapter has emphasized that the relationship between security and identity remains an important foundational basis upon which we can make sense of a state's preferences and visions of itself and the world. Yet if that understanding is constrained by gendered visions of identity, state, and security, the ability of middle powers to offer anything different is severely curtailed. Rather, gendered understandings color ideas of the state and what must be protected.

In the cases explored in this chapter, we see how identity can inform ways in which gendered protection and ideas of the state enact different policies that remain underwritten by masculinist impulses and conceptions. Sweden, in its efforts to discard its neutral past, deploys concepts of gendered protection to make permissible its new military engagements. The pursuit of a feminist foreign policy is also measured against the practicalities of "real world" politics. Australia's efforts to reassert sovereignty at the border speak to a longer legacy of external threat and a desire for protection. The enactment of efforts to reclaim the state are, nonetheless, reliant on militarized and masculinist notions of protection that promise to make the state safe. These examples point to the intricate relationship between gendered notions of identity, the state, and what it means to be secure, but also the challenges that remain for Elshtain's call for a postsovereign politics.

NOTES

1. I thank Swati Parashar for this suggestion.
2. Peterson notes that the masculinist Athenian polis conformed to a gendered pattern of state-making that became attached to the idea of the modern state, reflected in conceptualizations of citizenship, property ownership, and the domestic division of labor (1992, 35–37).
3. However, gender divides remain, with female peacekeepers allocated complementary roles in operations (Persson 2013).
4. Feminist approaches and the promotion of gender in foreign policy have featured in the UK with William Hague, the United States with Hillary Clinton, and among Nordic states (True 2015b).
5. Wallström condemned the public flogging of Saudi blogger Raef Badawi. Saudi Arabia then prevented her from delivering a speech on women's rights and democracy to the Arab League. Business visas were canceled for Swedes, and ambassadors were recalled.
6. This is not to say that all feminists would see the hard/soft power divide as problematic. True (2016) suggests that they combination of hard and soft power might defy gender stereotypes.

CHAPTER 6

Gendered State Assemblages and Temporary Labor Migration

The Case of Sri Lanka

SAMANTHI J. GUNAWARDANA

Within the political economy of migration there are actors, institutions, and relationships that "move" laboring bodies across borders (Xiang et al. 2012). The gendered state is a central actor with territorially distributed, negotiated, and renegotiated power resources (Sassen 2006). This chapter draws on "assemblage thinking" (Acuto and Curtis 2014) to understand the way in which states relate in seemingly contradictory gendered ways to transnational temporary labor migration[1] and migrant workers. I apply Michael DeLanda's (2006) conceptual refinements of assemblage and follow Saskia Sassen's (2006) usage of the term in a descriptive sense to the postcolonial state in the realm of global political economy. Extensive gender analyses are available on the gendered, racialized nature of migrant labor markets, worker experiences, migration policy, and employment systems (Yeoh 2016; Lan 2006). However, few accounts of labor migration have theorized gendered states[2] that further structure state and interstate relations (see chapter 1). Thus, this chapter aims to examine the gendered state vis-à-vis labor migration.

I argue that within the fractured logic of a neoliberal development agenda, three distinct but interrelated, and at times contradictory, gendered regimes have emerged to facilitate migration and address harm faced by workers.[3] Together they make up a gendered state assemblage that produces mixed results for migrant workers. In international political economy, the study of regimes has explained how states have cooperated with each other in a globalized world around common interests (Kranser 1983). The concept of "regime" is widely used to describe how various institutions, implicit and explicit norms, rules, principles, and procedures converge to build gendered regimes (Ostner and Lewis 1995). Multiple regimes operate simultaneously, so that the state as assemblage stretches across all layers of local life, from the household to training and national institutions governing migration processes. At the same time, the gendered state assemblage also expands across national borders into transnational spaces.

These three regimes can be classified as *regulatory, protectionist*, and *brokerage*. All involve multiple actors, processes, and institutions, spanning the local and global. *Brokerage* regimes emerge as countries turn to remittances as a viable development strategy. States attempt to create opportunities for citizens to migrate for employment. *Protection* regimes materialize to "protect workers" from multiple forms of harm, but the politics of protection (see chapter 5 in this volume) results in reinforcing gendered state regimes. *Regulation* regimes are formulated to manage migration and protect workers by influencing the actions of employers and the labor-hosting state. They are interlaced through the other two regimes.

The chapter is focused on the case study of Sri Lanka,[4] where for much of the late twentieth and early twenty-first century, women taking up employment, primarily as housemaids and nannies in the Middle East, dominated the out-flow of migrant workers. Because this pattern has been distinctly gendered, Sri Lanka offers a case study on how gender is reproduced through state action. The Sri Lanka case illustrates how temporary transnational labor migration is "mainstreamed" into national development policy as a poverty alleviation pathway (de Hass 2012). Although indebted workers may be exposed to exploitation (Piper et al. 2016), remittance flows make migration an attractive option for states. Across Asia, temporary labor migration is now a mainstay of livelihood strategies within neoliberal economic development discourse and policy by organizations such as the World Bank. In 2015, international migrants from the global South remitted $432 billion, of which 57 percent went to the Asia Pacific, outstripping foreign aid and investment (Ratha et al. 2016). In Sri Lanka, personal remittances (including worker remittances) accounted for 8.5 percent of GDP, or $US7 billion in 2015 (World Bank 2016). According to the Sri Lankan Central Bank, approximately 50 percent of remittances come from the Middle East (Daily Mirror 2016).

This chapter is structured as follows. First, the main ideas underpinning assemblage thinking are outlined. Second, an examination is made of how transnational migration is ordered through labor protection, regulation, and brokerage regimes. Within each regime, I highlight how officials, institutions, discourses, symbols, meaning making, and identity are bought together to enable migration and regulate migrant workers. Gender norms are embedded within these regimes, which in turn reproduce more gender norms. Third, conclusions are discussed, highlighting the way in which these regimes help to constitute the postcolonial gendered state.

THE GENDERED STATE AS ASSEMBLAGE

Once regarded as a failure in local development planning (De Hass 2012), this latest incarnation of the "migration-development nexus"[5] has focused on the transformation of citizens to self-reliant market actors.[6] Although "temporary" periods of migration are not defined cohesively in the literature, migration occurs for a predefined, limited amount of time with no associated settlement rights. Such workers are often citizens who occupy already marginalized material positions and identities within states (Frantz 2013). States are engaged in simultaneously facilitating migration and responding to (marginalized) citizens who are outside their territorial sovereignty.

An assemblage approach to the state involves recognizing the historical transformation of state power rather than the erosion of sovereignty (Sassen 2006). The state as assemblage creates new meanings and forms, recontextualizing and refashioning relationships, including relations of power (Mezzadra and Neilson 2013, 195). Importantly, assemblages have material outcomes for workers.

Deleuze and Guattari initially used the French term *agencement*, which is commonly translated as "assemblage" in English to focus on connection (or relations), and how those connections are arranged and rearranged in context to each other (Phillips 2006). Unity in the assemblage is found in harmonious relations between disparate elements rather than homogeneity. The notion of the assemblage has been deployed in international relations for its explanatory power relating to synergistic properties of the state, particularly during periods of rapid social change (Acuto and Curtis 2014, 2). Assemblage thinking takes on many styles, but at heart is an ontological stance as well as a repository of methods (Acuto and Curtis 2014).

Treating the state as a historically constituted assemblage means analyzing it as the arrangement of various economic, social, and political processes, institutions, authorities, power relations, people, networks, concepts, norms, organizations, and discourses. This vast conceptualization can be organized by referring to DeLanda's (2006) classification of components. They are material (e.g., bodies, organizations); expressive (e.g., language, topics on meeting agendas, symbols); territorializing/deterritorializing process of stabilization/destabilization; and coding (the practice of naming, establishing meaning, promoting homogeneity to build identity). Decoding, therefore, implies breaking these established meanings and supporting heterogeneity. Held together across a variety of territorial scales, recurring interactions within the different elements of the assemblage produce different impacts. The elements making up the assemblage can be dismantled and brought together elsewhere, in "relations of exteriority" (DeLanda 2006). These relations of exteriority are important in explaining how generated state regimes operate simultaneously in the case of transnational labor migration. Power relations emerge through the assemblage interactional processes (DeLanda 2006).

Explaining that she uses assemblage in "the most descriptive sense," Saskia Sassen (2006, 5) argues that the project of global restructuring is fundamentally one of disassembling the territory, authority, and rights of the modern nation state. States are then reassembled across multiple scales and reconfigured, enabling the globalized economy. Although the nation state provides the judicial framework for regulations, citizenship, and policies on employment and social reproduction, these are not fixed (Jayasuriya 2005). Indeed, the institutions that make up these frameworks may be reassembled beyond national boundaries, creating different material outcomes for various groups of workers (Sassen 2006).

Particular configurations of power relations within three core regimes that govern labor migration help to understand the gendered state. That is, by understanding how states craft/reinforce the norms, institutions, rules, and governance structures that enable ongoing transnational migration, I argue that the regimes operate simultaneously to produce a gendered state assemblage. To illustrate, I turn to the Sri Lankan case.

BROKERAGE REGIMES

The first regimes examined are brokerage regimes. A traditional brokerage employment relationship involves the mediation of a third party beyond the worker and employer. As Xiang et al. (2012) point out, there is a wide array of brokers in transnational migration, including state officials and migrant workers, highlighting the ambiguity between state and market, formal and informal (Endo and Afram 2011). Rodriguez (2010, x) argued that postcolonial states such as the Philippines take on brokerage role:

> Labour brokerage is a neoliberal strategy that is comprised of institutional and discursive practices through which the Philippine state mobilises its citizens and sends them abroad to work for employers throughout the world while generating a "profit" from the remittances that migrants send back to the families and loved ones remaining in the Philippines.

The place of remittances within this definition distinguishes brokerage from mere facilitation, whereby the state helps to justify labor migration as a necessary poverty alleviation route (Aguilar 2014).

In Sri Lanka, international labor migration is facilitated by the Ministry of Foreign Employment Promotion and Welfare. Under this ministry sits the Sri Lankan Bureau of Foreign Employment (SLBFE), the primary institution for overseeing migrant workers. The SLBFE was set up by the Sri Lanka Bureau of Foreign Employment Act No. 21 of 1985 (amended in 2009). Although noted for its lack of gender sensitivity[7] and its inconsistency with the ratified 1996 International Convention on the Protection of All Migrant Workers and Their Families,[8] the act gives far-reaching authority to the SLBFE. The SLFBE also oversees the Association of Licensed Foreign Recruitment Agencies (ALFEA), established under the SLBFE act. This agency oversees private recruitment agencies.

Over time, the institution has gone beyond collecting data, registering workers prior to departure, and promoting migration, to offering predeparture training programs via an island-wide network of training centers, overseeing welfare issues, setting minimum contractual standards, and providing guidelines for private sector employment agencies. The SLBFE deploys labor officers to the district level in-country, as well as attachés to Sri Lankan embassies abroad. When workers have issues, they can seek redress only through the SLBFE act of 1985, via a conciliation forum to handle the grievances of workers, and to prosecute local agents (not an overseas employer) (Gunawardana 2014).

The SLBFE oversees guidelines pertaining specifically to women including issuing guidelines on minimum monthly wages for those migrating on the housemaid category (Wickremasekara 2015). They set minimum age requirements for men and women, and they also require that women obtain a family background report before departure, as discussed in the discussion of protection regimes later in this chapter.

The brokerage regime extends from the local to international regimes. Potential migrant women workers who wish to migrate to Saudi Arabia as housemaids first encounter local rules around permission/legitimacy. This includes obtaining a medical report from approved medical centers (Samuels 2013 in Gunawardana 2014), undergoing training at a local training center that introduces workers to the norms of care work, and cultural context of Saudi Arabia.[9] They must obtain a police report, as well as the family background report. The latter entails encounters with community-level social/administrative institutions and norms from the household to local-level district secretariats (see discussion below). Following this, workers encounter broader state regimes that draw in the SLBFE, which monitors departure, an employment agent in Sri Lanka who liaises with the Foreign Employment Agency in Saudi Arabia, the Sri Lankan embassy in Saudi Arabia, and finally the employer.

The state through various bodies such as the SLBFE also mobilizes, reinforces, and reproduces gender norms and stereotypes to market workers to both internal and external audiences. The state draws on national and global gender narratives and norms to reproduce images of "ideal workers," women, and gendered and racialized ideas about noncitizens (Liang 2011).

In Sri Lanka, migration has highlighted traditional household relations and roles in broader popular critiques expressed in the media and by politicians, leveled at labor-receiving states and women migrants (Gamburd 2008). The introduction of protectionist policies (as discussed in the section below on protectionist regimes) can be understood within the context of regular reports of abuse, death, and exploitation among migrant housemaids in the local media. At the same time, the family background report, which was a response to local moral critique about women migrating alone, has centered on the social costs of migration, including alcoholism among spouses, child abuse, and overall social decay, including the breakdown of relationships as well as debts owed to loan sharks (Gamburd 2000, 2008).

Sri Lankan women have been primarily constructed as wives and mothers in relation to the nation state and venerated for their caregiver or social reproduction roles (De Mel 2001). These norms have been highlighted particularly in relation to patterns of women's participation in employment following shifts in the local economic structure with the introduction of economic liberalization policy in 1977. For example, Lynch (2007) examines how nationalist norms developed through anticolonial movements focused on respectability as a characteristic of "good" women, whose primary role was cast as wives and mothers. However, virtues such as domesticity, discipline, and restraint were upended by single rural women migrating to take up employment in urban free trade zones established as part of liberalization policy.

Gamburd's (2000, 2008) work on women workers migrating overseas as nannies and housemaids after 1977 similarly highlights popular critique women faced from the media and politicians for "abandoning" their children to care of others. While women's role in the economy has been acknowledged in recent policy platforms, policies continue to neglect the tensions between economic and social reproduction roles, including the lack of childcare (Gunawardana 2014). The use of the family background report is a material element of the regime that is also embedded within broader gender norms regarding women's responsibility for reproduction and childcare.

Yet social reproduction and gendered household roles are marketized within brokerage regimes. In marketing workers, labor-sending states utilize domestic narratives around nation state identities, as women are often also cast as reproducers of the nation state or symbols of cultural and national purity throughout South and Southeast Asia, including Indonesia and the Philippines (Silvey 2004; Rodriguez 2010). Using essentialized and feminized characteristics of reproduction and caregiving, states promote virtuous caregiving and caretaking identities for migrant women workers (Lan 2016). In general, states may construct a representation of ideal citizenship and nationalism centered on remittances and familial responsibility (Rodriguez 2010; Lan 2006; Gunawardana 2014). These narratives, however, omit narratives articulated by the women themselves, which focus on consumption, acquiring worldly experiences, or escaping social stigma or domestic violence (Constable 2014).

Internal domestic marketing is also important. Classifications of jobs are an important arena to counter poor valuation of migrant work and labor. In the Philippines, state institutions changed the terminology used to categorize entertainment workers to avoid criticism that the state was exporting sex workers disguised as entertainers (Encinas-Franco 2013, 100). In Sri Lanka, the deputy general manager of the SLBFE stated that housemaids would be known as "domestic housekeeping assistants" (Daily News 2013). Discussing the introduction of worker training in 2007, he reflected that training programs introduced after 2007 attempted to reorient how domestic work was viewed from unskilled to skilled workers:

> Time planning, scheduling, arranging their work schedules, daily timetable, weekly, monthly, seasonal timetable . . . as a domestic housekeeper they need to know about the seasonal timetable like festivals, when and where and how they [should] get ready for those things. . . . so they cannot no more [sic] be recognized as unskilled. They are to be recognised as skilled workers. Even NVQ [National Vocational Qualification training] is given.[10]

Heroism discourses are another form of classification that helps to justify labor export and migration (Encinas-Franco 2013; McKay 2007). The Sri Lankan state has sought to recast migrant workers as *rata viruwo*—'nation heroes.' In 2011–2012, the SLBFE introduced the Rata Viruwo Program. The state sponsors a Rata Viruwo televised global talent quest, lotteries, ongoing programs involving scholarships for children, a housing program for migrant families, and self-employment opportunities for migrant families as well as a reintegration program for workers, which includes working with trade unions and NGOs. The idea, again, was to reorient workers' public identity and highlight their contribution to the national economy through these rewards (Gunawardana 2014, 17). Yet, while these elements of brokerage can be helpful for workers, they do not address many of the underlying structural issues promoting migration or labor conditions in host countries.

In summary, brokerage regimes help to facilitate migration by setting up local structures such as the SLBFE or passing special laws to enable migration. Regimes made up of existing or specialized local rules and structures are invoked to ensure that the right workers are sent abroad (e.g., they are healthy, trained, and have "permission" from spouses). States internationally promote feminized identities for migrant women workers. However, states must respond to local contradictions between dominant gender norms that cast women primarily as wives and mothers and the essential transgression of those norms ("abandonment" of families) required to migrate. This has involved reorienting the image of work/workers from devalued to valued, as well as imposing strict requirements such as the family background report to ensure that women fulfill their primary role as per dominant gender norms.

REGULATION REGIMES

Regulation regimes function within the other two regimes mentioned here, and exist in a relationship of exteriority on their own. Domestically, states have relied primarily on passing legislation setting up institutions and processes. These elements are also found in the other regimes. In this section, I focus on diplomacy and nonbinding agreements covering the period of the labor contract to regulate migrant worker conditions in host countries. Although labor migration can become major diplomatic flashpoints between states, most sending states lack political and diplomatic clout relative to their wealthier, labor-receiving host countries (Elias 2013). As Piper, Rosewarne, and Withers (2016, 3) point out, structural inequalities in the global economy and institutional ineffectiveness mean that "migration governance is not matched by labour governance." Moreover, postcolonial feminist interventions highlight how women from the global South are embedded in broader relations of gender, race, class, and ethnicity— multiple relations of power alongside structural violence in the global political economy (Agathangelou and Turcotte 2016). Below, I outline key ways states such as Sri Lanka have participated in and shaped regulation regimes.

The first kind of regulation is through participation in consultative transnational platforms, including the Colombo Process, ministerial consultations, the Abu Dhabi Dialogue, the South Asian Migration Commission, and the Ramphal Commission on Migration and Development. These are all nonbinding, focused on information sharing and capacity building.

Legally binding bilateral agreements and non-binding memorandums of understanding (MOUs) with migrant-receiving countries are popular regulatory mechanisms (Lan 2006). Sri Lanka entered into bilateral MOUs with Italy, Bahrain, Jordan, Libya, Qatar, United Arab Emirates, Korea, Malaysia, and Saudi Arabia (Wickremasekara 2015). Most of the MOUs pertain to reducing irregular migration, training workers, permit systems, quotas, joint cooperation on technical matters, health insurance, or travel expenses.

As the above measures have been described as a symbolic gesture to signify good relations, they are critiqued for being ineffective and underutilized (Gunawardana 2014). A report prepared for the International Labour Organisation (ILO) (Wickremasekara 2015) reviewed 144 such agreements in Asia, Africa, Europe, the Arab states, and the Americas. The most common form of agreement in Asia were MOUs, where labor ministries or specialized agencies were the primary labor-sending country party to agreements. Key objectives included encouraging mutually beneficial cooperation, strengthening "existing friendly relations," coordinating "manpower" recruitment, and regulating the employment of migrant workers. Only a third of the MOUs mentioned worker rights relative to local workers. Some countries had specific MOUs for domestic workers and others (e.g., domestic gardeners) not covered in the destination country laws. Redressal action remained vague. The report concluded that in contravention of Guideline 4.5 of the ILO Multilateral Framework on Labour Migration, which urges states to ensure that labor migration policies are gender sensitive, the reviewed agreements lacked good practice provisions related to gender concerns and vulnerable migrants.

States may also ratify international conventions. Sri Lanka has ratified all core ILO labor conventions; however, it has *not* ratified Convention 97,

Migration for Employment Convention (Revised) 1949. The only countries in South and Southeast Asia that have are the Philippines and Malaysia, but both have opted out of Annex II, which outlines the conditions for recruitment and placement of labor under government-sponsored arrangements, including oversight of third parties. Convention 143, Migrant Workers (Supplementary Provisions), which covers protection of migrants in abusive conditions and equal opportunity, has been signed only by the Philippines. The 1997 Convention 181 on Private Employment Agencies has not been signed by any of the countries in Southeast and South Asia, while Convention 189 on Domestic Labour has been signed only by the Philippines.

In terms of monitoring and enforcing these agreements, local actors are important. Therefore, police become involved in the predeparture stage in cases of agency or broker fraud and trafficking. The Sri Lankan Women's Bureau and women development officers often handle individual complaints by families or workers, while the National Committee on Women runs a Gender Complaints Unit that receives complaints by workers and families. The Legal Aid Commission of Sri Lanka receives complaints on nonpayment of or lower-than-agreed wages, as well as harassment on the job. At the local village level, the *grama niladari*[11] handles complaints and may also intervene in disputes. Advocates have asserted, however, that these mechanisms only provide partial remedies, if any, for workers (Gunawardana 2014).

One of the key drawbacks of the above mechanisms is that they do not usually allow for worker voice. Although the global governance mechanisms recognize and often involve trade unions in consultations, the local mechanisms do not provide a space for representation of migrant workers. For Sri Lankan nationals, there is no room for independent representation, and workers must depend on negotiations and participation of either a Sri Lankan Embassy representative or any representative of the Sri Lanka Bureau of Foreign Employment (Gunawardana 2014).

In summary, regulation regimes are gendered through the omission of women's concerns in regulatory mechanisms and through the lack of gender-sensitization and representation of women's concerns in constructing regulations. Regulation regimes are a key aspect of the gendered state assemblage, and involve both local and international governance structures. In the transnational arena, labor-sending countries such as Sri Lanka have participated in nonbinding agreements making or ratified international rights conventions. The process involved is largely exclusionary of worker voice. At the local level, various institutions are involved in monitoring migration and receiving complaints to enforce and seek redress for violations of agreements and other regulations. Involvement in global regimes has meant the boundaries of the gendered state are extended beyond the nation state, yet influence is curtailed by structural inequalities. A partial response is the emergence of protection regimes, as discussed below.

PROTECTION REGIMES

While protection regimes aim to provide security for the worker, they are often premised primarily on regulating women themselves (Rodriguez 2010, 105). Constitutive elements of protection regimes can be found in both regulation and brokerage regimes. Making visible the politics at play in protection regimes highlights how women are constructed as a vulnerable group in need of paternalist protection that can only come from the masculinist state (Elias 2013). Young (2003, 2) argues that "citizens come to occupy a subordinate status like that of women in the patriarchal household." This involves distance from decision-making autonomy or agency, which can have various material impacts on women.

In postcolonial states such as Sri Lanka, directives such as the family background reports,[12] effectively ban some women from traveling overseas, although Sri Lanka is not alone in instituting such prohibitions (e.g., Nepal and Indonesia during various periods). Bans are often a reactionary policy aimed at the local public to address protest around violations of migrant worker rights, high rates of abuse, or unjust death penalties handed down in labor-receiving countries that could not be allayed via diplomacy (Pande 2014; Elias 2013).

In examining the reasons given for bans, state discourse and action reveal not only concern for women's welfare but gendered ideas about women's role in the nation state, as well as an essentialized understanding of women's vulnerabilities (Parreñas 2005). In Sri Lanka, the family background report applies directly to women migrating to work as domestic workers. Women's perceived "abandonment" of families has generated moral anxiety and critiques about women's role in Sri Lankan society. Reports on the social costs of migration, such as alcoholism among spouses and abuse of children, reinforce the ideological idea that migrant women contribute to overall social decay (Gamburd 2000, 2008).

"Unskilled" women workers such as maids are often seen as needing protection and surveillance, as they may be easily duped because they do not possess the "same level of academic and skill training or the requisite class status" as professional migrants (Guevarra 2006, 530). Thus, state apparatuses designed to protect women via brokerage elements such as predeparture education reproduce gendered stereotypes of docility and train workers to perform specific familial and national obligations. It serves the dual function of enabling the state to "represent [itself] as virtuous and caring" (Rodriguez 2010, xx). Being unskilled is often construed as not only being formally uneducated but also being unable to use the technology employed in domestic work or be adept at "modern" cleaning methods or childcare techniques. Training can be provided through state-run institutions to avoid strained relations between the employer and worker and avoid employer abuse (Guevarra 2006). Training programs attempt to discipline the worker herself, holding her accountable for her abuse; the idea behind this training is to remedy workers' social behavior, including sexual and gender relations (Pande 2014).

Another protection strategy in Sri Lanka is the attempt to proactively shift the profile of migration from unskilled to skilled workers, by reducing the number of women migrating as housemaids. In addition to announcing that housemaids would be known as "domestic housekeeping assistants" (Daily News 2013), the qualifying age was set for twenty-five years old, and it was stipulated that workers would need to undergo a twenty-one-day residential training course. Overall, the state announced it was committed to reducing the number of women workers migrating as housemaids "by at least 50%, and we need to divert their career to another profession, like alternative vocational skills to be introduced for girls coming out from schools" (Gunawardana 2014). It is yet to be assessed whether the vocational programs have targeted the same group of women. Without focused targeting, women considering migration may be forced into intermittent and low-wage forms of employment such as working for daily wages in agriculture.

The family background report requirement is an extension of this policy. At the village level, the *grama niladhari* confirms residence and civil status. At the household level, the assigned caretaker of the children (if not the husband) is required to sign the report. The husband is bound to sign, declaring "no objection to travel." The "sign-off" process involves inspections visits by development officers to the prospective migrant's home and, in some cases, discussions with neighbors and other individuals to ascertain the family situation. If women have children under five, the officers are obligated not to recommend them for migration, regardless of care arrangements. Women over fifty-five years of age cannot migrate. Those traveling to Saudi Arabia must be at least twenty-five years of age. Other Middle Eastern countries have an age limit of twenty-three and above, with all other countries requiring a minimum age of twenty-one years.[13]

There has been a marked drop in women migrating overseas as a result of this ban, with labor attaches such as the Sri Lankan embassy in Oman stating they would only accept maids with the no-objection certificate (Daily Mirror 2013). In 2013, a migrant woman worker challenged this rule in the Supreme Court with the assistance of civil society actors, filing a fundamental rights petition. However, the chief justice ruled that it was not gendered discrimination or in violation of human rights (Samath 2013). Nonetheless, the background report continues to be critiqued for the unfair burden of proof of childcare placed on women (Daily News 2016).

Not only does the report place the onus for childcare solely on women, the above bans are underscored by gendered assumptions about women's capacity for self-protection based on age. The assumption is that younger women need to be protected, but older women may be immune or at least mature enough to protect themselves from exploitation. This assumption is blind to the abuse women in the older age group have endured, and ignore structural conditions that contribute to violence, exploitation, and abuse. Such discourses implicitly hold migrant women responsible for their exploitation, and absolve the state and other actors from any responsibility (Cheng et al. 2015).

In postmigration contexts, embassies and consulates play a crucial role in providing advisory services, advocacy, safe spaces, and welfare centers (Frantz 2013). Consular, services such as those undertaken by labor attachés, are an essential element in the state, as they provide first-contact services for workers overseas. Sri Lankan consulates operate shelters for workers leaving their employer within their contract owing to abuse or harassment. Observing the exchanges at the Sri Lankan consulate in Jordan in 2006, Frantz (2013, 1080) noted that often consular staff acted as "brokers between workers and employers and helped to enforce the bondage relation." She observed that embassy staff members were sympathetic to workers, but felt conditions were justified owing to the workers' poverty. Moreover, rather than following official channels, such as going to the police in the case of gender-based violence, for example, sexual assault, they sought out unofficial channels for reconciliation. Thus, if an employer admitted fault, a financial settlement was made and the worker sent home. The staff felt this was the better option, as court cases could take years. While Frantz did not present the workers' reflections, this course of action has the impact of conveying that the state protected the interests of the workers, although such action takes decision-making power away from workers, including whether she would like to pursue the case through the court system, or indeed, to stay in the country with a new employer.

In summary, this section examines how states construct masculine protectionist regimes as a response to the inherent structural, gendered, racialized, and class power differentials in the global political economy of labor migration. In labor-receiving countries, consulates create protectionist spaces, such as the operation of shelters. However, they are also bound within the brokerage regime, making these institutions compromise regulatory or other processes designed to help workers seek redress. Locally, the sum result of the politics of protection is often the regulation of women themselves, resulting in limited mobility and, therefore, limited opportunities for income generation. Protection is directed at protecting women *from themselves*, as well as their children and households. Sri Lanka's family background reports are one response to local public protest around violations of migrant worker rights, as well as moral anxiety around women's perceived "abandonment" of families. The family background report involves extensive external surveillance that removes or stymies women's agency, reinforces her primary responsibility for social reproduction, and places this power in the hands of spouses. The protection regime, however, does produce variegated conditions for different types of workers (older versus younger women) depending on the intended host country. Women who are cleared for migration are assumed to be unaware and uneducated about the risks of migration. Protection regimes can also involve introducing predeparture instruction that ultimately transfers risk and responsibility to workers for their well-being in the destination country.

CONCLUSION

The case of Sri Lanka illustrates how three seemingly contradictory but interrelated labor migration regimes—regulatory, protective, and brokerage—constitute the assemblage that is the postcolonial gendered state. The three regimes cofunction symbiotically (e.g., protectionist regimes would not form without brokerage regimes), and elements of each of the regimes are found in others (e.g., regulatory mechanisms are found in protectionist regimes). Theorizing the gendered state as assemblage means that we can account for contradictory processes, norms, and actions across multiple scales, while accounting for the overlapping common elements that are found across all.

The concept of an assemblage enables us to understand the reassembly of the postcolonial gendered state within a neoliberal global political economy. In relation to transnational temporary labor migration, the gendered state reaches across multiple territorial scales, albeit within a context of limited power in the transnational realm. The gendered state extends its reach into the global space, cooperating with powerful host states, while deepening its relations of domestic interiority through the setting up of institutions and processes as well as the mobilization of gender norms and gendered processes.

The gendered state is constituted through three key regimes, each of which produces and reproduces gender through their simultaneous functioning. *Regulation* regimes provide a governance structure for the movement of labor across borders, and signal the contours of acceptable treatment of workers. However, nonbinding agreements are rarely inclusive of workers' voice, while ratified international rights conventions have been poorly reflected in national regulation. Regulation regimes have extended the territorial boundaries of the gendered state, yet influence is curtailed by structural inequalities within the global political economy. At the local level, in countries like Sri Lanka, regulation has focused on managing the migration process, through the establishment of various institutions involved in monitoring migration, receiving complaints to enforce, and seeking redress for violations of agreements. Elements of the regulation regime are found in both brokerage and protection regimes.

Brokerage regimes facilitate migration via institutions (e.g., SLBFE) or special laws. They ensure that "appropriate" workers are healthy, trained, and, in the case of the family background report requirement, have permission from spouses. These regimes overlap with regulation regimes. Importantly, they are imbued with local gender norms about motherhood, marriage, and feminized caregiving and caretaking identities for migrant women workers. Yet brokerage regimes have an in-built tension—migration involves transgressing local norms ("abandonment" of families). Thus, states must also internally broker transitional images of migrant workers to its citizens, from devalued to valued.

This highlights the failure of regulation regimes owing to inherent structural, gendered, racialized, and class power differentials in the global political economy of labor migration. In addition to transgressing norms, Sri Lankan migrant women workers have faced violence while being employed abroad.

The Sri Lankan state has evoked *protectionist* regimes as a response. Embassies and consulates create (much-needed) shelters. However, as a part of brokerage regimes, embassies have been found to informally compromise processes designed to help workers seek redress, reinforcing gendered harm. Locally, the politics of protection has resulted in the regulation of women, resulting in limited mobility and, therefore, limited opportunities for income generation. This aspect of protection regimes is designed to protect women from themselves, as well as their children and households. Sri Lanka's family background reports are a response to public outcry about the violence women aboard have faced, as well as moral anxiety around women's perceived "abandonment" of families. Surveillance stifles women's agency, reinforces their primary responsibility for social reproduction, and grants spouses greater decision-making power. The protection regime also produces different conditions for different types of workers. Finally, protection regimes also involve predeparture training to create ideal workers, which ultimately shifts the risk and responsibility for well-being onto women workers.

The ultimate—albeit unsurprising contradiction—is that the production and reproduction of gender through brokerage, protection, and regulatory regimes constitutes the gendered state assemblage, which ensures that labor migration is sustained even in the face of significant gendered harm for women.

ACKNOWLEDGMENT

I thank Jacqui True for comments on this chapter.

NOTES

1. The configuration of markets, mobilities, and border crossing encompasses trafficking, forced labor, asylum seeking, and marriage, making drawing fixed boundaries problematic. My concern in the chapter is to focus on transnational labor migration via state-sanctioned means.
2. Here understood as how patriarchal gender regimes that ascribe essentialized masculine and feminine attributes not to only personhood but to all aspects of social, political, cultural, and economic relations constitute the state.
3. Although gender regimes can be counted as a fourth, here I examine how gender is embedded across all three of the aforementioned regimes.
4. The chapter draws upon research published by the Solidarity Center (United States) for a larger project funded by the US Agency for International Development (Gunawardana 2014).
5. The migration-development nexus describes the relationship between migration, remittances, poverty alleviation, and the impact on families, communities, and the country. De Hass (2012) notes that attitudes toward this relationship have swung between optimism and pessimism over the past century.
6. Yet migration is often a forced choice, driven by conflict, dispossession, exclusion, and unemployment (Delgado-Wise 2015).

7. The act does not require gender mainstreaming of policy or programs for migrant workers.
8. For example, the family background report requirement for women, discussed in this chapter.
9. Training has included understanding how to operate appliances; simple lessons in Arabic; safety training, including how to respond to employer demands; respectful language; and hygiene and cleaning methods.
10. Mangala Randeniya, interview by the author, 2013.
11. Local-level village official.
12. Discussed in detail below.
13. As per Circular No. 13/2013, Circular No. 19/2013, and Circular MFE/RAD/1/3 of 12.2013 effective January 15, 2014. In 2013 and 2014 Sri Lanka adopted provisions outlined in the National Labour Migration Policy (2009) via two circulars that mandated a compulsory family background report be completed by all women seeking employment overseas as housemaids.

PART III
Troubling the Gendered State

CHAPTER 7

Mother Russia in Queer Peril

The Gender Logic of the Hypermasculine State

CAI WILKINSON

Following the collapse of the Soviet Union in 1991, the Russian state and its citizens experienced a profound crisis of masculinity as the nation struggled to cope with the practical and psychological consequences of the end of the Cold War. For both state and individuals the experience was deeply emasculating; the sudden loss of superpower status and ideological death of communism was compounded by a dramatic contraction of state capacity and decline in living standards. Virtually overnight, men were stripped of their Soviet-era role of public builders and managers of communism and found themselves largely unequipped to reassume "the traditional masculine roles of father and provider" now that the "universal patriarch" Soviet state was no more (Ashwin 2000, 1; Ashwin and Lytkina 2004). At every level of state and society, masculinity was left looking enfeebled, from the humiliation of the Russian army's defeat in the first Chechen war in 1994–1996 (Riabova and Riabov 2010, 57) and the embarrassing drunken antics of President Boris Yeltsin, to the high mortality rates among Russian men, whose already poor average life expectancy fell to just fifty-nine years in 2000 as political and economic collapse left the Russian state with even less capacity to improve the health and well-being of its citizens than the Soviet Union had possessed (Kay 2006, 6–8).

Yet despite the dramatic emasculinization of the 1990s, the 2000s has seen masculinity become not just a central feature of the Russian state, but arguably its defining characteristic. This has not been accidental. Rather, it has occurred via a deliberate process of "remasculinization" designed to restore national pride and dignity by "creating a positive collective identity of Russians with the help of gender discourse, particularly by promulgating masculine images of Russia" (Riabov and Riabova 2014, 23). Central to this process has been the carefully managed creation of what Sperling (2016) describes as "macho personality cult" around President Putin. By portraying him as the all-action epitome of a "real man" who, it is implied, is capable of restoring Russia's national pride and status in a way that less manly men could not (Riabova and Riabov 2010), the Kremlin's media advisers have sought to exploit the intimate linkages between embodied masculinity and nation-state building that have long been shaping politics and ensured that states are fundamentally "masculinist projects" (Nagel 1998).

The success with which Putin has used masculinity to legitimize his rule is indisputable (Sperling 2015), in spite of the obviousness of Putin's (frequently staged) performances of manliness. Indeed, in an unusually direct conflation of state and individual, the first deputy head of the presidential administration went so far as to comment in 2014 that "if there's Putin, there's Russia; if there's no Putin, there's no Russia" (Sivkova 2014). The public expression of such sentiment, which is by no means unique given the "jaw-droppingly high" level of public support Putin enjoys (Birnbaum 2016), points to the fact that under Putin the Russian state has not just been remasculinized, but become *hypermasculine*, with the performance of hegemonic masculinity becoming "a strategy for creating not just legitimacy, but also a scenario of power itself" (Wood 2016, 330). In other words, Putin's ongoing performance of extreme masculinity, which began as a political strategy to facilitate his hold on power, has become an integral feature of contemporary Russian political culture that directly affects the character and behavior of the state thanks to the "muscular equation of himself and the Russian state" that Putin has created (Wood 2016, 330).

Russia's highly visible performance of masculinity under Putin has captured the attention and imaginations of the international community and Russian public alike, as adroitly demonstrated by Valerie Sperling (2015, 2016). However, a gendered analysis of the state must take into account that masculinity—particularly in hypergendered forms—cannot be performed in isolation. Rather, as Peterson (1992b, 9) explains:

> The terms of man-woman and masculine-feminine are related. Rather than categorically separate, independent categories, the terms are mutually constituted and interdependent: they presuppose each other. The appropriate metaphor is

not "A and B," or "A1 and A2", but "A and not A." "Man," "masculinity," and "male worlds" are defined by their exclusion of (and disdain for) that which constitutes "woman," "femininity," and "female worlds."

As a result, she continues, "masculine constructions . . . *depend upon* maintaining feminine ones" (Peterson 1992b, 9). At a basic level, therefore, the feminine functions as a passive "other" that provides a way to demarcate the superior male from the inferior "not-male."

Recognition of this interrelationship and hierarchy invites us to consider the role of the feminine in constituting Russia's gendered statehood. For the practical purposes of regime legitimation, femininity serves mainly as a passive foil to either enhance masculinity though the misogynistic sexualization of women or to delegitimize male opponents by homophobically feminizing them (Sperling 2015). For the production of a hypermasculinist national and state identity, however, a hyperfeminine other is required, reflecting the fact that hypermasculinity occurs "when agents of hegemonic masculinity feel threatened or undermined, thereby needing to inflate, exaggerate, or otherwise distort their traditional masculinity" (Agathangelou and Ling 2004, 519). Viewed through Peterson's (1992c, 50) "lens of protection," this "reactionary masculinity" (Nayak 2006, 43) thus creates an imperative for the state to make good on its promise of protection—something that, at least for the hypermasculine state, is best achieved by riding to the rescue of a worthy damsel in distress in an act that simultaneously (re)confirms the state's masculinity and femininity's subordinate and dependent status.

Given the shortage of damsels waiting—and willing—to be rescued in the contemporary world, however, this is not an easy task. Nevertheless, reflecting the performative nature of gender (Butler 1990), which means that damsels are made rather than born, the Russian state has solved this problem by creating its own damsel, Mother Russia, and an accompanying narrative that explains both her distress and how the Russian state will save her.

The basic plot of this deeply gendered tale is that Mother Russia, a long-standing national personification of Russia, has been rescued from a decade of post-Soviet neglect and ignominious destitution, and is now once more being supported by the manly Russian state and his aides to fulfill her natural womanly destiny of (re)producing and caring for the nation (her children). However, a pernicious "Unholy Queer Peril" is stalking Mother Russia, aggressively trying to tempt her with feminism, unnatural gender roles, and secular Western decadence in order to distract her from her maternal and wifely duties and break up the traditional

Russian family. The Russian state must therefore take all necessary measures to protect Mother Russia and her children (the nation). Failure is not an option: at stake is not just his honor, but the very future survival of Russia.

In the rest of this chapter I explore why rejection of the Russian state's hypergendered norms is perceived as such a serious threat to Russian state identity and power via an analysis of the relationships between Mother Russia, the Russian state, and the so-called Unholy Queer Peril. In the next section, I provide an overview of Mother Russia as the Russian state's "feminine side" that highlights the gendered work "she" performs for the Russian and Soviet state as its leading female personification and symbol of national identity, both setting the standard for norms of femininity and providing an "other" against which masculinity can be defined. While her long history as the object of national affection and reverence makes her a logical choice as a masculinist Russia's leading lady, a backstory is nevertheless required to cast Mother Russia a convincing damsel in distress. Thus, in the third part of the chapter, I consider the Russian state's rapprochement with Mother Russia as it recovered from the emasculating failure of the Soviet Union, demonstrating how a narrative explaining the need to "save" Mother Russia and restore her to her "natural" role was created, thereby enabling the newly remasculinizing Russian state to successfully perform the role of patriarchal protector. Then, in the penultimate section, our attention turns to the villain of the piece, the Unholy Queer Peril. Here I describe how the Russian state has successfully portrayed feminists and homosexuals as an existential threat to Mother Russia and thus as a matter of national security, since deviation from the hypermasculine and hyperfeminine gender roles demanded by "traditional family values" constitutes an intolerable challenge to the hypermasculinist Russian state.

The chapter concludes by reflecting on what the tale of Mother Russia in queer peril tells us about its author and main narrator, the Russian state, and about the hyper-gendered state more widely. I argue that hypermasculinity's reactive nature not only makes the Russian state's promise of protection conditional on the performance of gender in accordance with the state's norms of masculinity and femininity, but also renders it coercive by creating an imperative for punishment of transgressions of gender norms. Thus, the queer peril reveals how the hypermasculinist state can only ever fulfill its promise of protection to itself, rather than to its citizens, since the failure to actively perform hypermasculinity—for example, by tolerating gender deviance—represents the failure of the state, meaning that the protection of the state must take precedence over protection of citizens.

Instances of Russia performing masculinity are rarely hard to find, from displays of military might such as the annual Victory Day parade held on Red Square in Moscow, which in 2016 included ten thousand participants and an extensive array of military hardware,[1] to action man President Putin's well-documented and frequently bare-chested "fighting, hunting, shooting and fishing" activities (Foxall 2013; Sperling 2015).[2] Such visible demonstrations of strength and power fit well with Russia's historical image as a belligerent and brutish bear, whose enemies, Putin suggested in 2014, want to put him on a chain and rip out his teeth and claws (RIA Novosti 2014).

What is perhaps less visible to Western eye and ear, however, is that Russia also has a very definite feminine side. Gender is literally as well as symbolically written into Russian national identity, beginning with the very words that are used to describe Russians' relationship to Russia. Rosamund Bartlett (2007, 1) explains:

> [Russian has] as many as three words denoting "native land." *Otechestvo* is the literal word for "fatherland," but it sounds high-flown and official to Russian ears, and is used mostly in poetry. *Otchizna* is a word that suggests fatherland and motherland together, cleverly combining the root-word for "father" (*otets*) with a female ending, but is also little used. Like *otechestvo*, it has a role in the rhetoric of nationalist politics.
>
> By contrast, *rodina* (motherland) is used by every section of the population, and its associations are far more intimate. If *otchizna* and *otechestvo* relate to the country in which one is a citizen, *rodina* is the place where one is born—a familiar place which has always been there. It is where one feels a sense of belonging, the warm hearth to which one returns. *Rodina* is identified, moreover, with the nation's soul.

The word *rodina*, commonly translated into English as "motherland" but literally meaning "birthplace," Bartlett goes on to comment, is potentially "the most emotive word in the Russian language" due to its associations with motherhood, belonging, and the land.

The national personification of Mother Russia (*Rodina-mat'*) provides one of the clearest illustrations of the affective power of the word *rodina* for Russian collective identity (Riabov 2006). The image of Mother Russia has a long history in Russian culture that extends back to medieval times and intertwines multiple images of motherhood, including Mother Earth, the motherland, and the Mother of God. In the case of the latter two, Suspitsina (1999, 117) observes that "the two images . . . merged in the collective consciousness in a curious way, creating a new symbolic relation-ship. [As a result, the] Mother of God came to be perceived as the pro-tector of Russia, while Russia acquired the epithet 'holy' (*svyataya Rus'*)." Reflecting these deep and powerfully emotive origins, Mother Russia has become inextricably linked to Russian and Soviet patriotism and national identity, functioning as an affective symbol that is used to mobilize people in the service of the nation state and define the boundaries between what is Russian and what is not (Riabova 2015; Ryabov and Ryabova 2016).

Internationally, arguably the best-known representation of Mother Russia is in the form of a Soviet propaganda poster from 1941 by Iraklii Moiseevich Toidze entitled "Rodina-mat' zovet," or "The Motherland Calls." Created at the start of the Great Patriotic War,[3] the poster portrays a serious-faced woman against a background of rifles with bayonets, one arm raised as if beckoning to those behind her, the other thrust forward toward the viewer with a piece of paper printed with the military oath in her hand.[4] Within Russia, meanwhile, the 85-metre-tall, 8,000-ton statue *Mother Russia Calls* that was erected on Mamayev Kurgan in Volgograd in 1967 to commemorate the Battle of Stalingrad bears particular mention as an iconic representation of Mother Russia (BBC Russian Service 2009).[5] Such visual representations of Mother Russia provide Russia's feminine side with a physical embodiment that enjoys additional affective power among Russians due to historical associations with war and patriotic sacri-fice for one's country. In contemporary Russia, however, Mother Russia is most frequently found as a rhetorical symbol in attempts at political mobi-lization, with political actors "exploit[ing] the image in multiple forms" in order to encourage Russians variously to vote, "to participate in anti-government actions, to support a certain candidate, [and] to defend the Motherland against external and internal enemies" (Riabova 2016, 125). Ignoring an invocation of the Motherland is closely associated both popu-larly and politically with a lack of love and respect for one's country, mean-ing that Mother Russia has an almost unrivaled capacity to successfully call Russians to action.

In addition to her ability to mobilize people, as the definitive ideological feminine representation of Russia (Ryabov and Ryabova 2016, 99), Mother Russia plays a central role in articulating norms of femininity and female-ness. In this capacity she performs a positively Stakhanovite amount of gender(ed) work for the Russian state, fulfilling all five of the major roles identified by Anthias and Yuval-Davis (1989, 7) for women's participation in practices of nation-statehood: first, she is the "biological reproducer" of the Russian nation and the reproducer of the boundaries of Russian national (ethnic) identity (functions a and b); second, Mother Russia is a central figure in "the ideological reproduction" of Russian collectivity, serving as both figurehead and archetype for motherhood in the Russian context (function c); third, when juxtaposed with the Unholy Queer Peril, Mother Russia functions as a ideological signifier and symbol of Russia's distinctiveness, signaling its alignment with and defense of traditional family values (function d); and finally, Mother Russia exemplifies women's participation in "national, economic, political and military struggles" (function e) as gendered citizens who fulfill their "natural" feminine roles of wives and mothers for the good of the masculine state and its nation, thereby becoming the defining and definitive feminine representation of Russia (Ryabov and Ryabova 2016, 99).

As a performance of imagined femininity, Mother Russia is a "monumental and heroic figure" who during the Soviet period set "an exacting standard against which the citizen-children were measured (and inevitably found wanting)" (Issoupova 2000, 44). Accordingly, she also sets the standard for the performance of masculinity by the state and its citizens—a logic that underpinned the Soviet gender order. Sarah Ashwin (2000, 1) explains how in the Soviet Union "gender became the basis on which the duties of citizens to the new polity were defined," with women expected to take on the role as "worker mothers who had a duty to work, to produce future generations of workers, as well as to oversee the running of the household" while men would assume the roles of "leaders, managers, soldiers, workers" who "were to manage and build the communist system." Significantly, Ashwin also notes that this gender order positioned the Soviet state as a "universal patriarch" that "assumed responsibility for the fulfilment of the traditional masculine roles of father and provider." Consequently, although men's roles were of higher sociopolitical status, they were also circumscribed, since masculinity "became socialised and embodied in the Soviet state," as a result of which individual men's masculinity was "officially defined by their position in the service of that state," rather than more broadly through the performance of roles at home as well as at work (Ashwin 2000, 1).

With the end of the Soviet Union in 1991, it was optimistically assumed by many that this Soviet gender regime would change to reflect new post-Soviet realities, becoming less monolithic in the absence of a state-driven vision of gender relations (Ashwin 2000, 2). In practice, this hope was short-lived. Any new gender order that emerged in the 1990s was driven primarily by harsh post-Soviet economic realities, which compelled women to assume new gender roles in order to feed their families and maintain the household even as the government attempted unsuccessfully to convince women to leave the public sphere and "return to their 'purely womanly mission' in the home" (Albanese 2006, 108). Men, meanwhile, often found it hard to navigate the loss of professional status on which their masculinity depended. This contributed to widespread media discussion of the "crisis of masculinity" among Russian men, with their responses to the challenges of post-Soviet life characterized as "increasingly apathetic and irresponsible" rather than vigorously entrepreneurial (Kay 2006, 5, 20). With Russia's remasculinization in the early 2000s, however, the logic of protection could once more be reasserted to justify a return to a traditional gender order, and the scene was set for the Russian state to ride gallantly to Mother Russia's aid and simultaneously restore both individual and national masculine pride and feminine virtue after the "unnaturalness" of Soviet-era gender roles (Kay 2000, 20–21) and the humiliations of the 1990s.

THE DAMSEL IN DISTRESS: SAVING MOTHER RUSSIA

In contrast to the effort required to locate a preexisting damsel, only minimal work was required to make Mother Russia's portrayal of one highly convincing. As noted earlier, the consequences of the Soviet Union's collapse were experienced both collectively and individually as a sudden and visceral loss of masculinity. For Mother Russia, this national emasculation meant the loss of masculine protection. Previously revered, celebrated, and provided for by the Soviet state, the 1990s saw her, and the Russian nation she represented, deserted by the state and left largely unsupported, rendering her "suffering, weak and unattractive" (Issoupova 2000, 44). State provision of benefits and resources for mothers and children declined dramatically (Issoupova 2002, 24); she was physically deserted as male suicide rates rocketed;[6] and symbolically she fell from being a mother to being represented as a "woman of easy virtue" as "prostitution became a metaphor for the country's foreign policy" (Riabov and Riabova 2014, 25).

Mother Russia's fall from grace was compounded by her "barrenness" in the face of a growing demographic crisis. In short, since 1992, the Russian population has decreased from a peak of just under 149 million to approximately 144 million in 2015.[7] Even allowing for factors such as high mortality rates, a key reason for the decline of Russia's population has been low fertility levels. The upheaval and uncertainty caused by the Soviet Union's collapse resulted in Russia's fertility rate being among the lowest in the world in the 1990s, reaching a low of 1.16 children per woman in 1999 (Perelli-Harris and Isupova 2013, 144). Reflecting the central role that control of reproduction and sexuality plays for the gendered state (Anthias and Yuval-Davis 1989), increasing the country's birth rate became not just a priority for the newly remasculinizing Russian state, but an imperative for survival (Chernova 2012) and, from 2006, an official matter of national security (Erofeeva 2013, 1931).

In order to achieve the required increase in the birth rate, in 2006 Putin launched "one of the most ambitious family policy agendas ever," with a particular focus on incentivizing women to have a second child through the provision of extended financial benefits (Perelli-Harris and Isupova 2013, 148). However, without addressing the structural reasons why most women stop at one child, which include a lack of family-friendly infrastructure and services in Russian cities as well as a shortage of affordable housing for young couples and widespread discrimination against mothers in the workplace (Orlova 2014; Perelli-Harris and Isupova 2013, 149–150), the impact of financial incentives was always going to fall short of what was desired. Recognizing this, policymakers increasingly sought to frame fertility as an issue of ideology (Chernova 2012), with the result that "gradually parenthood began to be conceptualized not in terms of being a responsibility and duty to the state and nation, but principally as a moral value" (Pecherskaya 2013, 93).

This shift formed part of a wider effort by the Russian state to actively promote a moral regime of highly conservative pronatalist, patriarchal, and heteronormative "traditional family values" that was presented as the only way to save Russia from a loss of human dignity and eventual inevitable extinction, as Vladimir Putin explained in 2014 at the final plenary of the Valdai International Discussion Club:

What else but the loss of the ability to self-reproduce could act as the greatest testimony of the moral crisis facing a human society? Today almost all developed nations are no longer able to reproduce themselves, even with the help of migration. Without the values embedded in Christianity and other world religions, without the standards of morality that have taken shape over millennia, people will inevitably lose their human dignity.[8]

For women, the new "traditional family values" agenda has meant that they are viewed first and foremost as the mothers of Russia's future (i.e., children). The masculinist state therefore views itself as being responsible for their protection from all forms of potential harm, even if such "protection" is at the expense of bodily autonomy. Tangible consequences of this logic have included the imposition of restrictions on access to abortions (Erofeeva 2013) and proposed legislation requiring tattooists to warn women that lower-back tattoos may complicate the administration of epidurals (Rothrock 2014). Despite the heavy-handed paternalism of such measures, by reframing reproduction as being primarily a matter of morality, it became possible for the Russian state to reassert the logic of masculinist protection by demonstrating its ability to protect Mother Russia and her future children. In addition, with women returning to their natural and sacred role, Mother Russia would once more be properly feminine, and thus provide a worthy and stable—but still subordinate—"other" for the masculine state.

One question still remains, however. What exactly is Mother Russia in need of protection from? More obvious suggestions would seem to include domestic violence, widespread sexual harassment, or even restrictions on reproductive healthcare. But these answers do not fit with the specific gender performances required to enact the hypermasculinist logic of protection. Even worse, such answers risk suggesting that hegemonic masculinity might be part of the problem rather than the solution to Mother Russia's woes. So instead, the Russian state identified a far more terrifying threat: an Unholy Queer Peril.

THE UNHOLY QUEER PERIL

The appellation "Unholy Queer Peril" describes a range of actors that have collectively been portrayed by the Russian state as posing an existential threat to Mother Russia and hence to the Russian nation state due to their failure or unwillingness to conform to the strict norms of gender and sexuality that are central to the ideology of "traditional family values." The name is designed to highlight the key characteristics of the groups it purportedly describes *from the perspective of the Russian state*. First, the term "queer" is utilized here to denote not only nonheterosexuality and gender variant identities, but also deviations from state-sanctioned gender norms such as being childless or unmarried (especially in the case of women), and/or rejection of highly gendered and sexed patriarchal family and societal structures. It thus recognizes that while lesbian, gay, bisexual, and transgender (LGBT) people are one of the main groups that have found themselves positioned as a threat in recent years, as is discussed in more detail below, feminists and other heterosexual and/or cisgender people who reject the Kremlin's "traditional family values" have also been cast as gender deviants.

This use of "queer" reflects one of the central aims of queer theory, namely "to reveal how power operates in normative codes and normalizing practices [and] 'make strange'—disrupt, destabilize, deconstruct, effectively *to queer*—what is considered normal, commonplace, taken-for-granted, or the 'natural order of things'" (Peterson 2014, 604), especially in relation to gendered hierarchies of sex and sexuality. Importantly for an interrogation of the gendered state, this usage also emphasizes the performative nature of gender as something that is constituted via repeated and repetitive acts (Butler 1990). Second, use of the adjective "unholy," reflects the centrality of religion, and specifically a dogmatically conservative version of Russian Orthodox Christianity, to the Kremlin's hypermasculinist national identity project, with opponents being portrayed as godless and immoral enemies of the God-given natural order. And third, "peril" is borrowed from Gayle Rubin's conceptualization of a "domino theory of sexual peril" whereby a clear line must be maintained between "good" (that is, acceptable) and "bad" sexual (that is, unacceptable) practices. For those subscribing to the theory, "The line appears to stand between sexual order and chaos," making its maintenance imperative, lest the "barrier against scary sex . . . crumble and something unspeakable . . . skitter across" (Rubin 1984, 152).

Although Rubin's analysis of normative sexual hierarchies deliberately did not extend to gender, when combined with an understanding of queer as the transgression of gender(ed) norms of behavior, it becomes evident that while not synonymous, "bad" sex and "queer" sex have much in common—not least the ability to provoke extreme anxiety and fear in a hypermasculinist state that perceives the maintenance of a strict gender order to be vital for its identity and survival. Nonconformity and opposition to the state's moral and gender regime, therefore, must be clearly identified, and then even more clearly repelled and, ideally, eliminated. Although opposition to the state can potentially come from a wide variety of groups, for the purposes of constructing the Unholy Queer Peril as an existential threat to Russia's future that can only be neutralized by a wholesale embrace of "traditional family values," the Kremlin has focused on two "gender deviant" groups in particular: feminists and "homosexualists,"[9] each of which is discussed below in order to highlight how the Russian state constructs its gendered identity and that of the Russian nation in opposition to them, especially by contrasting their performance of gender roles unfavorably with that of Mother Russia and the Russian state.

Feminists

Following seven decades of demonization by the Communist Party of the Soviet Union, during which time feminism was "painted as a 'bourgeois' movement, accused of splitting the working class by highlighting women's interests, and outlawed" (Sperling 2015, 49), it is perhaps unsurprising that feminism remains not just unpopular but strongly stigmatized in post-Soviet Russia. As Voronina (2009, 252) explains, feminism is widely perceived as deviant and unnatural, a perversion of woman's "natural" role:

> Popular culture keeps voicing the idea that feminism, as a Western phenomenon, not only leads to a war with men but even poses a threat to Russian national values. The media creates the image of feminists as masculinized, sexually unsatisfied, and/or morally degraded women whose core values are rights, power over men, and money—not family and children, which a "normal" woman is expected to prefer.

Associations between feminism and lesbianism compound the stigmatization, meaning that "you will immediately be seen as a butch ball-buster" if you call yourself a feminist, in the words of one of Sperling's interviewees (2015, 53). In short, at least in the popular imagination, to be a feminist is to be a transgressor of gender and sexual norms or, in other words, to be queer. Given such stereotypes, it is unsurprising that women are reluctant to identify with feminism, especially as doing so openly is likely to provoke hostile and deeply misogynistic reactions.

While this view of feminism may already seem quite extreme, for the hypermasculinist Russian state and its supporters—most notably the Russian Orthodox Church—the problem with feminism runs far deeper. In addition to being unattractive and abnormal, it is argued that feminism is an outright threat to the country's future due to the challenge it poses to the traditional gender roles espoused by the Kremlin and its supporters. Patriarch Kirill, the head of the Russian Orthodox Church, made this exceptionally clear in comments to a meeting of the Union of Orthodox Ukrainian Women in 2013 that were widely reported (Elder 2013; New York Times 2013; News.com.au 2013; The Telegraph 2013):

> It is entirely evident that women are the homemakers, the very centre of family life. No-one would dispute this. Men have their gaze turned outwards—they must work and earn money, but women must be focused inwards, on where her children are, where her home is. If this incredibly important function of women is destroyed, then everything else will be destroyed—the family and, in the broad sense, the motherland. It is no coincidence that we refer to Russia as the motherland, but precisely because women are the homemakers. . . .
>
> I consider the phenomenon known as feminism to be very dangerous, because feminist organisations proclaim the pseudo-freedom of women, which,

in the first place, must manifest outside of marriage and the family. At the centre of feminist ideology is neither family nor raising children, but some other function for women that frequently contradicts family values.[10]

Such staunchly traditionalist views also provide an insight into the harsh sentences received by three members of Pussy Riot, a self-identified feminist punk band, following their performance, subsequently titled "Punk Prayer—Mother of God, Chase Putin Out!," in front of the altar of the Cathedral of Christ the Savior in Moscow in 2012. While Rutland (2014, 581) argues that the Kremlin "cannot seriously have believed that the women's actions constituted a threat to the stability of the Russian state" but rather "cynically exploited the Pussy Riot punk prayer to advance its neo-traditional values agenda," this conclusion underestimates the extent to which the hypermasculinist state perceives violations of its normative order as existential threats that must be eliminated. Indeed, in sentencing the three members of the band to two-year jail terms for "hooliganism motivated by religious hatred" (BBC News 2012), the court's verdict explicitly noted that "feminism is incompatible with social relations in Russia that are historically based on a religious worldview" (Sharafutdinova 2014, 616), thus positioning feminism—and feminists—as alien and threatening to Russia (Sperling 2015, 291–293). Once this othering is factored in, it is possible to see why the Russian state's reaction, especially initially, was so unforgiving. Not only were the members of Pussy Riot deviant by virtue of their identification with feminism and violation of behavioral norms in a sacred space, but their performance was understood as a direct challenge to both Putin and the Russian state's masculine authority and legitimacy, sacrilegiously imploring the Virgin Mary (a figure of motherhood that is beyond reproach) to actively reject Putin—an act that would both emasculate Putin and leave Russia without his protection.

Homosexuals

In contrast to feminists, who threaten the hypermasculinist Russian state by rejecting their designated gender role as represented by Mother Russia, homosexuals have been portrayed as a more direct threat to Mother Russia in that they allegedly deprive her of her children. This argument is based on three main claims, all of which are used to justify why "traditional family values" are vital for the nation's survival (Wilkinson 2014).

First, it is asserted that acceptance of homosexuality and other "nontraditional" sexual practices is contributing to Russia's demographic decline as people in nonheterosexual (and by implication nonheteronormative) relationships allegedly do not procreate. Elena Mizulina, chair of the State Duma Committee on Family, Women and Children's Affairs, has explicitly articulated this logic in explaining the need for antigay laws, noting that she believes that they are necessary to tackle Russia's falling population (Queerussia 2013). President Putin subsequently openly endorsed this view in 2014 when commenting on efforts to improve Russia's birth rate, observing that "anything that gets in the way of [population growth] we should clean up" (Aljazeera America 2014).

Second, homosexuality has been portrayed as a threat to Russia's children's psychological and moral health. Reflecting the fact that homosexuality remains widely understood as a disorder or illness, it is argued that minors must be protected from information that could lead to the perception that homosexuality or other nonheterosexual behavior is normal. They should not be exposed to such information when they are still developing psychologically because they are particularly vulnerable to corrupting influences. This line of argument, which is evident in the wording of the federal "antigay" law introduced in June 2013 that officially outlaws "propaganda of non-traditional sexual relations to minors" (Wilkinson 2014, 366) is further underpinned by popular conflation of homosexuality and pedophilia, and the belief that homosexuals and bisexuals aggressively seek to "recruit" young people to their way of life. As Putin commented in response to questions about whether LGBT people would be welcome at the Sochi Winter Olympics, "You can feel relaxed and calm [in Russia], but leave children alone please" (Walker 2014).

Finally, homosexuality and gender variance is viewed as a Western imposition that is aimed at infiltrating Russia and dooming it to the same fate as the decadent and morally corrupt West. The image of "Geiropa," or "Gay Europe," is especially salient in this respect (Riabova and Riabov 2013), being starkly contrasted with images of Russia that reference Holy Rus,[11] the notion of Moscow as the Third Rome, and Putin as the new defender of Christianity (Galstyan 2016), and also the Great Patriotic War and the country's fierce fight against fascism. Similar to the outrage generated by Pussy Riot's "Punk Prayer," failure to accord such imagery respect can lead to violent retribution. Internet personality Alena Piskun experienced this firsthand following the release of a video of a photoshoot in which, as Russian media outlet Life.ru (2013) described it, "gay freaks imitated a sexual act above the Eternal Flame in the Pantheon of Glory in Mamayev Kurgan," which is part of the memorial complex surrounding "The Motherland Calls!" statue in Volgograd. In addition to numerous demands to prosecute her for hooliganism or desecration of graves (Vershinina 2013), Piskun received death threats "almost daily," and an attack in a Moscow café left her with second-degree chemical burns to her eyes (Life.ru 2013). While anyone engaging in such behavior could reasonably expect to be widely condemned, in a hypermasculinist state that has made homophobia a defining feature of national identity (Wilkinson 2014), Piskun's queerness almost certainly intensified people's hostility towards her, reflecting her transgression of gender norms as well as social ones.

For both feminists and homosexuals, their status as a threat to Russia is reinforced in the public imagination through references to Mother Russia (Riabova and Romanova 2015). In addition to intensifying anti-Western sentiments, Mother Russia's role as a marker of Russianness tacitly implies that being feminist and/or LGBT is fundamentally incompatible with being Russian. Consequently, even before their transgressions of the moral and gender regime are explicitly articulated, queers have already been cast as "foreign agents" whose very presence in Russia is alien and dangerous.[12] The association is further strengthened in the case of homosexuality through discourses surrounding LGBT rights that present advocates of LGBT rights as "homofascists" who are seeking to impose their demands for special rights on Russian society (Reveal News 2016)—a discourse that implicitly references the defense of the Motherland against Nazi Germany as well as suggesting that LGBT rights are in contravention of democratic norms and processes in prioritizing the rights of a minority over those of the majority (Wilkinson 2014, 369).

Combining group-specific narratives of how the gender transgressions of feminists and homosexuals threaten (Mother) Russia's future with homophobia-tinged xenophobia has made the Unholy Queer Peril a very persuasive villain. Moreover, even if one is unconvinced by the Kremlin's narrative of Mother Russia in queer peril, it is virtually impossible to challenge, for to do so is in itself a violation of the gender regime of "traditional family values," simultaneously representing a treacherous failure to love and honor Mother Russia as well as a lack of confidence in the state's ability to fulfill its central protective function—or in other words, its masculinity.

CONCLUSION: PERFORMING GENDER, PROTECTING THE STATE

In creating the narrative of Mother Russia's queer imperilment, the hypermasculine Russian state was motivated by the need to demonstrate its manliness and in particular its ability to fulfill the logic of protection. However, as the analysis in this chapter has demonstrated, achieving this aim fundamentally relies not only on specific and extreme performances of masculinity, but also on idealized and highly traditional articulations and representations of femininity. The Russian state has implicitly recognized this dynamic in its efforts to promote and protect "traditional family values" at home and abroad. In international fora, Russia's efforts have focused on opposing moves to further gender equality or extend human rights protections to LGBT people (Filipovic 2013; Wilkinson 2014), often in cooperation with other "profamily" states such as the Holy See and organizations such as the World Congress of Families (Montgomery 2016).

Domestically, meanwhile, the Kremlin has sought to rehabilitate femininity—as represented by Mother Russia—and put it back to work in the service of the state to justify and uphold a traditional gender order that demands women's participation in the reproduction of the nation. In the absence of effective material and financial incentives for Russian women to take up this gender role, however, and facing the potential failure of being unable to control the reproduction of the nation, the remasculinizing Russian state resorted to presenting femininity as being existentially threatened by the Unholy Queer Peril—a narrative that has, perhaps surprisingly, demonstrated considerable and sustained persuasive power, as demonstrated by the passing of a federal anti-homopropoganda law in 2013 (Wilkinson 2014), and the decriminalization of "moderate" domestic violence in February 2017 (Walker 2017).

Yet as the analysis in this chapter has shown, the Kremlin's apparent saving of Mother Russia has been motivated primarily by the need to ensure the continued performance—and hence existence—of the hypermasculine state, which requires the contrast of hyperfemininity in order to be recognized and indeed to recognize itself. This points to a paradox not just for Russia, but for any hypermasculine state: while "queer" is reviled and rejected, it is also a vital component of its extreme gender order, providing an "other" against which the performance of both masculinity and femininity can be measured and corrected. This dynamic reveals the continued defining role of masculinity in practices of statehood and how, when gender norms are rejected, the logic of hypermasculinity can rapidly transform the state's already coercive promise of protection (Peterson 1992c, 32) into a promise of punishment that simultaneously affirms and undermines the state's masculinity. In the end, it is not Mother Russia that is saved, but the state itself.

NOTES

1. http://en.kremlin.ru/events/president/news/51888. Accessed March 27, 2017.
2. See, for example, http://www.telegraph.co.uk/
   news/picturegalleries/worldnews/9446015/

Fighting-hunting-shooting-and-fishing-with-Vladimir-Putin-Russias-man-of-action.html. Accessed March 27, 2017.

3. The Great Patriotic War began in 1941 and ended in 1945.

4. https://sovietposter.blogspot.com.au/2007_08_07_archive.html. Accessed March 27, 2017.

5. Volgograd was known as Tsaritsyn until 1925, when it was renamed Stalingrad in honor of Joseph Stalin. It was renamed Volgograd in 1961 as part of efforts under Khrushchev to dismantle the cult of personality that had developed around Stalin.

6. Male suicide rates in Russia increased from 43.9 per 100,000 in 1990 to 72.9 per 100,000 in 1995 and remained elevated at 70.6 per 100,000 in 2000 before declining to 58.1 per 100,000 in 2005 and 53.9 per 100,000 in 2006 (World Health Organization, http://www.who.int/mental_health/media/russ.pdf).

7. http://data.worldbank.org/indicator/SP.POP.TOTL?locations=RU. Accessed March 27, 2017.

8. http://en.kremlin.ru/events/president/news/19243. Accessed March 27, 2017.

9. "Homosexualist" and "homosexualism" are direct translations from the Russian and are used in contrast to "homosexual" and "homosexuality," both of which also exist in Russian, in keeping with the terms used by opponents of LGBT rights in Russia.

10. http://www.patriarchia.ru/db/text/2899463.html. Accessed April 9, 2017.

11. "Holy Rus" is an epithet that has been used to describe the Russian state and its predecessors since at least the fifteenth century (Cherniavsky 1958). The phrase evokes an Orthodox Christian empire of faith that has its origins in the ninth-century eastern Slavic state of Kievan Rus' and which continues to be have currency as part of the Russian Orthodox Church's contemporary geopolitical imagination (Suslov 2014).

12. While beyond the scope of this chapter, this xenophobic othering reflects a wider political trend that is most clearly evident in the Kremlin's adoption of a so-called "foreign agent" law that requires nongovernmental organizations to register with the Ministry of Justice if they receive any funding from foreign sources or engage in "political activities." Among those fined under the law have been LGBT organizations Side by Side and Coming Out (Human Rights Watch 2013), and as of December 2016 more than 145 organizations have been registered as "foreign agents" (Human Rights Watch 2016).

CHAPTER 8

A Global South State's Challenge to Gendered Global Cultures of Peacekeeping

LESLEY J. PRUITT

This chapter draws from and builds upon feminist (re)conceptualizations of the state. While peacekeeping is generally seen as an international activity, in practice it works as a federation of individual state troop contributions that remain mostly under state direction. Recognizing that *Gendered States* focused mostly on the liberal state and American and European trajectories, I reflect on and adapt the ideas from that book in considering how global South states may offer differently gendered contributions to international peacekeeping. I analyze an example of a state—India—creating spaces for women to participate in peacekeeping by developing the first all-female formed police unit (FFPU) deployed in United Nations (UN) peacekeeping. In doing so, this chapter analyzes gendered dynamics of the Indian state's role as a postcolonial state of the global South acting as a peacekeeping provider offering new avenues for women's participation. This influx of women into the historically male-dominated sphere of peacekeeping makes visible the gender of peacekeeping practice and poses complex questions around how states pursue international peace and security.

Given that in international peacekeeping men and masculine institutions remain the dominant actors and decision-makers, the FFPU represents innovation. However, in my research I found that at the UN a particular aversion arises when it comes to embracing solutions proposed by states of the global South—including postcolonial states such as India, deemed a "rising power." Such states are looked on suspiciously, and often assumed to be incapable of leadership on gender equity. Uncovering such assumptions and the logic underpinning them is important for better understanding and addressing intersecting inequalities that undermine women's access to peace and security. Globally such differences include the state or type of state in which one is born or situated, while in India in particular these differences include, but are not limited to, "class, caste, region, and religion" (Singh 2010, 169). Such differences intersect with and have significant implications for gender-based discrimination (Narain 2001).

The status quo of peacekeeping marginalizes the skills, needs, abilities, and perspectives of many women and maintains a hierarchical arrangement in which behaviors and traits associated with masculinity are seen as the "right" way of doing peacekeeping. One reason for continued masculinism in peacekeeping is that, while narratives around the need to incorporate women in peace and security have proliferated, dominant approaches to women's participation in peace and security tend to rely on discourses of individualism that deny or reject approaches that sometimes offer additional avenues for women's participation or entice more women to participate. Such discourses coincide with an aversion to, or the outright rejection of, changes to the structures of peacekeeping. Likewise, I suggest that such efforts may be curtailed or marginalized when they are understood to sit outside global culture, that is, global norms, around peacekeeping and/or gender equity at the UN. This may especially be the case when initiatives such as the FFPU come from countries that are assumed to be "behind" on gender equity as opposed to supposed "leaders" on the UN's Women, Peace and Security (WPS) agenda.

Despite the declaratory policy of countries supporting the WPS agenda (for more on WPS see True 2012; Shepherd 2011; Davies 2013), which sees gender equity and women's participation as crucial for sustainable peace, global implementation of the WPS agenda has been slow or staggered. In this context, the global culture of peacekeeping, as understood at the UN, may actually limit the ability of women to participate and their interest in doing so. Indeed, around the time of the FFPU's initial deployment, Conaway and Shoemaker (2008) noted, that UN peacekeeping missions had "failed to attract, retain, and advance the most qualified talent in leadership positions, threatening the implementation of demanding peace operations," and the absence of women, particularly women from non-Western states, in the staff and leadership of these missions was commonplace. Yet this chapter shows how states—following women's domestic activism and advocacy—may provide alternative pathways that could sidestep some of the "blue tape" to achieving increased participation by women.

INDIA'S "PEACEKEEPERS OF THE NATION" GO GLOBAL

In 2007, the first all-female formed police unit (FFPU) was deployed to the UN peacekeeping mission in Liberia. The contingent included 105 Indian women peacekeepers. These recruits came from a special paramilitary section of India's Central Reserve Police Force (CRPF)—an organization tasked with containing domestic insurgencies. Likewise, Indian media has referred to the CRPF as "the peacekeepers of the nation" (see, e.g., Staff Reporter 2008). The first FFPU contingent was declared a success, and was replenished annually until their final departure in February 2016 (Dickinson 2016).

The context and reasons behind how and why India developed the FFPU are more complex. However, in brief, the concept for the FFPU was made possible through a history of Indian women's activism and state support for all-female stations and units. Moreover, during his tenure as UN police adviser for the UN Department of Peacekeeping Operations (DPKO), Mark Kroeker aimed to recruit more women. In discussing this with Indian Permanent Mission staff, Kroeker learned about all-female police units operating in India. He inquired whether it might be possible to have such a group deployed as a formed police unit in UN peacekeeping. Around the same time, Kiran Bedi, a former UN DPKO police adviser, was also working to ensure India's women police could access opportunities for contributing to peacekeeping. To do so, she used her persuasion skills to draw links between the contributions Indian women police could make to peacekeeping and Indian state identity as coconstructed in an international system. She spoke of negotiating with Indian officials, explaining to one:

> Sir, if you send a formed unit . . . India would make a splash. . . . Indian women cops would stand out. . . . They've delivered. They're very good, and it will be very good for the country and the world over . . . you've got your strength, why hold it back? (Pruitt 2016, 39)

Such selling points appear to have been particularly important in getting the FFPU up and running. Moreover, as Walsh notes, "Obtaining outside funding for a state institution is a way to make the institution itself more valuable to the state, because elected representatives get 'credit' in the public eye for developing institutions that in fact cost the state very little" (Walsh 2008, 58).

It seems the FFPU did show it could deliver and make important contributions that reflected well on India. The FFPU's key role was providing security in Liberia. The intense schedule included long shifts six and a half days per week, filled with activities like quelling riots and patrolling with and training local Liberian police officers. My research on the FFPU, including fieldwork in Delhi, New York, and Monrovia, Liberia, has explored the key responsibility of the FFPU—providing security—and how the FFPU officers have taken on and carried out this role in Liberia. It appears that, while facing many challenges, the FFPU has succeeded in doing a great deal to break down barriers to women's participation in peacekeeping (Pruitt 2013). The FFPU officers' actions and public recognition received for them indicate that women, including those working in all-female units, can not only meet, but at times exceed, expectations around security provision, both in the traditional "law and order" sense of policing and in responding to gender-based crimes. This is significant, for women who may wish to take on careers as peacekeepers, for women in postconflict zones, and for women who may wish to have the option of reporting to female security personnel.

Yet my research also suggests that UN rhetoric around women in peacekeeping relies on a narrative of women peacekeepers as "naturally" good at what they do and expects them to be "superheroines" (Shepherd 2011) who can solve seemingly unsolvable problems by sheer willpower while taking on extra tasks at which they "naturally" excel. Relying on such gendered stereotypes may actually hinder women's participation in providing peace and security, as the expectations of them are magnified compared to their male peers. Indeed, FFPU members frequently take on a "second shift" where they serve, including providing dance workshops, hygiene training, and career fairs for women and girls (Pruitt 2016). These activities no doubt benefit local women where the FFPU is deployed. At the same time, in comparison to their male counterparts, women peacekeepers face a burden of extra expectations on their time in order to perform such activities. This is significant considering their already extensive standard working hours.

While the original FFPU was deemed a success and the unit was replaced annually for eight years, the UN remains hesitant about encouraging further FFPUs or even visibly supporting those that already exist. Why might that be, and what are the implications for participation by women from global South states in particular? States can institutionalize masculinist systems of domination, but can states also contribute to interrupting and disrupting them? These questions are particularly significant in the global system when this apparent disruption comes from the global South, given that these states have been positioned as "behind" on gender equality.

As Spivak (1995, 166) notes, the state can be both medicine and poison, so it is worth looking holistically at India's approach. Sometimes in India women have been instrumentalized to achieve the Hindu Right's goals, which Hasan (2010) argues have sidelined the agenda of women's rights. Likewise, in reference to issues like India's skewed sex ratio, Menon argues that Indian government officials and policymakers have focused solely on the numbers, without due care to the "actual lives of women and girls," which are seen as incidental in comparison to "the embarrassing figures," and also seen as "unbefitting of an 'emerging global power'" (Menon 2015, 5).

At the same time, several feminist scholars suggest that, for the many not able to effectively contest marginalization solely through individual action or will, the state may provide another avenue for posing challenges and (re)gaining some power and respect. After all, Spivak (2013) argues, the state is still the sole weapon the citizen, impacted by gender, race, and class, has to fight against the degradations brought by globalization. Moreover, states are increasingly seen as possibly buffering the negative impacts of global capitalism and neoliberalism. They may do so, for example, by providing a social safety net, and/or through asserting the rights of workers, in both paid and unpaid roles. Likewise, Tickner (2014, 69; see also Tickner in this volume) says women have often been able to access more power through states than through markets.

A key contention here is that when it comes to peacekeeping contributions, it appears that women need to be packaged not only as "adding value" but as doing so in ways that do not require significant changes to institutions or challenge the dominance of men and masculinity in existing structures. The case of the FFPU highlights that when initiatives incite significant change in gender dynamics, critics tend to resort to pointing to the state's perceived inability to "do gender" the "right" way. These perceptions of the "right" way may marginalize important contributions from the global South and postcolonial states more specifically, but the case of the FFPU also shows how a postcolonial state of the global South has been able to develop and maintain differently gendered approaches to peacekeeping that have had clear benefits, both for local women where they are deployed and for the women peacekeepers themselves.

What might a postcolonial state of the global South bring to peacekeeping and gender equity? The state here is understood "as an evolving site of struggle which represents gender relations as well as reconstructs them" (Walsh 2008, 50). In this way, the state is not a fixed entity or object, but rather a project in an ongoing state of flux including changing aims and engagement with and disengagement from inside and outside social forces; hence contextual analysis accounting for space, time, and cultures is required (Peterson 1992b, 4). Likewise, states are always susceptible to transformation; in studying states it is crucial to examine and acknowledge practices of opposition and resistance within and across them (Peterson 1992b, 4). It is not enough to categorize states as simply coherent or unified; instead, the parts that make up the state face blurred boundaries, push and pull factors, and prospects of domination, just as other social organizations do (Peterson 1992b, 3). So while the state may embody unique prospects and characteristics, such claims must necessarily be tempered.

Having been hailed as "the 'backbone' of UN peacekeeping" (Gowan and Singh 2013, 183), India has been a major contributor to UN peacekeeping since the 1950s, and is consistently in the three top troop-contributing countries. Having served in forty of sixty-five UN peace operations, India has made peacekeeping participation one of its clearest contributions to the UN (Gowan and Singh 2013). This can be understood in relation to India's positioning itself through its own constitution as a state with a clear "commitment to international peace and security" with a post–World War II commitment to contributing to decolonization (Banerjee 2013). Thus, India can be understood in the context of its being a postcolonial state of the global South with self-declared interest in leading on issues that affect other postcolonial states and the global South more broadly.

As Basu convincingly highlights, despite widely held notions that the global North has been responsible for developing and executing the UN Women, Peace and Security (WPS) agenda, it is crucial to identify and analyze the significant contributions that have been made by global South actors, including governments, NGOs, and other international and civil society organizations. As she notes, participation in peacekeeping, including the deployment of women peacekeepers, can be seen as one way the global South also "writes" the WPS agenda and takes ownership of implementing WPS and contributing to its evolution (Basu 2016b).

The point here is not to claim that the Indian postcolonial state is inherently better at providing security for women (or women better than men at providing security) but rather to suggest that overlooking or denying the prospects for significant and valuable contributions from such states and the women peacekeepers they deploy can have serious implications. These implications include, but are not restricted to, limiting options for achieving gender equity along with sustainable peace at a global level. Moreover, such marginalization of postcolonial states and global South states may more broadly lend itself toward neocolonialist assumptions or practices.

Scholars have often theorized in terms of the need for protecting women from the state, or the frequent occurrence of states failing to protect women (see, e.g., Walsh 2016; Nduka-Agwu 2009). At the same time, there is a need for understanding alternative roles states may play, including in changing discourses in ways that may situate women as capable of providing security and simultaneously improve women's access to security (see, e.g., Agius in this volume). As Harrington argues, since states create, focus, and condense political power, they may be understood as "the best friend, not the enemy, of feminists" because states can significantly disrupt "the patriarchal/economic oppression of those in the lower reaches of class, sex, and race hierarchies" (1992, 66).

While Harrington refers specifically to the liberal state and her work is situated predominantly in discussions of European and American contexts, the Indian case of the FFPU shows a postcolonial state of the global South—and one widely considered an emerging power—attempting just such a disruption in the realm of global security. Indeed, following Harrington's points, one might interpret the FFPU case as evidence of the state acting as a "political power close to home" that can "create spaces of freedom" for women (Harrington 1992, 76).

Since Harrington wrote those words over two decades ago, the world arguably has seen numerous examples of states adopting women-friendly policies or policies aimed at transforming gender. For example, Sweden has championed what Foreign Minister Margot Wallström referred to as a "feminist foreign policy," while Hillary Clinton, during her tenure as US Secretary of State, took a similar direction, with policy documents stating the explicit intention for the State Department to integrate "women and girls into everything we do" (Basu 2016, 263).

The Indian FFPU likewise represents an example of the state creating spaces for women to participate in peacekeeping. Here the state is not merely doing so at the state level, but acting as an entrepreneur in taking the idea out to the global context of international security. Despite limits on states remaining the key actors in providing international peacekeeping, the fact that the FFPU was implemented and remained deployed for so long suggests that peacekeeping is open to transformation and that through their peacekeeping policies and practices states may significantly change the ways peacekeeping occurs.

The FFPU highlights how states can propose unique directions and succeed in implementing a variety of approaches to the shared goal of international security. Indian options for policymaking and practice are different from those of states of the global North, or states most often seen as "leading" on gender equity internationally. This might not be such a bad thing. In fact, postcolonial states and/or global South states like India may be able to sidestep some of the limits states situated as "leaders" on advancing gender equity in peacekeeping face due to the norms these "leaders" already have in place. After all, these norms appear to allow only a very limited range of approaches to fit into what is deemed legitimate or appropriate participation by women and may be unnecessarily restrictive.

The FFPU's presence is the result of a state process in which male domination of violence and protection is challenged and made visibly political. Typical peacekeeping, relying on the dominant male protector model, represents a framework in which "when the state *does* intervene [in violence against women], it typically does so from within a patriarchal ideology that at best 'protects' women while simultaneously reproducing masculinist givens that ensure women's "need for protection" (Peterson 1992c, 46). Hence Peterson and others have insisted on the need for "asking structural questions about the processes by which male domination and violence are reproduced" (Peterson 1992c, 46).

The FFPU may challenge existing norms around gender, peace, and security and make space for new norms in which the presence of women as security providers and protectors is seen as legitimate and acceptable. This is a significant contribution. It occurs in the international normative environment wherein states can be seen as the chief managers of gendered power relations and where states use power through state actions, approaches, customs, and procedures that make up and control "acceptable forms and images of social activity and individual and collective identity" (Peterson 1992c, 45).

Including more women in peacekeeping through an FFPU may be a complex, sometimes contradictory approach, but it critically makes space for much-needed thinking around broader political questions of gender, peace, and security. If we are to recognize power dimensions in unequal social relations and different cultural forms and acknowledge "the complex and sometimes contradictory interaction of systems of power . . . what is required is *not* simply the addition of women to masculine abstractions but a transformation in our understanding of politics, power, and political identities" (Peterson 1992c, 55). The introduction and continuation of the FFPU continuously challenges dominant understandings, including around how postcolonial states of the global South, often seen as "lagging behind" on issues associated with the Women, Peace and Security agenda, can take on significant leadership roles, contesting existing norms to advance more gender-inclusive notions of global security and protection.

ADVANCING GENDER EQUITY IN PEACE AND SECURITY:
THE CONSTRAINTS OF GLOBAL CULTURE

I suggest that the FFPU represents a divergence from norms of "global culture." Paris (2003, 441–443) argues that the international normative environment—"global culture"—significantly influences the way peace-keeping is understood and carried out. Furthermore, he contends that peacekeeping institutions are prone to designing and putting in place strategies that reflect norms conforming to global culture (Paris 2003, 441–443). At the same time, Paris says, peacekeeping institutions reject strategies that differ from existing norms, even when said strategies might have a greater chance of achieving the goals of peacekeeping. Likewise, he suggests, "Global culture limits the range of possible policies that peace-keepers can realistically pursue," as "peacekeepers are effectively precluded from pursuing these strategies, regardless of how effective such approaches might be at promoting peace" (2003, 441, 443). Paris proposes that the log-ics of appropriateness (in light of global norms) and effectiveness are not mutually exclusive. In focusing on how the "appropriateness" logic shapes peacekeeping, he highlights that looking deeper at how global culture affects peacekeeping can improve our bases for understanding reasons for behavior of those charged with peacekeeping (Paris 2003, 444).

The character of peacekeeping is not "determined" by global culture; rather, global norms significantly and repeatedly shape the way peace operations are designed and conducted, though those charged with peace-keeping could also opt to resist existing norms by implementing policies and practices that challenge them (Paris 2003, 462). As global norms are evolving concurrently with international behavior, shifts in norms could over time lessen concerns about particular policies or practices that are currently seen as normatively unacceptable (Paris 2003, 463). Paris (2003, 451) suggests that peacekeeping institutions will apparently dismiss out of hand strategies seen as contravening existing global norms without refer-ence to chances of enhancing effectiveness or peacebuilding, as sometimes worries about norm adherence will be prioritized over reflections on oper-ational effectiveness.

Analysis of the FFPU suggests such initiatives—those that contest existing global culture around gender equity and peacekeeping—may make inroads to challenging norms while also facing obstacles to more wide-spread adoption. While a range of international conventions and resolu-tions suggest that international agreement exists between states around women's rights, women's ability to access these rights is contested locally and globally, within and between states. States can and do operate in multifaceted ways domestically and internationally—they may act to limit women's access to their rights at home or abroad, but at the same time the state may function as a promoter of women's rights in the global community.[1] For example, states may challenge global cultures of peacekeeping and the gendered norms they represent.

In my interviews with UN officials and staff, it appeared that the creation and deployment of the FFPU brought up a number of gendered fears, concerning both women's participation in security and more specifically their participation as women in all-women units. The latter highlights the concerns relating to a global culture of peacekeeping in which the participation of women is commonly seen as "appropriate" or "legitimate" only if women participate in units predominantly populated by men. One former official discussed encountering attitudinal barriers to the FFPU's deployment, saying:

> I think when the discussion was there and the idea of the FFPU emerged the question was, Can the Indian government actually produce it? Do they have the right equipment, qualifications, and is the mission willing to have them? . . . The questions started coming: Are you sure an all-woman unit is really appropriate?

The response, the official said, was simply to state, "They're either capable or they're not. If not, they shouldn't deploy. But not only are they capable, they are excellent. No one ever asked if we should have an all-male unit. Why should we ask if all-female?" Delving into and critically engaging with the logics underlying those questions of whether all-female units are appropriate (especially as they are posed without asking the same questions about all-male units) is crucial for fostering sustainable peace in which women can take part in peace and security initiatives and access peace and security in their own lives.

Adhering to a narrow view in which women must participate in existing male-dominated structures to be seen as "appropriate" or "legitimate" overshadows one key way women's inclusion in peace and security initiatives is limited. A former high-ranking UN official who served in Liberia noted that, although the FFPU was professional and successful, the official still

> heard the FFPU of India was not one of the best we have professionally. People say it's just because they're women and not on par and I think it's dangerous. . . . That's why I underline they are very professional. I don't want them to be a token of gender parity.

Statements like this indicate a problem wherein women—without basis in evidence but rather solely due to their gender—are often assumed to be tokens, less qualified, and less professional. Such assumptions do not tend to be made about male peacekeepers on the basis of their gender. Moreover, a common assumption that somehow women's being situated in single-sex units makes them less relevant, qualified, or appropriate—when that assumption has not been made of all-male units—serves to disclose the hierarchical gendered assumptions still present in peacekeeping operations.

This "appropriateness" narrative undermines greater understanding of the ways women may enhance peace and security when deployed as peacekeepers. Sticking to existing global culture around women's involvement in peacekeeping, without engaging critically with other possibilities, may actually stall or limit prospects for advancing peace and security and gender equity. Breaking down such limiting attitudes will require both men and women at the UN and beyond to challenge the existing global culture when it comes to gender norms.

Moreover, effectively advancing gender equity in peacekeeping requires recognizing and challenging the dominance of approaches that individualize gendered barriers women face to participation. After all, restricting women's participation mostly to individual women willing and able to deploy in mostly male units has clearly not led to significant advances in women's participation. Significant changes may be realized when states refuse to accept the individualizing narrative that says women need to fit into mostly male units and instead offer the option of participating in women's only units.

INDIVIDUALIZATION, RANKINGS, AND WHAT WE MISS OUT ON UNDER NEOLIBERALISM

When theorizing on state contributions to peacekeeping and individualizing narratives of gender equity, it is worth investigating the broader social, political, and economic context that has facilitated and reinforced such narratives. After all, the global culture of peacekeeping reflects assumptions that situate individual women fitting into existing structures as the only appropriate or legitimate way for women to take part in peacekeeping operations. This can place constraints on how many women will participate, which women will participate, and how they will participate. Likewise, this limits the range of options for conducting effective peacekeeping, which necessarily involves contributions from both women and men. So how did this individualizing narrative of gender equity emerge?

I propose that in this context understanding the spread of neoliberal economic policies and related discourses is crucial. These policies and discourses have eroded the power and centrality of the state, while spreading a dominant discourse of individualized, market-based solutions that ignore structural impediments. Since the late 1970s, neoliberalism has grown and developed as the dominant model of how economies should work to promote growth. Endorsed by the World Bank and International Monetary Fund, neoliberal approaches became more widespread in the 1980s, when economic crises and war led many developing countries to request loans from these two Western-based organizations, which provided the financial assistance "on condition that the neoliberal model was implemented" (Jacobson 2013, 228).

This neoliberal view has come into favor with geopolitical elites, economists trained in wealthy countries, and policymakers working for related global institutions. The framework relies on the assumption that politics and culture can be separated from economics, and that any emerging issues will best be resolved by free-market initiatives. However, while advocates of neoliberalism define it as a technical economic approach, scholars have noted that it is actually impossible to separate out neoliberalism and a specific ideological lens (Peterson and Runyan 2010). Hence, the term "neoliberalism" is used here to refer to the hegemonic political discourse that envisions interactions in the world and the world itself as typified by the neoliberal ideals of privatization, freedom, choice, and individualization (Couldry 2010).

Neoliberal approaches deny or ignore structural adaptations to deal with structural inequalities such as those related to class, race, and gender (Duggan 2004). Thus gender inequality is rendered personal, with individuals expected to overcome obstacles by making the "right" or "best" choices in how to navigate the ostensibly free marketplace of ideas and opportunities. This marginalizes questions around how the structure of institutions, or institutional policies and practices, may exclude women from participation. In the case of peacekeeping, for example, through the neoliberal lens, women as individuals are expected to seek out opportunities within existing structures, rather than push states to create new structures or adapt old ones to better accommodate them—as India has done with the implementation of the FFPU.

I suggest that existing global cultures of peacekeeping incorporate neoliberal discourse, as institutions such as the UN tend to favor a position in which they legitimize the strategies they are taking—in this case talking a lot about needing more women in peacekeeping but expecting them to fit into the male-dominated status quo. At the same time, they tend to discount strategies that diverge from existing global approaches—like the FFPU, a women-only space for women to participate in peacekeeping—as not the "right" kind of feminism for institutionalization. Of course, not all UN staff I interviewed opposed FFPUs, but it did appear to be the dominant view at the UN in terms of the global culture of peacekeeping, or dominant norms around legitimate or appropriate ways to involve women in peacekeeping.

As one former senior official said, "We were on one hand pleased, but it really wasn't what we were on about with gender mainstreaming. We'd rather see a mixed-gender contingent like the Nigerians." His lauding Nigerian efforts to demonstrate a more appropriate or successful approach is particularly interesting, since, according to a formed police unit coordinator in Liberia, the "Nigerian peacekeeping force at the time was 80% male and 20% female, but the women cooked, cleaned, and did administrative work, not policing" (Pruitt 2016, 110). These limitations have been corroborated by UN reports, which describe Nigeria's inclusion of women peacekeepers in mixed-gender battalions as "a *potential* best practice, not as a best practice. The reason is that these peacekeepers hold supportive as opposed to direct impact roles" (UNMIL 2010, 46).

There exists a hierarchy of ways in which women might be "appropriately" involved in peacekeeping, and individually choosing to take part in mostly male units is situated as best by many observers. Notably, this is the way the few women from the global North who participate in peacekeeping tend to do so, since, as Hautzinger notes, these countries are less likely to have gender-specific policing, because they tend to see its disadvantages as greater than its advantages (Hautzinger 2007). FFPUs are compared unfavorably and treated with skepticism often relating back to the type of state offering the initiative. As one European female officer working in the UN Mission in Liberia stated of the FFPU,

> You've even got to look at the culture of the countries that they come from— and it's like safety in numbers, sending the women over together. . . . We've had very few, if any, Indian IPOs [individual police officers] here that are females. . . . I think that I'd rather see more [of those] actually than [them] coming as a safe pack.

When it comes to gender equality and the status of women, such mind-sets that deny contributions from India appear to be based at times on assumptions that "women in postcolonial societies are by default oppressed, whereas those in the Western countries are liberated, echoing [Gayatri Chakravorty] Spivak's sarcastic observation that it requires white men to save brown women from brown men" (Liebowitz and Zwingel 2014, 374–375).

One way this hierarchy of appropriateness gets constructed is through international institutions' widespread practice of measuring and ranking states on gender equality (Liebowitz and Zwingel 2014, 374). In 2013, for example, India ranked 101st in in the World Economic Forum's Global Gender Gap Report (World Economic Forum 2013). The following year saw an apparent decline, with India ranked 114th (World Economic Forum 2014). Developing and analyzing data in this way "serves to reinscribe neocolonialist understandings of gender (in)equality, where Europe is nearly 'perfect' and the barbarism of the 'others' has created poor, uneducated, abused women" (Liebowitz and Zwingel 2014, 375). Overall, the most common approaches to measuring gender equality "tell—directly and indirectly—a limited, misleading, neocolonialist story about what gender equality is and to what extent and where it has been realized" (Liebowitz and Zwingel 2014, 369).

These ways of constructing gender equality predominantly as a measurable outcome where only certain approaches count seriously impacts understandings of what still needs doing, where, and how (Liebowitz and Zwingel 2014, 369). For example, one might assume from the European countries' rankings[2] that they have solved the problem of gender inequality, yet many of them deploy consistently small numbers of women in peacekeeping themselves and they certainly could not be seen as having solved the problem of women's inequitable access to postconflict peace, security, and justice. As it stands, women continue to make up a very small proportion of peacekeepers deployed in UN missions globally. Take Sweden, for example, with the self-declared feminist foreign policy noted earlier. In 2012, of Sweden's sixty-nine uniformed UN peacekeepers deployed, only twenty were female (Heldt 2012)—while this proportion is still significantly greater than what most countries have managed, at less than 29 percent, it is far from gender parity.

I do not suggest that the measures taken into account in global rankings are unimportant. Certainly most, if not all of them, deserve significant attention and action. However, when positioned as comparing countries, such rankings can perpetuate the discourse of hierarchy that suggests in some places the goal of gender equality has been or is nearly completed and that it is possible or even easy to "measure just how close a country is to this goal" (Liebowitz and Zwingel 2014, 374). The rankings thus render invisible the ways in which these measures are often inadequate, partial, and address only a very small range of issues relating to gender equality (Liebowitz and Zwingel 2014, 374). They inspire criticisms and commentaries like the one from the European officer above without equivalent reflection on how limited progress toward gender equality in policing and peacekeeping has been in global North states.

Such rankings are fostered by neoliberal logics that deny the diversity of women's experience and limit what actions might be taken to foster gender equity in peace and security. In particular, approaches like the FFPU, which are seen as failing a "legitimacy" test of the global culture of gender equality, are written off without consideration of further application. Such approaches overshadow innovations from states from the global South, including postcolonial states, as they are frequently positioned as not measuring up when it comes to knowledge and ability needed to advance gender equity in peacekeeping or otherwise. Within this context, it appears that decision-makers and other security actors tend toward skepticism of contributions to gender equality from "low ranking" states like India, despite their widely accepted position as leaders in some senses in peacekeeping.

Common assumptions exist around who can "do" gender the "right" way, with the assumed right way being the way women from the global North tend to participate, though they do so infrequently. Some women in the United States and Europe might also be willing to join peacekeeping missions if they had the option of participating in an all-women unit, but since only one model of women's participation (as a minority in a male-majority, typically hypermasculine environment) is seen as legitimate or "real," those women remain excluded, too. Likewise, the aversion to adding further women-only units may actually hinder the participation of women from around the world in peacekeeping.

While hierarchical discourses situate Western or global North approaches to gender equity in peacekeeping at the top, as the problem-solving leaders, research suggests that women peacekeepers from these states often face dangers from their own male colleagues (Simić 2010). Nonetheless, the presumption is made that some countries have solved these problems. At the same time, norms uncritically valorizing global North solutions to gender equality have overshadowed important contributions being made by global South states and postcolonial states, which tend to be written off as bad places for women's rights, as compared to "good" approaches reflecting neoliberal individualism.

CONCLUSION

Effective moves toward implementing UN Security Council Resolution 1325 and the broader WPS agenda will not be served by assumptions that only some states, or only certain kinds of states, can contribute. Rather, a plurality of approaches are needed and useful. My research suggests that the FFPU has led to important outcomes around women's participation in peacekeeping. The potential for such contributions by postcolonial states or global South states more broadly should not be overlooked. After all, investigating the FFPUs suggests that this Indian approach may offer useful insights while providing significant opportunities for women, outcomes that could be easily missed if we looked only through the "western eyes" (Mohanty 1988) of individualized, marketized approaches to measuring the impact of peacekeeping or outcomes of gender equity initiatives.

This chapter focused on the introduction of the Indian FFPU in UN peacekeeping, while engaging in a broader critical analysis of approaches to pursuing gender equity in peace and security. I propose that approaches to implementing the WPS agenda may be limited by an overreliance on dominant global discourses that presume existing equality, treat equality as sameness, and see gender equity as a quantifiable good that can only be legitimate or appropriate when conducted in ways that align with particular, global North approaches while denying the way differences that intersect with gender can influence gendered participation. This approach universalizes experiences of a small minority of women in the global North, and does so in a way that likely hinders prospects for more gender equitable participation in peace and security. Scholars, policymakers, and practitioners could all stand to back away from the rankings obsession and instead recognize the need for complexity, nuance, and attention to differences both within and between states, cultures, and genders.

NOTES

1. Consider, for example, the "feminist foreign policy" approaches noted earlier, including from the United States, where women's rights also remain restricted in several areas and women make only $0.78 for $1.00 earned by a man.
2. In 2015, for example seven of the top ten countries were European states. See World Economic Forum (2015).

CHAPTER 9

The Gendered State and the Emergence of a Postconflict, Postdisaster, Semiautonomous State

Aceh, Indonesia

KATRINA LEE-KOO

Amid the devastation wrecked upon societies by disaster and conflict lies opportunity. As states begin the task of rebuilding, the foundational values and structures of the state can also be reimagined. This creates a chance to reshape gendered social and political relations. Yet this opportunity is frequently missed. Instead, recovery from disaster and conflict is premised upon a discourse of urgency. This discourse permits the dismissal of values such as gender equality in favor of more "urgent" needs. Seeing equality as something that can wait for later, or as an indulgence in a crisis, political power-brokers at local and global levels instead focus their attention on familiar, formidable, and traditional state-based agendas and practices. These agendas and practices are patriarchal in design and leave unchallenged preexisting social and political values regarding gender. Instead, this discourse seeks to replicate and repair them in a rapid return to normalcy. As "state formations constitute power relations" (Peterson 1992a, 39), this normalcy reproduces a gendered hierarchy of power that disempowers women and uses state-making processes to constrain their ability to pursue equality. This has been noted across the world: in East Germany after the collapse of the Berlin Wall (Bleiker 2000), amid crisis in

Kashmir (Parashar 2011), in the aftermath of the 1983–2001 hostilities in Sri Lanka (Harris 2004), and in the recovery from the 2010 earthquake in Haiti (Duramy 2014, 137–152).

Aceh—at the northernmost tip of Indonesia—offers another such missed opportunity. Aceh became a semiautonomous region in 2006 in the wake of a three-decade-long conflict and the devastating 2004 Indian Ocean tsunami. Aceh did not become a fully independent state; rather it is classified as a special territory of Indonesia. Under the 2006 Law on Governing Aceh, Aceh can undertake independent local elections, create local laws, undertake administrative arrangements, and retain majority ownership of its natural resources (Miller 2009, 170–182) while still remaining part of Indonesia. The establishment of these arrangements in the aftermath of the tsunami gave Aceh an opportunity to enshrine women's equal participation in its governance. However, this did not occur. Instead, a set of postconflict, postdisaster political arrangements steeped in patriarchal values was established. This form of patriarchy prioritized masculinist structures, cultures, and identities. In doing so, it reinforced traditional gendered divisions between public and private space, and gendered constructions of roles and responsibilities in society (Walby 1990). This has seen the exclusion of women as legitimate political actors and deems women's experiences as largely nonpolitical events. The cementing of these values in the foundation of the emerging governance structure of Aceh has—in turn—made it difficult for the nonetheless strong women's rights community to make significant progress for women in key areas of political and social life.

With a focus on Aceh, this chapter demonstrates how the discourse of crisis and urgency facilitates the reinstatement of gendered state logics. More specifically, this chapter identifies two types of cooperative patriarchal values that enable this. The first is *local patriarchal values* that have reasserted themselves in Aceh in the wake of the tsunami. These are based upon persisting conflict masculinities, emerging patronage politics, and renewed religious paternalism (Afrianty 2015). The second is *international patriarchal values* that this chapter describes as pragmatic patriarchy. Openly, it remains rhetorically committed to global frameworks of women's participation, but it is nonetheless regulated by a discourse of crisis and urgency, which allows gender to be de-emphasized and places it as a lower-order priority. In combination, these forms of patriarchy have become the lifeblood of Acehnese governance, running through every major political and social organ. In the decade since peace, such patriarchal values have been difficult to challenge. The long-term consequence is that Acehnese women remain excluded from political processes.

To demonstrate this argument, this chapter begins with an examination of the peace process and early relief and recovery programs in the months after the tsunami. The failure to include gender equality at its conception meant that women particularly were marginalized from the reconstruction of the state. Second, this chapter illustrates the difficulty of challenging patriarchal structures once they are established. Examining women's participation in recent elections, the evolution of sharia law, and the politics of international development assistance reveals these gendered dynamics.

FROM GENDERED CONFLICT TO PATRIARCHAL PEACE

The experiences of men and women during the civil conflict in Aceh reflect the culturally and socially constructed gendered roles of the Acehnese population. The conflict itself was a bid for independence from the central Indonesian government in Jakarta that began in 1976 and ran with sporadic levels of intensity until the tsunami hit in 2004 (Aspinall 2009). While it is often described as an independence struggle, several factors were at play (see Miller 2009, 3–9). These included economic and resource exploitation—particularly of the natural gas and oil reserves, Jakarta's repressive approach to dealing with Aceh, and the presence within the province of a strong regional and ethnic identity that was independent of Jakarta (see Schulze 2003). Rizal Sukma sums it up as follows: "At the risk of oversimplifying, the sources of the problem can be grouped into four basic aspects: economic exploitation, centralism and uniformity, military repression, and the politics of impunity" (quoted in Human Rights Watch 2001, 23). Passing through three phases, the conflict had periods of intense fighting and major human rights violations (see Drexler 2006). The overall death toll of the conflict is contested. Aspinall (2009, 2) suggests it sits somewhere between 12,000 and 20,000 people, while the Aceh Reintegration Agency suggest that around 33,000 Acehnese were killed, or around 0.75 percent of the population (quoted in Aspinall 2008, 8).

The contestation regarding the number of deaths is indicative of a broader lack of data regarding the experiences of civilians in the conflict. While there remains both individual and communal knowledge, there is nonetheless a public shroud over it. This has been facilitated by a number of factors. First, there is a lack of independently recorded data on the conflict, largely because of the difficulty for researchers or observers in access to Aceh during the conflict period. Jakarta tightly controlled information about the conflict, and access to the region by international humanitarian workers, journalists, or researchers was extremely difficult. Second, there was little outside willingness to intervene in the conflict to seek a peaceful resolution. Regionally, neighboring states like Australia instituted a blanket policy of supporting Indonesia's territorial integrity that also included West Papua and East Timor (see Burke 2008). While there are a few reports from nongovernmental organizations (NGOs) such as Amnesty International and Human Rights Watch, there is a lack of consistent reporting throughout the conflict.

The available research on gender-based experiences of the conflict is even thinner. While men were the primary combatants, it has been reported that 79 percent of women experienced combat (IOM et al. 2007, 30). There are reports of widespread sexual violence against civilian women, including accusations that the Indonesian military engaged in rape and sexual slavery (Siapno 2010, 172). Amnesty International reported in 2004 that there had been "a long-established pattern of rape and other sexual crimes against women in [Aceh]" (2004, 37). Gendered violence also included the illegal detention and imprisonment by Indonesian forces of women suspected of providing support to members of the Gerakan Aceh Merdeka (Free Aceh Movement). Similarly, female relatives of GAM members were held hostage in attempts to lure male combatants out of hiding (Amnesty International 2004, 37–40). There have also been claims that GAM used Acehnese women as human shields during security sweeps by Indonesian forces, or abandoned them to face Indonesian interrogations (Siapno 2010, 187). Moreover, women were targeted for gendered physical and sexual violence, abduction, torture, and forced movement; had property confiscated and destroyed; and frequently witnessed violence against others (see IOM 2007). In the wake of the death of their husband, women became solely responsible for families. Between 1989 and 1998, Amnesty International reported, three thousand women were widowed. Against this backdrop of violence, Kamaruzzaman (2008, 15) points to women's resilience as central to maintaining communities throughout the conflict period:

> Acehnese women played strategic roles, generated bright ideas and were able to find unique ways to survive. They were able to become agents for change, performing negotiations between the two parties involved in the conflict or engaging in efforts to save their husbands, sons or their community. When insecurity forced men to flee their villages, women became the main breadwinners and decision-makers and took over most of the social roles played by men in their community life.

There remains, however, a strong social stigma attached to women talking publicly about their conflict-related experiences. Against the backdrop of a densely patriarchal culture, Acehnese women have reported that they consider their conflict experiences as being less significant than men's, or less significant than the losses endured during the tsunami (see Siapno 2001). Moreover, women reported being concerned about social backlash for reporting incidents such as sexual violence. For instance, a sixty-year-old woman reported:

> Nobody has reported about the rapes here, as if it never happened, when it actually happened to us. This is unfair. The village head and other officials said, "Don't ever let us hear that someone reported these rapes. It brings shame to all our people and the village government. Don't spread such nonsensical shame."
> (Quoted in Clarke 2008, 21)

Reporting of gendered violence that took place during the conflict becomes even more precarious in the wake of the introduction of sharia law, which will be discussed in further detail below.

In addition to civilian experiences, a number of Acehnese women engaged in combat and performed combat-related functions. While there is little formal or published information, estimates suggest that there were about three thousand female GAM fighters, known as *Pasukan Inong Balee*. Shadia Marhaban suggests that as part of these forces, women performed an important role as intelligence gatherers, arms and personnel smugglers, and logistics and networking agents in supporting GAM's struggle against the Indonesian state (Marhaban 2011).

There was also a strong movement among Acehnese women to pursue peace. Women were among the first groups to speak formally and collectively for an end to the conflict. In February 2000, 486 women participated in the first All Acehnese Women Congress to discuss their wartime experiences and plan for peace (Kamaruzzaman 2008). This meeting was among several stop-start movements toward transitioning the conflict. In a more organized capacity, women also actively spoke out against the violence. Organizations such as Flower Aceh and the Acehnese Democratic Women's Organisation negotiated their way through conflict to support women, provide basic necessities to communities, and demand peace. Women's groups engaged in a number of tactics such as peaceful campaigning, lobbying, information dissemination, distribution of emergency relief, negotiation between conflicting parties, and data collection for the purposes of documenting human rights abuses. Their activities were undertaken in extremely precarious circumstances. As noted above, many of these women faced intimidation, terror, and sexual and other physical violence in order to carry out their programs.

This brief overview demonstrates that the civil conflict in Aceh followed patterns that are familiar to feminist scholars of armed conflict. Women performed multiple functions, often simultaneously: victims as well as agents of violence, combat supporters, advocates of peace, and heads of households and communities. However, gendered cultural constraints, biases, and difficulties in reporting these experiences have meant that they have largely gone unacknowledged in the public sphere. Instead, the social history of the conflict remains dominated by patriarchal themes of male combatants and territorial claim. The important relationship between the gendered experiences of the conflict and the gendered politics of the Indonesian and Acehnese states remains largely unexplored by participants and observers. This lack of feminist curiosity, as will be discussed further below, is reflected in the peace process that took place in the immediate aftermath of the tsunami.

Aceh was the epicenter of the tsunami that hit countries bordering the Indian Ocean on December 26, 2004. It killed over 165,000 Acehnese (UNORC 2009, 4), constituting a majority of the estimated 250,000 deaths in eighteen countries. As a poor, developing, and conflict-ridden area, it had little capacity to anticipate or resist the tsunami's sudden impact. The gendered consequences of the tsunami were immediately evident. The fatality rate of women was disproportionate in comparison with men killed by the tsunami's initial impact. Oxfam reported that in four villages surveyed in the Aceh Besar district, male survivors outnumbered women survivors by a ratio of almost three to one (Oxfam 2005). A number of explanations have been offered to account for this imbalance, which reflects the gendered roles and responsibilities in Aceh: women were more vulnerable because they were not taught to swim; as primary caregivers they were attempting to save children and the elderly; their quick movement was restricted by their traditional clothing; at home on a Sunday morning, they were unaware of public announcements; and many men in coastal areas were out at sea and did not experience the impact of the wave (Oxfam 2005; True 2012, 168–172).

Women remained vulnerable in the period immediately following the tsunami. In 2005, the United Nations Population Fund (UNFPA) reported that the most common problems facing women resulted from a lack of gender-sensitivity with regard to emergency relief arrangements. Women faced a lack of feminine hygiene products, limited access to maternal and reproductive health services, a shortage of proper latrines and bathing facilities, a paucity of clean water in the camps, and inadequate access to humanitarian aid. Added to this was the increased vulnerability to gender-based violence during the emergency period. This included trafficking, sexual assault, domestic violence, and harassment (UNFPA 2005, Felten-Biermann 2006, 82–83). Gender-based violence also included verbal and physical attacks by radical Islamic clerics who held Acehnese women's "impious" behavior (such as a failure to wear head coverings) as the cause of the tsunami (Meo 2005).

The extent to which gendered needs were adequately addressed varied depending upon the interrelation of local political and cultural idiosyncrasies within the context of aid provision. Felten-Biermann (2006, 83–84) argues that "the different needs of men and women during crisis intervention and reconstruction were not taken into account . . . by most of the foreign non-governmental organizations involved in the tsunami relief. Many times, women are not even mentioned as a target group." While there is also evidence of good practice, there is sufficient evidence to suggest that gender awareness was inconsistent and poor. Furthermore, as there were 3,645 registered NGOs working on the ground in Aceh—many of which worked independently or in loose coalition with one another—a coordinated approach to emergency relief was lacking that could effectively mainstream gender in the overall approach (see Mazurana et al. 2011). This is true not just during the emergency, but also in the longer-term humanitarian operations.

As the emergency subsided, women became primary caregivers to children, the elderly, and the injured in extended families. Women also took on greater responsibility for household work, now undertaken in cramped conditions (such as temporary camps that had been established by local and international agencies) and often without access to water and household facilities. Many women did not see the camps as safe for themselves and their families, and this led to a higher rate of female-headed households among those internally displaced within towns and villages (Mazurana et al. 2011, 18). As a result, women's workloads dramatically increased. Women had less time to engage in public sphere programs such as receiving aid, or providing representation in decision-making processes regarding the distribution of aid. Unless they were directly targeted for aid, women's access was limited and reliant upon redistribution by male family members. A general (though not universal) failure to target a gender-specific aid program toward women in the early postemergency period saw the social exclusion of Acehnese women by limiting the physical capacity of women to participate in public sphere activities, such as attending meetings and creating a benchmark for post-tsunami activities. In short, a culture of women's inclusion had not been established, either in the discourse or in the practice of emergency relief. This both sidelined women and encouraged the embedding of a patriarchal culture in the peace process.

The tsunami provided a catalyst for the peace process, but it was not the only precursor. Peace and peace processes had begun with a failed "humanitarian pause" in May 2000 and a failed Cessation of Hostilities Agreement in 2002 (see Aspinall 2008). While these failures were interspersed with periods of violent conflict, the election in 2004 of Susilo Bambang Yudhoyono and the weakening of GAM forces as a result of the introduction of martial law had facilitated ongoing negotiations (Jones 2008, 7). Movements toward peace had already begun. However, the tsunami created "an undeniably tragic 'window of opportunity' for conflict transformation in Aceh" (Le Billon and Waizenegger 2007, 422). In the wake of the tsunami, the urgent need for peace had two imperatives: first the unfathomable loss of life caused by the tsunami placed the ongoing civil conflict in an unacceptable moral context (Schulze 2003, 23). The idea that conflict should be ongoing amid those circumstances—particularly as they world watched on—was untenable. Second, there was also a pragmatic imperative. The international humanitarian community was primed to begin relief efforts, and conflict complicated their capacity to function both politically and logistically in tsunami-affected areas. Humanitarian actors were influenced by a number of concerns: consideration of the safety of their staff, the capacity for free and unimpeded movement, the moral and political issues associated with providing aid to potential combatants, and the unwillingness of humanitarian actors to become involved in political machinations. These circumstances made peace an urgent necessity.

Former president of Finland Martti Ahtisaari mediated the 2005 Aceh peace process. Within nine months of the disaster Ahtisaari had led five rounds of peace talks in Helsinki that concluded with the signing of a memorandum of understanding. These talks agreed to the standing down of GAM fighters, the establishment of local security arrangements, and the removal of a majority of Indonesian security forces. Following this, the European Union established the Aceh Monitoring Mission with the support of the Association of Southeast Asian Nations. Its role was to ensure the demobilization and disarmament of GAM fighters. In terms of political arrangements, the memorandum of understanding did not give Aceh sovereign authority; however, it created a mutually acceptable arrangement for an expanded autonomy for Aceh. In 2006 the Indonesian national parliament passed the Law on the Governing of Aceh, dividing power between central and provisional governments. At the December 2006 regional elections a former GAM strategist, Irwandi Yusuf, was elected Aceh's governor. A second regional election was held in 2012, with another former GAM fighter taking over the governorship. There have also been two Indonesian legislative elections in the postconflict period—in 2009 and 2014—where parties within Aceh contested for representation.

The peace process established a patriarchal peace with a near complete exclusion of women. The sudden, urgent, and devastating tsunami was responded to through a language of crisis: international action was required, and fast! Peace needed to be immediate and therefore sharp, focused, and minimalist. Negotiators, including the lead negotiator, made it clear that the urgent need for humanitarian access meant that the ongoing conflict was an irritant that must be swiftly addressed. Ahtisaari's view, as characterized by one observer, was that "the agreement should be brief, and general in content, if it was too detailed, then they would never reach results" (quoted in Aspinall 2008, 14). The negotiators took this as a cue to minimize the agenda and rely upon familiar patriarchal peace models. Men become the default negotiators and masculinist/militarized negative peace concerns were established as the sole and limited agenda. The negotiations thus focused upon public sphere concerns: the transitional role of combatants and the arrangements of power sharing between Jakarta and Aceh. The memorandum of understanding consisted of six substantive provisions: governance arrangements, dispute settlement, the establishment of the Aceh Monitoring Mission, security arrangements, amnesty and reintegration of GAM combatants, and issues of human rights. The issue of human rights, which might directly include consideration of women's experiences, had three provisions—the establishment of a human rights court (2.2), the establishment of a Commission for Truth and Reconciliation (2.3), and a commitment from Indonesia to adhere to the UN's International Covenant on Civil and Political Rights and on Economic, Social and Cultural Rights. However, there have been no concrete moves toward fulfilling either the provision for a human rights court or a truth-and-reconciliation commission (Crisis Management Initiative 2012, 20).

The exclusion of women and gender considerations was evident throughout the peace process. Men conducted the five rounds of peace negotiations in Helsinki, with one woman, Shadia Marhaban, joining the GAM delegation late in the process. Kamaruzzaman (2008, 71) points out that this was not simply the case during the 2005 negotiations but that women had been largely excluded from the previous five years of peace discussions, showing a disregard for women's parallel peace activism. Similarly, women were underrepresented in the drafting of the Law on Governing Aceh (Cunliffe et al. 2009, 19; Crisis Management Initiative 2006, 19). One of the two women involved in the drafting process claimed: "In all of these processes—from peace-building, transition, reconstruction and rehabilitation, institutions building—none of them (women) have been included" (quoted in Siapno 2010, 166). Similarly, issues affecting women were a mere afterthought in the Aceh Monitoring Mission. One women's rights organization reported being asked to comment on the peace-monitoring process as the mission was departing (Siapno 2010, 168). In addition, women have been sidelined in the demobilization, demilitarization, and reintegration programs, in the compensation programs, and in the debates on justice (see Clarke et al. 2008; Lee-Koo 2012).

Both the international mediators and the Indonesian and Acehnese negotiators are responsible for the failure to include women and a gender perspective in the peace process. Under the United Nations Security Council Resolution 1325 (Women, Peace and Security) and CEDAW (Convention on the Elimination of Discrimination against Women), all parties had a responsibility to ensure consideration of the conflict's impact upon women and women's participation in the peace processes. However, neither Acehnese nor international actors insisted upon it. Acehnese actors continued a tradition of patriarchal politics that had dominated throughout the conflict, and this was reflected in the peace agenda. Emphasis upon the inclusion of women, or of issues uniquely impacting women, would disrupt existing gender hierarchies and social arrangements and challenge local masculinities and patriarchal power. Meanwhile, international mediators saw the introduction of such concerns as a stumbling block to a peace deal and therefore exhibited a pragmatic patriarchy that allowed it to be "left until later." The failure to insist upon the inclusion of gender equality set a standard—a pattern of behavior—that became further entrenched. In its follow-up to the peace process, the Crisis Management Initiative acknowledged:

> The role of women in Aceh, both as peacemakers but also as combatants during the conflict, has been underestimated. Women have been largely sidelined from the relevant bodies and initiatives that substantially deal with the peace process. Women, including former combatants, struggle to find their way as participants and actors in political life in post-conflict Aceh. (2012, 32)

The transformative moment in the immediate aftermath of the tsunami offered an opportunity to promote a gender-aware approach to peace and recovery. However, that opportunity was lost because of the dominance of preexisting and default masculinity, which was reinforced by the determined need to act swiftly. As a result, the culture of peace that was negotiated marginalized women's experiences as irrelevant, and treated women's participation in public sphere life as abnormal. Efforts to address the neglect of women's participation in the postdisaster reconstruction phase

of Aceh's state-building program were therefore more difficult, as propo-
nents of gender equality faced an already legitimated culture of local and
international patriarchy.

BUILD BACK BETTER: FROM PATRIARCHAL PEACE
TO GENDERED RENEWAL

The peace process enabled the arrival of a substantial international presence to provide immediate post-tsunami relief, followed by longer-term
development programs. Partnerships between local, national, and global
actors undertook rescue operations, clean-up processes, distribution of
food and medical assistance, family reunification, environmental assess-
ments, temporary and longer-term accommodation, economic growth, and
sustainable political institutions. In the aftermath of the tsunami, US$8
billion of aid was pledged for the province by international donors, and
within one month of the relief operation, the UN had registered 3,645
NGOs to operate in the local context. In short, this was a sudden, major,
and unexpected humanitarian operation, followed by a longer-term development project. While organizations pursued independent agendas, the
paramount international commitment to Aceh was to "build back better."
This was the slogan adopted by former US president Bill Clinton in January
2005 when he took on the role of UN special envoy for tsunami recovery.
This goal was ambitious. It was not simply to get people back on their feet,
but to reshape Acehnese society through facilitating relief and recovery,
development, new governance structures, and the promotion of human
rights. Clinton summed this up by promising:

> We will work to restore the livelihoods of the survivors; to finance new economic
> activities to raise family incomes above the pre-tsunami levels; and to increase
> the capacity of local governments, non-governmental organisations and busi-
> nesses to undertake the gargantuan reconstruction effort. (Clinton 2005)

Thus the "Build Back Better" campaign was not simply a humanitarian
operation. It was also a political program to construct a new Aceh. But the
new visions of Aceh pulled in several different directions: Indonesia sought
to retain some control (politically, as well as over natural resources); the
international community moved toward introducing liberal governance
structures and values in addition to recovery; and local actors were vying
for control in a new political system, while also wanting to differentiate
themselves from both Indonesia and the international community. Of

course, crossing all of these were feminist re-visions of Aceh, based on combinations of local, global, liberal, Muslim, and Western visions of what women's rights would and should look like in the Acehnese context.

As the language of crisis was replaced by one of renewal, slightly different forms of patriarchy emerged. At the local level, the focus was upon establishing an independent Acehnese identity, commensurate with the new semiautonomous political arrangements and distinct from both Indonesia and the international presence. For international actors, pragmatism continued with a preference to adopt minimalist frameworks that empowered women in economic and political spaces, but without fundamentally challenging gender roles (Jauhola 2013). In this sense, the promotion of a gender equality framework was only considered legitimate if it was justified within traditional social, cultural, and, importantly, religious patriarchal discourses. The constraining nature of this is evident in the debates on sharia law, and the issue of women in elected political office.

Religion plays an important role in Aceh. Known as "the veranda of Mecca," Aceh dates its conversion to Islam back to the ninth century, making it the earliest conversion in Southeast Asia. More recently, the introduction of sharia law in 1999 was embedded in the politics of the conflict between GAM and the government of Indonesia. However, it was after the peace process that sharia law began to have a more significant impact upon the region. Since then, it has become an important aspect of Aceh's postdisaster identity, facilitated by the establishment of semiautonomous arrangements that allowed local authorities greater capacities to make and enforce local laws. However, the resurgence of this form of identity-making is also seen as a reaction to the international presence in the region and as a purposeful contrast to the often secular or Christian agendas of international NGOs (Grossman 2012, 104). For many Acehnese who interpreted the tsunami as a punishment by God, sharia is seen as "a means to protect the community from calamity" (Feener 2013, 1–3). Its amplification during this period is intertwined with the local patriarchy discussed earlier in this chapter. Consequently, the introduction of sharia is a site of contestation over gender equality and women's rights. These debates coalesce around interpretations of religious texts, and the introduction of regulations that discriminate against women.

The local government has the power to create *qanun* (provincial regulations) that govern everyday activities in accordance with Islam. These occur in areas of faith and worship, dress and behavior, and religious education. There are a number of *qanun* that have raised the concerns of women's rights advocates in Aceh. Perhaps the most controversial of these is Qanun 14/2003, which governs close proximity. "Close proximity" is described as "any activity carried out by two or more individuals of opposite sex who are not bound as a family nor legally bound under marriage" (quoted in Afrianty 2011, 40). It makes it difficult for women to report rape, allows intrusive monitoring of their associations, actions, and movements, and increases their vulnerability to predatory or violent men, particularly in familial relationships. Specifically, it has been used to patrol women's behavior and movement and in some parts of Aceh has led to a style of mob or vigilante justice (see Grossman 2012, 103–105; Afrianty 2015, 72–76). A number of cases have been reported throughout Indonesian and Western media that demonstrate this. In 2015, for example a twenty-five-year-old woman and man were sentenced to nine lashes of the cane for being found in a house alone together. According to reports, a group of ten villagers near the rural town of Langsa broke into the house to find the couple, tied the woman up, and took turns in raping her. The couple were then reportedly marched through the town (see Bachelard 2015). Two of the rapists were sentenced to two to three years in prison. For women's rights activists, the concern is not only the behavior of local men and the lack of justice, but also the heavy-handed tactics of the sharia police (see Grossman 2012, 104).

Women's rights groups have struggled to critique and reform these laws. The uneven targeting of laws and subsequent (in)justice has meant that women must tread very carefully when voicing concerns. Within this context, women's insecurities cannot be easily heard and are subsumed under public national and religious state-making practices (see Hansen 2000). Critiques must be carefully managed for fear of accusations of blasphemy (Grossman 2012, 105), though Afrianty (2015, 145) has pointed out that "Acehnese women have demonstrated that they have been able to manoeuvre to advance women's interests [by] appearing in public and challenging the local government." Much of this challenging, however, is done within the sharia framework. While international frameworks obviously support women's rights, for Acehnese women the complaint must come from within the Islamic tradition itself. Afrianty (2015, 2–3) notes the importance of returning to Islamic teachings, traditions, and texts to demonstrate that the discriminatory intent evident in laws is not inherent in Islam. Rather it is the product of modern reading from a perspective of patriarchal cultures. Women's rights activists have therefore focused their activism on submitting requests for the redrafting of qanun based on alternative readings of Islamic texts. They have also sought the introduction of new qanun to provide greater protection for women. This has met with limited success (see Grossman 2012, 105–106). However, while these qanun have sought to address issues such as rape and crimes against children, they do not challenge the original regulations, and they do not bar provisions that criminalize homosexuality and impose the death penalty by stoning for convicted adultery (Grossman 2016, 87).

These discriminatory sharia practices are underpinned by the patriarchal leadership and governance structures established in Aceh after 2005. In this sense, women's absence from governance roles has produced a legacy of institutionally embedded gender inequality. A decade on, it has curtailed the ability of women to launch effective challenges against an entrenched religious patriarchy. Furthermore, the limited capacity for international organizations to render significant assistance to women demonstrates the closed and impenetrable nature of these patriarchal structures. It also demonstrates the pragmatic patriarchy that sees international actors unwilling to offer strong condemnation of the practices of sharia law that contravene global norms around women's rights. Thus Acehnese women find themselves struggling within and against an increasingly entrenched patriarchal and religious culture.

In the political sector, the patriarchal patronage culture creates similar difficulties for women's widespread and transformative engagement. Affiat's (2011) research exploring the causes of women's low representation in Acehnese politics finds that patriarchal culture pervades all aspects of Acehnese political life, from views about the appropriate roles of women, to the process of political participation and the structures of government. She argues that "Aceh's current political context is a mixture of patronage, masculinity, communality, ideology, and vested interests," further noting that "it is men, with their strong grassroots connections, cultural, economic and political access, who hold the majority of political positions" (Affiat 2012, 5). She further argues:

> Generally speaking, men [believe that] . . . women can actively participate in the public sphere but they should not be in leading positions as decision-makers, or at least they are less favourable for these positions. A commonly shared view amongst men also holds that women are actually given the space and opportunities to participate but it is the women themselves who do not take those chances, because they lack confidence, capacities or initiative. (Affiat 2011, 35)

This highlights the institutionalization of the patriarchal structures that dominate Acehnese political institutions. Moreover, international interventions that call for the greater inclusion of women (see Crisis Management Initiative 2012) appear to adopt a "just add women and stir" approach to political representation, believing that increasing the number of women will eventually cause a cultural shift. However, as critical feminist scholars have outlined (see Peterson 2004), such an approach neither confronts nor restructures the masculinist political architecture that inhibits women's political participation.

To some extent, Acehnese women's civil society groups have undertaken this restructuring of politics. In this instance, local women's rights activists rely upon a greater array of gender-based infrastructure to provide a counterpoint to patriarchal discourses and practices. A cornerstone achievement in this regard is the release in November 2008 of the Charter of the Rights of Women in Aceh. Produced by the Women's Committee for the Revival of Aceh, the Charter's main themes reinforce the rights of women's equality in all aspects of political and social life. It also reaffirms women's rights over key issues pertaining to their lives: reproductive health; access to education; rights within the family; rights to own land; and the right of women to be treated with respect. The signatories to the Charter included the governor of Aceh, the chairman of the regional parliament, representatives of the government, judiciary, and police, representatives of Islamic institutions, and NGOs. While the Charter has been contravened in numerous circumstances—not least of all in the implementation of sharia discussed above—its widespread rhetorical support has generated greater awareness of its principles.

The Charter is supported by preexisting stipulations on women's rights by the government of Indonesia. The Convention on the Elimination of All Forms of Discrimination against Women (CEDAW) was signed by the government of Indonesia on July 29, 1980, and ratified on September 13, 1984. Similarly, in October 2000, Indonesia, as already noted, adopted Security Council Resolution 1325, acknowledging the importance of the role of women in preventing and resolving conflicts. Presidential Decree 18/2014, National Action Plans for the Protection and Empowerment of Women and Children during Social Conflicts, has more recently reinforced this. In addition, the Presidential Instruction No. 9/2000 on Gender Mainstreaming in National Development obliges all heads of national and subnational government institutions to implement gender=mainstreaming strategies in all of their activities. In Aceh the BRR (Reconstruction and Rehabilitation Agency for Aceh and Nias) launched, in September 2006, its own strategy paper on gender mainstreaming entitled "Promoting Gender Equality in the Rehabilitation and Reconstruction Process of Aceh and Nias." This provided its own commitment to the "full engagement of women and men as equal partners in social, cultural and economic development of Aceh and Nias."

Unlike the example of sharia discussed earlier, these frameworks have supported some progress on women's participation in public life. Since 2005 there have been numerous initiatives to increase the number of women in political roles, including the introduction of a quota, and training programs and support for women to contest elections, though NGO intervention in this regard is often seen as haphazard (Crisis Management Initiative 2012; Affiat 2011). In terms of political representation, Article 75 of the Law on Governing Aceh requires local political parties to have 30 percent of its candidates be women. This has contributed to the slow, but determined, improvement in the number of women that have been elected to Aceh's legislative body—Dewan Perwakilan Rakyat Aceh—since its creation in 2005. In the most recent 2014 legislative elections, 14.8 percent of seats were filled by women, which marked a significant increase from 7.25 percent in 2009. Yet, as Affiat notes, one of the key impediments to women's greater participation remains sociocultural views of women's and men's roles in society. As she notes: "Women who wish to enter this world of modern politics must be ready to rub shoulders [with those in power] and fight" (Affiat 2012, 13). This demonstrates that many of these gains in political representation have been won despite the limits of a patriarchal system. Moreover, their capacity to be politically transformative remains constrained.

CONCLUSION

As 2005 dawned, there was an opportunity to infuse gender equality into the foundations of the newly emerging semiautonomous state of Aceh. From a crippling civil conflict and a devastating disaster emerged an opportunity to rebuild a new state based upon mutual and equal respect for men and women, which was, however, sadly missed. At the local level, the Acehnese men responsible for building the postconflict, postdisaster state chose to protect their privilege and reinforce the culture of patriarchy that dominated public sphere activities. At the international level, actors adopted a pragmatic patriarchy that did not push gender equality as a necessary concern. The context of disaster and conflict created a discourse of urgency and crisis that apparently excused all actors from their obligations to gender equality. The supposed need to promote peace, relief, and reconstruction *first* (as opposed to mainstreaming gender into them) set a powerful standard that allowed gender issues to be excused and sidelined. Once they were sidelined, it became more and more difficult for Acehnese women and their supporters to challenge the entrenched patriarchy. This has meant that movement for women's rights is limited by the gendered state.

These findings in Aceh are not new in terms of what feminists already know about the gendered state (Tetreault 1992; True 2012). What is alarming is that after over two decades of feminist theorizing and global promotion of gender equality frameworks, gendered states are still being constructed. Aceh is an example of this. This case demonstrates that the creation of gendered states in the twenty-first century requires the following ingredients. First, it requires local patriarchies where women's experiences have been marginalized and political participation is restrained. Second, it requires an international pragmatism that will negotiate women's rights away in preference for a stable agreement on supposed core issues. This pragmatism itself constitutes a form of patriarchy. Third, it requires an enabling discourse. In the case of Aceh it was the discourse of crisis and urgency that justified a minimalist and masculinist agenda and promoted women's rights as an indulgence. This does not preclude feminist challenges, but it makes them dangerous and difficult for those within the gendered state.

PART IV

Gender in Troubled States

CHAPTER 10

The Postcolonial/Emotional State

Mother India's Response to Her Deviant Maoist Children

SWATI PARASHAR

Fear against hope, hope against humiliation, humiliation leading to sheer irrationality and even sometimes to violence – one cannot comprehend the world in which we live without examining the emotions that help shape it. (Moisi 2009, xi)

Although the study of emotions has gained recent prominence in international relations (IR), social theorists have long paid attention to the political impact of emotions on the construction of the self, other and the social world (Ahmed 2004; Fortier 2008; Marcus et al. 2002; Butler 2004). Scholars have highlighted how dominant emotions (positive and negative) exist and acquire collective dimension shaping political and social processes in the international system. Expressing an emotion itself constitutes a political act and emotions shape geopolitics (Moisi 2009; Bleiker and Hutchison 2008; Åhäll and Gregory 2015). Martha Nussbaum (2001) argues that emotions are important forms of knowledge and evaluative thought. Emotions are linked to cultural responses and reactions, and scholars are increasingly recognizing and accounting for the "emotional" turn in global politics. Emotions are ascribed to individuals, identity groups, and communities that are constituted through particular experiences. The subjective emotional experience is shaped by language and culture, and, as Nussbaum argues, "Differences in normative judgments affect experience itself" (2001, 160). Individual or cumulative emotional experiences (of individuals and societies) constitute political community and enable political existence.

Emotions as political utterances have now begun to interest feminist IR scholars, although much has already been written about the gendered politics of emotions and the gendering of emotions itself by feminist theorists (Lloyd 1993; Ahmed 2004; Jeffery 2014). One could think of two aspects to the question of emotions and politics. One pertains to the negotiations with emotions that are inherent in research work. The pressure to suppress emotional responses, particularly when studying conflict situations, has been discussed by feminist scholars (Sylvester 2011). They have pointed out the perceived association of emotions with weakness, to prevent which, experiences and responses of the researcher are often carefully kept out by her. This not only changes the nature of research work that is produced (Parashar 2011a), but also brings out issues of masculine objectivity being hegemonic in academia that censures emotions as irrational (Sylvester 2011). The other aspect of this methodological problem of not embedding emotions in research is the gaps it can create in grasping any political context. Bleiker and Hutchison (2008) use the example of 9/11 to make this point. The repeatedly displayed images of the collapsing towers of the World Trade Center compounded the emotional and traumatic impact this attack had on Americans, which went on to also become the justification of the US invasion of Afghanistan and Iraq and torture and human rights abuses, carried out in the name of defending "against forces of evil." This also demonstrates the ways in which identities are constructed around emotions, and for purposes of this chapter, the identity of the state.

The state as the predominant political and cultural institution globally is not passé; it facilitates identity politics but is far from relinquishing its power and sovereignty (Gandhi 1998; Hasan 2000; Nandy 2003). States perform emotions and ascribe emotions to the bodies of their citizens (sympathizers and dissidents); the state of the "state" can be known through its affective presence communicated by the ruling elite, through militarized institutions, and through governance policies and decisions. Public displays of tears, outrage and emotions are no longer limited to the few celebrity artists and sportspersons; many politicians and heads of state have made it a trend. The deeply embedded affective relationship between individuals and the state determines the nature of identity politics prevalent in contemporary states. States are grappling with competing nationalisms, political ideologies, wars and peacebuilding, truth and reconciliation, as well as developmental challenges, most of which are rooted in identity politics and, as I argue, driven by emotions. Communities (ethnic, religious, sectarian, national, and international) are fostered around emotions. If the

9/11 attacks were a calculated but emotional response to American hegemony, the 'global war on terror' was launched from an emotional platform of hurt and anger.[1] This is also visible in many other conflicts between states and insurgent groups, such as the Maoists[2] in India.

In this chapter I discuss how we can "know" the state through its emotional language and appeal and how "affective citizenship" is a necessary precondition for the creation and sustenance of postcolonial statehood. This emotional language used by the state to communicate with all (consenting and nonconsenting) citizens within its territorial boundaries is highly gendered. Postcolonial states use gendered emotional language to reject colonial emasculation/feminization and reclaim masculinity through demonstrating particular kinds of emotions and conferring particular kinds of affective citizenship. This reclaiming of masculinity is juxtaposed with the state's feminine maternal instincts and nurturing narrative, which privilege certain kinds of attachments and allegiance to the state.

The chapter studies the affective ontology of the state by analyzing the Maoist conflict in India, where the state retains its postcolonial legitimacy and power through gendered emotions. I demonstrate how the Indian state uses affective language in its political and policy discourse to construct its national and historical narrative, to confer rights and privileges on compliant citizens, and to police and punish the deviant insurgents/antinationals who challenge its power and authority.

AFFECTIVE CITIZENSHIP, AND POSTCOLONIAL STATEHOOD

In affective economies, emotions do things, and they align individuals with communities—or bodily space with social space—through the very intensity of their attachments. Rather than seeing emotions as psychological dispositions, we need to consider how they work, in concrete and particular ways, to mediate the relationship between the psychic and the social, and between the individual and the collective. (Ahmed 2004, 118)

If emotions form an economy because they become attached to material objects that create self, community, and "other," states are part of those affective economies. They are at the helm of decision-making, and although some scholars argued that globalization in the post–Cold War world had weakened the traditional state system, the hegemony of the idea of the modern nation state is retained (Nandy 2003; Hasan 2000). The state system thrives in the global North as a raison d'être for its existence. The election of Donald Trump in the United States, with his slogan "Make America great again," signifies that there is anxiety among the people whenever the state is perceived to be soft, weak, and feminized. Public intellectuals and voters in India similarly alluded to the weak feminized state under the Congress led regime that needed to be fixed, after the electoral victory of Narendra Modi and the right wing Bharatiya Janata Party (BJP) in 2014 (Basu 2016). The rise and popularity of ultraright nationalist parties and leaders in the United Kingdom, United States, India, Australia, Turkey, and elsewhere who advocate a strong state demonstrates the crises of masculinity that requires the patriarchal state to take control and embody strong masculine emotions. This is evident even in the rise of the proto-state ISIS, as Katherine Brown discusses in this volume.

In *Gendered States*, Spike Peterson demonstrated that feminism is at the heart of the shift from "women as knowable" to "women as knowers" and that this has a significant impact on knowledge claims (1992b, 9). This was the first attempt within feminist IR to understand the politics of states from a gendered lens that rejected knowledge claims based on the partial experience of elites. Peterson and other contributors to the volume argued that knowledge about social realities must incorporate a wide range of human experiences, particularly of the marginalized (1992a, 11). Extending this feminist understanding to the current ontological foundations of states, one must ask how the gendered state can be "known," and the ways of "knowing" it. I posit that the state can be "known" through the emotional language it speaks, through its policies, and by developing particular norms of citizenship. Consider, for example, the 2017 decision of the Supreme Court in India to enforce the singing of national anthem in cinema halls to demonstrate "committed patriotism and nationalism." The Court ordered that "all the cinema halls in India shall play the national anthem before the feature film starts and all present in the hall are obliged to stand up to show respect to the national anthem" as part of their "sacred obligation" (Anand 2016). A national outrage followed this diktat as public intellectuals queried the rationale and the constitutional validity of this decision (Mehta 2016). This was an attempt to enforce a norm around patriotic allegiance to the state and nationalism while imagining that through the singing of the national anthem, every citizen would experience emotional bonding with the nation state based on love for the motherland. The notion of "affective citizenship" is endorsed in such decisions.

The concept of "affective citizenship" is a permanent fixture of postcolonial statehood through which we can "know" the state and grasp its culture, character, and its deeply embedded relationship with diverse peoples and communities. It is "affective nationalism" of anticolonial struggles that gets transformed into "affective citizenship" with the creation of the postcolonial state. This affective citizenship is gendered in the differential public acknowledgment of emotional claims, rights, and obligations to the state. For Johnson "affective citizenship" explores "(a) which intimate emotional relationships between citizens are endorsed and recognized by governments and (b) how citizens are encouraged to feel about others and themselves in conceptions of the 'good citizen'" (2010, 496). She focuses on issues of sexuality, gender, race, and religion, and argues that the politics of affect has major implications for determining who has "full citizenship rights and protections" (Johnson 2010, 497). This argument can be further extended to suggest that affective citizenship is a mode of being for citizens that is both recognized and directly governed by the state. The state enables conditions for this affective citizenship to be realized and derives its legitimacy from it. It is the enforcing of this affective citizenship that creates conditions for people's resistance and armed rebellion against the state.

Mookherjee (2005) sees affective citizenship as a means to overcome the limitations and violence of unitary citizenship, recognizing the emotional relations through which identities are formed. Social disadvantages create experiential human bonds beyond the immediate family (Simpson 2000). These experiences are often constituted through direct or remembered pain, loss, humiliation, or even the psychological disorientation that postcolonial writers associate with the effects of colonial domination (Fanon 1967a, 78). Affective citizenship follows their lead by requiring that emotional connections and dispositions support citizens' most important reasons for action. Such connections may also explain, therefore, the basis for a set of difference-sensitive rights. Crucially, affective citizenship presumes that citizens' structural autonomy is formed not through just one set of affective bonds, but rather through commitments to multiple, intersecting communities. It, therefore, becomes important for purposes of this chapter to recognize that studies of affective citizenship indicate that "ideals of citizenship are grounded in emotions and emotional relationships" (Zembylas 2014, 6). The affective basis of citizenship is achieved by "governing through affect," feelings developed in relation to the nation and fellow citizens who can be both similar and different (Fortier 2010).

Political language and discourse of the ruling elite play an important role in promoting affective citizenship, through policies (such as making national anthem compulsory), emotional utterances in political speeches, public symbolism, and performances. The prime minister of India, Narendra Modi, otherwise known for invoking masculinity and macho values (through comments such as a fifty-six-inch chest is a prerequisite for bringing about significant policy changes and development), is one world leader who has made emotions a powerful mode of communication. His speeches and utterances are laced with tears and visual expressions that demand from the citizens an affective engagement, invoking strong emotions among his supporters and detractors and drawing them into an affective dialogue. India's first prime minister, Jawaharlal Nehru, in his "tryst with destiny" speech talked about the birth of the postcolonial nation state of India, whose long-suppressed soul was finding expression. On the eve of independence (August 15, 1947) he said, "At the stroke of the midnight hour, when the world sleeps, India will awake to life and freedom. A moment comes, which comes but rarely in history, when we step out from the old to new, when an age ends, and when the soul of a nation, long suppressed, finds utterance" (Nehru 1961). If the nation is the soul, the state is the institutional embodiment that encapsulates it. Martha Nussbaum (2015) reads Nehru's speech as a highly emotional speech that does not demonstrate resentment, hatred, or even fear of insecurities. There is compassion and determination, she argues, as Nehru was very keen that the newly attained state should embody the values that had been instrumental throughout the anticolonial movement. Since then, Indians have reposed unwavering faith in the state to address the problems faced by the postcolonial nation; affective citizenship has been actively promoted by the state to address the anxieties after the 1947 Partition and to accommodate differences and diversity.

The state, as the enabler of this affective citizenship, endorses a hierarchical set of allegiances and bonds, prioritizing some people's emotional claims over others. Dalit and Adivasi[3] voices and emotional claims have been consistently overlooked in the development narrative of the state in India, which caters to the rising middle classes and their anxieties. In postcolonial states this affective citizenship is also gendered. Ashis Nandy pointed out more than three decades ago that, "while the economic, political and moral results of colonialism have been discussed, its emotional and cognitive costs have been ignored" (1983, 71). If colonialism enabled emotional responses from the colonized, it also allowed the colonizers to feel emotionally committed to the civilizing mission. A complex coexistence of feminizing and hypermasculine tropes is made possible in the postcolonial state, as it replaces the colonizers' governance and institutional structures using similar idioms and practices, and also attempts to embody the values of the national movement, invoked in the anticolonial struggle. The affective citizenship model of the Indian state has been complex and subject to different ideological interpretations and endorsements by the ruling elite.

If statehood itself is a product of gendered emotional encounters, how does the sovereign postcolonial state, with its distinct history and territorial and cultural identity, manifest gendered emotions? How does the state confer subject status and citizenship rights to individuals based on emotional hierarchy (emotions of some privileged over others)? How does the gendered emotional language of the postcolonial state, in conflict with its own citizens, challenge its legitimacy? Does the state always perform masculinist emotions of outrage, hurt, aggression and domination, or does it demonstrate feminine attributes and emotional vulnerabilities? This chapter makes emotional sense of the armed resistance that postcolonial states are grappling with from their own discontented citizens who experience denial or subordination of their affective citizenship. I discuss the "state" of India in the next two sections.

MOTHER INDIA'S MAOIST CHILDREN

Little did I imagine until 1965—no, not even in a nightmare—that at some time the state would be all things to me: my darling, my friend, my mother, my child, my close relative. Then I became a Marxist, dreaming that the state would wither away and these emotional relationships would become real without its intrusion. (Rao 2010, 55)

As mentioned earlier, the masculine-objective perspective, which can only see emotions within the frames of "irrationality," has long overshadowed the theorization of politics (Sylvester 2011). Such a methodological frame can do little to grasp the strategic deployment of emotions, particularly in wars between states and insurgent groups (Åhäll and Gregory 2015). While history is rife with examples of reason's triumph over emotions (that being the eternal human dilemma) and over the display of appropriate emotions at different times (like patriotism in times of war; grief and mourning in times of loss; anger and revenge in times of conflict; forgiveness in times of reconciliation), Sara Ahmed reminds us that emotions are not mere psychological states, but social and political practices. "Emotions are not 'in' either the individual and the social, but produce the very surfaces and boundaries that allow the individual and the social to be delineated as if they are objects" (Ahmed 2004, 10). This becomes all the more evident as one studies the performance of emotions in wars and how war bodies are constructed through affective understandings of the "self" and "other" (Parashar 2015).

I now turn to the playing out and conscription of emotions in the war between the Indian state and the Maoist guerrillas. Since the armed peasant uprising in the village of Naxalbari in West Bengal in 1967, Naxalites or Maoists have been in an armed struggle to overthrow the Indian state and establish a people's democracy. After years of various groups continuing this armed struggle, in 2004 two major Naxalite factions—People's War Group and Maoist Communist Centre—together formed the Communist Party of India (Maoist) (Banerjee 2006). The Party's armed campaign is carried out in the Adivasi areas of central and eastern India, across the states of Chhattisgarh, Jharkhand, Bihar, Odisha, Maharashtra, Madhya Pradesh, Andhra Pradesh and Telangana. The Indian state has been carrying out sustained and organized action against these guerrillas, which intensified from 2005 onward, leading to the full-scale military onslaught called "Operation Green Hunt" launched in 2010. Thousands of lives have been lost, injured, or displaced, and yet the conflict continues to haunt the rural hinterland (Roy 2011; Shah 2010; Sundar 2016).

The formation of the Maoist party, its armed and non-armed political work in the Adivasi regions, and the intensified operations of the state against the insurgents, have unfolded in a specific socio-economic and political context. The region of central and eastern India, which is often referred to as the "red corridor," signifying the areas where the Maoists are active, is a mineral-rich region. Legally these areas, inhabited by Adivasis, are protected under special acts when it comes to landownership. For example, Jharkhand has the Chhotanagpur Tenancy Act in operation, which protects the lands owned by Adivasis from being easily commercialized but, which is seen as an impediment to development (Sharan 2005). This also comes in the backdrop of communal ownership of property in Adivasi communities. Added to this vulnerability is the economic stagnation and absence of state support in these regions.

Till not so long ago, the Koraput-Bolangir-Kandhmal belt of Odisha was known as the poorest region of the country, although these are mineral-rich areas, where mining of coal, bauxite, and other resources has been crucial to the Indian economy (Roul 2016). The neoliberal shift in economic policy has meant that private companies have also found an entry into these resource-rich regions. The wealth of these lands is in stark contrast to the poverty of the communities living on them. It is against this acutely unequal backdrop and state negligence that the support for armed left-wing politics has consolidated. The post-independence Indian state has in many instances left little space for people to voice their grievances peacefully; it has been the state's nature to suppress demands brutally—initiating a cycle of violence that finds no end (Banerjee 2015).

Nandini Sundar writes that the Maoist war is about how "emotions are mobilised, conscripted and engendered by both sides" (Sundar 2012). She mentions the denial of emotional citizenship to the Adivasis while the state performs "outrage, hurt and fear-inducing domination, as part of its battle for legitimacy" (Sundar 2012, 701). "Intrinsic to this is the privileging of certain kinds of emotions—fear, anger, grief—and the emotions of certain kinds of people over others. Subject populations are distinguished from citizens by the differential public acknowledgement of their emotional claim" (Sundar 2012, 701). Sundar highlights that emotion is an important ingredient in the civil war in India and that outrage and righteous anger are invoked by the state, while the Maoist guerrillas embrace martyrdom and heroism. Even winning hearts and minds, which is considered essential in the counterinsurgency operation, conveys that this conflict is about the display of public emotions (Sundar 2012, 701).

My field research reveals how individual experiences of oppression and injustices with several years of government neglect have resulted in collective anger among the Dalits and Adivasis; anger that is targeted against the representatives of the state, such as the police, government officials and security forces. The excesses of collective anger in armed insurgencies may appear to be less terrifying if located within the context of the material conditions that produce such strong collective emotional responses. It could be argued that "collective action frames not only provide an intellectual account of the injustice of certain situations but they also legitimate the expression of moral indignation and righteous anger directed toward the source of injustice. The centrality of anger to collective action stems from its link with action" (Hercus 1999, 36).

For the Indian state, its actions in the region which often have constituted gross human rights violations (Sundar 2016; Banerjee 2015), require legitimacy in the "rest of India." In 2009, a planned military campaign was launched by the Government of India against the Maoist insurgents, who were identified as one of the biggest security threats to the country. Known by the name of "Operation Green Hunt," this military campaign involved heavy deployment of armed auxiliary forces and support to local armed and nonarmed vigilante groups. A particularly notorious vigilante group supported by the state, *Salwa Judum*, was disbanded by the Supreme Court in 2011 after prominent citizens and human rights activists appealed against it.

Aside from the direct armed confrontation, the state and the Maoists have been engaged in propaganda wars against each other in which emotions, especially of fear, play a major role in enhancing their support base and mass appeal. In fact, the gendered emotional landscape of this conflict is made intelligible through the reporting of and propaganda around incidents of violence (from both sides), and also in how policies of the state and political campaigning of the Maoists are created and implemented (Guha 2007).

To elaborate on this "emotional war" Sundar (2012) draws on the example of the 2010 ambush in which seventy-six personnel of the Central Reserve Police Force (CRPF), an auxiliary armed force of the state, were killed by the Maoists in Tadmetla, Dantewada (Chhattisgarh). This incident became a flashpoint for the state to heighten its use of force in response to the actions of the Maoists. The ambush in April 2010 generated responses from the government that expressed a state of siege, not just for this region but for the whole nation. Two kinds of simultaneous reactions, amplified by the media, formed the discourse around this incident. At one level, the grief of the families of the slain and the bravery of the martyred soldiers were projected. At another, the terror of the Maoists and the state's iron fist against them were highlighted.

> The "Dantewada martyrs" became symbolic not just of the "butchery" and "savagery" of the Maoists, but of a political community—"India"—under siege, a message reinforced by the ubiquitous TV images of flag-draped coffins, last seen in the Kargil war against Pakistan. Headlines like "The outraged nation," "Government outraged over Maoist massacre—BJP wants fight to the finish" (Hindustan Times) and "War between India and the Maoists" (Times Now television channel), struck a note of infuriated anger, while others emphasized the pathos and sacrifice of the slain men: "Country bids farewell to Dantewada martyrs" (NDTV), "Amid heart-rending scenes 42 bodies reach Lucknow" (The Hindu), "Brave and helpless" (Outlook magazine). (Sundar 2012, 705–706)

Similar reactions were visible after the Maoist attack in Sukma (Chhattisgarh) on April 24, 2017, which resulted in the deaths of twenty-five CRPF personnel. Frenzied media coverage involved reports of draped coffins and emotional appeals by family members, with political leaders offering public tributes to the slain soldiers who died so that the 'nation' could live. Public legitimacy was being created for a stronger and more militarized response to deal with the insurgents (Pandey, *Indian Express*, April 26, 2017).

Through an urban-centric media, images of the conflict are flashed to the population outside of these areas—an urban, middle-class population. It is with them that the legitimacy of the state is affirmed by revealing the "barbaric" nature of the Maoists. But the locals who are caught between endless cycles of violence do not seem to be the target of this legitimation. Prime-time television discussions paint the Maoists as irrational extremists, and argue that controlling them is a matter of operating procedures in which governments can be blamed for their lack of action and decision-making. The actions of the Maoists are, at best, preventing the development of the nation, and at worst they are acts of pure terrorism. Nowhere in this narrative do we hear about the Adivasis living through this war. While acts of human rights violations do not make it to big-media publications, the "swift" actions of the state, the "bravery" of the security forces, and the exoneration of state or security forces from any charges of culpability are circulated widely, reinforcing the idea that demands of action against excesses of state agencies are propaganda to prevent the state from doing what is right. In this discourse, those from the civil society who speak for the Adivasis are deemed criminals or antinationals, like the Maoists themselves—an example of this was the arrest of, and charges of sedition against, Binayak Sen, a doctor and civil rights activist. On the other side is the local, rural media, mostly reporting in Hindi or other vernacular languages, with limited outreach and impact compared to the urban-centric media. The alternative discourse that reveals the scale of violations against locals and the economic plunder of the region exists only in local and some civil society circles (Ghosh 2016).

The propaganda of the Maoists, on the other hand, visible in their pamphlets and writings, targets the locals as their audience. It is to them that the Maoists are exposing the nature of state violence and the intent behind it. It is important for them to affirm their roots in the Adivasi community. For example, in their statement on the killing of a guerrilla commander in April 2015, which was published in Hindi, they talk about the modest origin of their comrade, who could not even complete his primary education. He was, however, attracted to the politics of the Maoists and eventually joined them as he believed that the exploiter class had to be defeated militarily. The statement is rife with militaristic language, and the deceased commander's proficiency in military struggle is spoken of in glorified terms. The appeal to the audience is to pay respect to his martyrdom by intensifying the "people's war" (Bannedthought. net 2015a). Another public statement issued in 2015, which appeared in Hindi and Telugu, addresses the police and paramilitary *jawans* (soldiers). It urges them to remember that they also come from similar origins as the locals that they are seemingly at war with—that, among them are Dalits, Adivasis, poor and exploited. It calls upon them to recognize that the government is exploiting them to forward its own agenda and is filling their minds with false notions of patriotism. In these statements and more, the investment of the Maoists in their immediate context, which goes along with the wide dissemination of their ideology, is apparent. The statement reminds of the local Adivasi livelihoods and culture that are being plundered and, in the same breath, speaks of militaristic action and Bolshevik ideals. An affective appeal is made to the *jawans* to reflect on their experiences of exploitation and poverty, even as they are recognized as enemies and agents of the state (Bannedthought.net 2015b).

The emotional appeals and propaganda wars that the state and the Maoists are engaged in, open up the vast terrain of the role of emotions in politics. Butler (2009) argues that frames within which a war is "affirmed" and "practiced" are as material as the ideals for which these wars are fought. The Maoist war is over resources, livelihood, and dignity on the one hand, and security and development on the other. The costs of this war are material too, almost crudely so, in terms of loss of life and property. However, the (ideological) frames within which the two sides are located are also essential to the war. The role of emotions is crucial precisely in the making of these "frames."

However, it is not enough to point out the emotive content and the affective nature of these wars; it is imperative to address the gendered nature of the deployment of emotions. Both the state and the Maoists appeal to a hypermasculinist, militaristic bravado when it comes to their operations and fighters. The might of their weapons and the bravery of their soldiers and guerrillas are the dominant images produced to speak of the strength of their camps. For the state, this masculinist glorification is juxtaposed with, and produced in response to, the fear and siege brought about by the Maoists. The emasculation, for instance, felt by the state in the killing of seventy-six soldiers, resulted in public announcements of strong retaliation. The shame and fear of "weakness" against the "irrational, barbaric Maoists" who are regularly demonized on television channels, are addressed through brute militaristic action, which is then hailed by the same urban media—all addressed to the urban citizenry (Sundar 2012).

From the Maoists' point of view, the plunder of resources, lives, and livelihoods of Adivasis is framed in terms of the plunder and devastation of a pure, innocent way of life, alluding to frames of sexual violence and rape. The analogies of sexual violence are far too common in histories of plunder and occupation of lands and societies. Against this violation (penetration) is the masculine protection of the rebels. The glorification of military action emerges in the context of such violence as protecting and avenging. Here again, a sense of weakness is responded to by hypermasculine frames of violence. Roy (2009), in her discussion about revolutionary violence and feminist ethics, argues that all forms of violence are embedded in a patriarchal logic. The expressions of weakness are equated with feminization and emasculation, which must always be responded to with masculinist power. This cycle of violence in the Adivasi heartland in central and eastern India is, thus, framed and legitimized by gendered emotive practices, as the next section further highlights.

MATERNAL INSTINCT AND MASCULINE EMOTIONS?

In a place where
I don't know whether
It is a wounded path
Or a soft cradle of life's secret emotions
I translate the ancient anguished cry
As "mother"! (Rao 2010, 74)

Ashis Nandy believes "that the ideal State [in India] is perhaps not mod-elled on maternity but on a fortunately distant, frequently absent father who does not want to live through his children but finds them amusing and fascinating in themselves and leaves them alone to work out their own destinies."[4] However, the figure of the "mother" enjoys an exalted status in South Asia/India in different cultures and traditions. Any powerful femi-nine form that must be venerated or even feared is symbolically invoked as the mother; hence *Bharat Mata* (mother India), *Ma Ganga* (mother Ganges),[5] *Go Mata* (mother cow), *Badi Mata* (big mother or small pox), *Chhoti Mata* (little mother or measles), *Dharti Mata* (mother earth), and so on. This is further enhanced by the powerful status of the goddesses in the Hindu pantheon, who are worshipped as benign mothers who can wage wars and kill to protect their children. In my previous research on militant movements in Kashmir and Sri Lanka, I have argued that armed resist-ance in different contexts in traditional societies derives legitimacy and mass appeal from the mothers' mobilization of grief and sacrifice (Parashar 2014). If motherhood is the prime feminine role and virtue that gets rec-ognition and legitimacy in patriarchal societies where otherwise masculine values dominate, how can it be understood in postcolonial contexts where the narratives of emasculation and hypermasculinity play out?

In the case of India, colonial masculinity resulted in the rejection of both emasculation anxieties and the aggressive reclaiming of masculinity by the anticolonial, nationalist movement (Gandhi 1998). There were ade-quate challenges to these binary gender narratives when colonial masculin-ity was countered by indigenous androgeneity and femininity. In colonial discourse, the language around the body was accepted as a way of explain-ing the inferiority of the subjected races and giving content to the ideas of "civilizing mission" and the "white man's burden." The colonized subject was an incomplete man and an incomplete or lapsed adult, which in the Gandhian vision, became a strength (Nandy 2003). Gandhi responded to the nationalist appeals to maleness in two ways: by offering a systematic critique of male sexuality and his self-conscious aspiration for bisexuality and by the desire to become God's "eunuch" (Mehta 1977, 194; Nandy 1983). In Gandhi's worldview, female virtues and femininity had an equal share in the construction of colonial subjectivity (Gandhi 1998, 100). Gandhi's femininity had a special meaning, for he often seemed to stress maternity at the expense of conjugality; his androgyny was colored primarily by motherliness and was a subversive project. It also became the basis of the gendered identity of the postcolonial nation-state, where the nation is venerated as a mother and the state demonstrates maternal instincts. Mother India is the benign protector and nurturer who looks after all her children, embraces adversities, and remains virtuous and pure.[6] The postcolonial nation-state embodying maternal sacrifice was adequately represented in Mehboob Khan's 1957 film *Mother India*, where the ideal Indian woman and mother was represented on screen. We shall return to this analogy later.

The ongoing Maoist conflict between the state and guerrillas demonstrates the maternal narrative of the state's protective and nurturing impulse. Take, for example, the carefully crafted "surrender policies" and public campaigns that appeal to the Maoist guerrillas to return to the mainstream and give up their path of armed resistance. In publicized appeals for the return of the prodigal sons and daughters to the path of righteous citizenry, the figures of Gandhi, Gautam Buddha, and Ganga (river Ganges) are invoked to uphold virtues of nonviolence, compassion, truth and purity, ideals embodied by Mother India.[7] These appeals are issued by state governments, local police, and the central Home Ministry, mostly through the local vernacular media. They also report emotional stories from the perspective of Maoist cadres, who express regret at joining the path of armed violence and the life of chaos and confusion that they wanted to escape from.[8] The publicity campaigns call upon the state and the "good" law-abiding citizens to work together to bring those who have lost their way, back to the right path. The Adivasis, long seen through the colonial lens of "emotionless savages," especially need cajoling to come back to the fold of the nation. There is an assumption here that not only does the state enable pathways for the return of its deviant citizens but also, like the good benign mother, forgives and embraces the children who once spurned her.

This maternal instinct of the state that treats its insurgent population as deviant children who must return "home" can be contrasted with the reclaiming of masculinity through militarized responses manifested in "Operation Green Hunt." The political discourse labels the Maoist resistance as an armed insurgency that deserves a strong military (masculinized) response. A crucial part of this masculinist emotional expression, moving beyond the machismo of the security paradigm, is the role of "outrage."

Sundar (2012) outlines how revenge and outrage formed the core of the state's frames, as it responded to the Dantewada ambush of 2010; the state performed the "outraged community." She argues, "Indeed, outrage might be said to be central to performances of stateness. While state violence is normalised as expressions of sovereignty, affronts to this monopoly over violence become punishable acts, thus coding outrage into the everyday act of ruling" (2012, 716). Further, this outrage is driven by a "righteous anger" that needs instigation and perpetuation. The ambush attack on 24 April 2017 that killed twenty-five personnel of the Central Reserve Police Force (CRPF) provoked a statement from the Home Minister that it was "cold blooded" murder (Das 2017). The central government announced that its anti-Maoist strategy will be revised, indicating a more aggressive approach. Emotional frenzy continues to be whipped around the figure of the martyred *jawans*, who died fighting the "enemies" of the state. The ruling Bharatiya Janata Party (BJP), which won a massive majority in Delhi's municipal elections in April 2017, dedicated its victory to the Sukma martyrs who died serving Mother India (*Times of India* 2017).

Sundar (2012) discusses how the instigation of fear of the Maoists is accompanied by blaming the inadequacies of governance on the Maoists. When the poor condition of basic infrastructure in the conflict areas is questioned, the regular government response is that it is unable to carry out developmental work due to Maoist attacks on public infrastructure, including schools and hospitals. This rules out any form of critique since, at the outset, weakness and vulnerability overshadow any other flaws in the way the state governs. The state, thus, keeps at its center the "imagined community" of citizens, to which it produces graded and differentiated responses. The parallel play of revenge, outrage, weakness, and vulnerability is a performance for the India outside of conflict areas that needs to be shown strength, as well as the specter of Maoist "infestation."

The dilemmas of the postcolonial state in situations where it faces armed insurgency from its own citizens include a desire not only to eliminate the challengers but also to ensure that its legitimacy remains intact and unaffected. Revengeful anger is helpful to eliminate the challengers, and maternal instinct, nurturing and sacrifice enable both legitimacy and postcolonial continuity. The emotional language makes visible the state's political existence and its impositions of affective citizenship. This complex emotional subterfuge, which embodies both maternal appeals and militarized masculinity through expressions of anger, revenge, and outrage, is profoundly captured in the film *Mother India*.[9] Radha is the lead character whose husband abandons the family after his disability makes him feel emasculated. She brings up her two sons alone enduring tremendous hardship, without compromising her virtuous purity and values. Eventually one of her sons, Birju, turns a rebel *dacoit* (bandit), unable to bear the exploitation and injustices his mother experiences. Radha, who had worked so hard to raise her sons and protect them from the cruelties and vagaries of the world outside, kills her rebel son in a moment of outrage and anger, to protect the honor of her people and society. The struggles of Radha's lives are the struggles of the postcolonial state, left to fend for itself since its independence from colonial rule. Radha's response to her rebel son (product of class exploitation and injustices), which shifts from maternal protection and nurturing to cold-blooded murder, is the most suitable analogy to understand the affective relationship between the postcolonial Indian state and its deviant Maoist children. The benign mother must take charge, must kill her deviant children for the greater good, for the honor of the nation and country.

CONCLUSION

I am not prescribing wholesale rejection of the modern state. I am aware that in the modern world, most international institutions and much of international law are organized around nation-states. I am recommending the desacralization of the nation-state. So that we can experiment with the format of the modern state and can acknowledge its limitations and explore the possibilities of other kinds of states. (Ashis Nandy in Nandy and Darby 2015, 105)

The state as a political and cultural institution continues to have tremendous influence on human life and community building in postcolonial contexts. In the absence of strong civil society, the state performs multiple functions to govern the lives of its citizens; both its presence and its absence in people's lives constitute a source of their anxieties and conflicts. This chapter tried to demonstrate that the state can be imagined and experienced through gendered emotions. The embeddedness of emotions in the political and cultural life of the postcolonial state and their co-constitutive relationship was analyzed through the affective impact of and responses to the Maoist conflict in India. The chapter tried to comprehend the state (considered the rational actor in IR) particularly through its fostering of affective citizenship that addresses its postcolonial anxiety and identity.

The postcolonial state has a gendered affective presence in which its political "self" is enabled through a cumulative emotional bonding among various people and communities. The state sees any challenges to its power and sovereignty (such as the Maoist insurgency) as an act of ultimate rebellion and expects the insurgents to embrace its benign maternal protection or face the wrath of its militarized masculinity. The state responds to the insurgency through emotional utterances where any efforts to draw attention to its failures can be marked as antinational or even treason. Gendered emotional utterances, thus, acquire great significance in legitimizing the state's control and authority over both its compliant and its deviant citizens, particularly in postcolonial contexts where shared histories of oppression and marginalization continue to engender popular armed revolts.

NOTES

1. Both George Bush and Osama bin Laden made emotional appeals to their constituencies in their speeches. Both whipped up frenzied nationalism (based on secular, liberal, democratic, and modern values in the case of the former, and based on a radical, fundamentalist version of Islam in the case of latter). Both played on the same set of emotions (nationalism and identity) and same kind of politics of us vs. them, although they had different objectives and outcomes.
2. Also referred to as Naxalites. Naxalite and Maoist are used interchangeably although they refer to different temporal dimensions of the popular revolt against the state in India.
3. Dalits are the untouchable or the lowest ranked and most marginalised caste group in the caste hierarchy of South Asia. Adivasis are tribals or indigenous people. Both Dalits and Adivasis have experienced socio-economic marginalization and violence from the state and fellow citizens.
4. This quote is taken from an interview of Ashis Nandy by Livio Boni for the International Psychoanalytical Association. https://www.ipa.world/ipa/IPA_Docs/FinalLivio%20Bobi_Ashis%20Nandy.pdf, accessed December 21, 2016.
5. Every river in India except Brahmaputra (son of Brahma) is referred to as the mother.
6. This is the same as Mother Russia and the role that she performs, as Cai Wilkinson describes in her chapter in this volume.
7. A public interest advertisement on the surrender policy of the Jharkhand Government was published in *Dainik Hindustan* (*Hindi Daily*) on August 11, 2011, prior to the celebrations of Independence Day on August 15. These advertisements by the state governments and police departments are common in Maoist conflict affected areas.
8. These stories are not identifiable experiential narratives of 'real' people. They come with a generic picture of a man or woman with some text.
9. The film *Mother India* was made by Mehboob Khan in 1957, and famous actors like Nargis, Sunil Dutt, Rajendra Kumar, Raj Kumar, and Kanhaiyalal made this film memorable. Some believed that the film was a response to American author Katherine Mayo's 1927 polemical book *Mother India*, which painted a negative picture of Indian society and culture. The lead character, Radha (played by Nargis) was seen as a metonymic representation of the good virtuous Indian/Hindu woman and an exemplary mother through self-sacrifice.

CHAPTER 11

Violence and Gender Politics in the Proto-State "Islamic State"

KATHERINE E. BROWN

The so-called Islamic State, also known as Daesh, highlights the fragility of statehood as a construct for international relations. While scholars have developed ideas about quasi-states (Jackson 1993), failing states, weak states, and collapsed states (Rotberg 2011), postcolonial states (Clapham 1996; Chatterjee 1993), and de facto states (Pegg 1998) to explain forms of political organization that do not fit neatly into the standard Westphalian story of statehood (Sharma and Gupta 2006), these concepts fail to account for the "Islamic State." Islamic State rejects statehood at two levels. First, statehood is "man-made" as opposed to divine, and therefore an illegitimate and insufficient mode of governance, and Islamic State offers the alternative of the caliphate. Second, statehood depends upon false identities of race and nationality; instead Islamic State asserts a globalized claim for loyalty based upon the idea of the *umma* (community of Muslims). It therefore proposes a worldwide borderless mode of governance that is distinct from a "world government" or "world state." Preexisting terms that qualify statehood and are rooted in territory are therefore insufficient in this case, but despite Islamic State's actions and propaganda that assert a transnational mode of political organization, at the level of the everyday and the domestic there are clear institutional attempts at state building. In an arena of extreme competition for loyalty and authority, its policies on policing, taxation, marriage, and education build clearly specified identities of membership in the group and demonstrate its authority, in ways that mimic statehood. Such practices might lead us to revisit ideas about "good governance" and "ungoverned spaces" given these locations are seen to generate terrorism and regional insecurity (Clunan and Trinkunas 2010). Yet Daesh governs a territory; it is not lawless or unorganized. An alternative is to see Islamic State as rebels, insurgents, guerrillas, or terrorists, regardless of its state-like capacities or claims to territorial control. Islamic State certainly terrorizes and threatens the stability and security of those who do not, or cannot, submit to its rule—both globally and locally—and therefore might be conceptualized as simply a violent rebellious nonstate actor. But its globalized agenda is not merely transnational in operational violence (as al-Qaeda aspired to project) but offers an alternative vision of everyday living and politics (Brown 2015). Seeking an explanation for Islamic State in ideas about governance or rebellion therefore seems incomplete. Instead I propose understanding Islamic State as a "proto-state."

The term "proto-state" has recently entered the lexicon of international relations and security studies to describe Islamic State (Lia 2015; Belanger-Mcmurdo 2015; Gaub 2016). However, analysts are simply using the term as a synonym for "nascent" or "emerging" state, with little understanding of the term's anthropological and etymological roots (Giustozzi 2003). This chapter explores these origins. In anthropology, the term "proto-state" denotes a highly unstable and yet cohesive environment (Diamond 1996). Within a proto-state, emerging centers of power are antagonistic to local and traditional ways of life, and are seeking to wrest authority and wealth away from existing structures to new ones. Charrad (2001), for example, has shown how in the Middle East, nation building and state formation involved a contest for power between patrilineal-based kinship networks and centralizing postcolonial states. Importantly, this contest was not to the advantage of women in the region. In a postcolonial environment, where this battle for power was presumed, new emergent centers of power also challenge formal state structures (Araoye 2012). In violent competition with both the local and national, these emerging centers of power manage to coalesce and cohere, much like the nucleus of an atom. They develop a structural integrity while being in a perpetual state of flux. These entities occupy the conceptual space between states and nonstate actors (Szekely 2016) and become proto-states, permanently "emerging" and never truly fixed. Indeed, were they to achieve permanence or apparent viscosity, they would collapse. One limitation of existing work on proto-states is that there is little explicit consideration of how gender affects these processes, given substantial feminist insights into the operation of statehood in international relations (Weber 1994; Peterson 1992a). In the original *Gendered States* volume, we see how feminist interrogations of state creation revealed the importance of gender patterns in the interlocking imperatives of state-making: centralization of political authority, accumulation, militarism, exploitation, and legitimation (Peterson 1992a). Additionally, we can see how gender inequality is sustained by the core ideas that legitimate the state—sovereignty, the distinction between domestic and international politics, and the fiction of the state as a person (Kanatola 2007). What is interesting is how these insights differ or are reflected in the proto-state, especially one that challenges so many of these principles and processes, as does Islamic State.

I argue that Islamic State, as an example of a proto-state, is "Schrödinger's state"[1]—simultaneously both a state and a not-state. This chapter demonstrates how Islamic State is forced into an existential paradox—namely the tension between territorial and worldwide claims to authority. Second, and essential to understanding and exposing this existential paradox, are the ways in which gender shapes Islamic state as a proto-state. I am introducing a more refined and gender-informed working concept of the proto-state to the field of IR, and introducing gender critique to the concept as it is understood in other disciplines.

DEFINING ISLAMIC STATE

The origins of Islamic State are in the Jamaat al-Tawhidwa al-Jihad (The Group for Jihad and God's Oneness), founded in 1999 and later merging with al-Qaeda and other Sunni groups in Iraq, but it really took the form we know today during the "Arab Spring" and the accompanying regional uncertainty of 2011. Then it evolved into the Islamic State of Iraq and the Levant and, through establishing Jabhat al-Nusra, expanded into Syria. Attempting to merge this latter group back into its structures, in 2013 it became the Islamic State of Iraq and Al-Shams (greater Syria). Alongside this evolution and expansion, however, were disagreements with al-Qaeda. Consequently, in 2014 the two groups formally split, leading to a final rebranding as "Islamic State" (Lister 2016). In June 2014, a speech by the group's leader, Al Baghdadi, signaled its ambitions (and importantly how it differs from al-Qaeda) by declaring it "the caliphate." In 2015, its opponents coined the name "Daesh," an acronym of its earlier Arabic name (Mapping Militants 2017). Acronyms are not widely used in Arabic, and it implies the group is "nonsense," like the neologism. The term sounds similar to *daas*, which means to trample underfoot, suggesting a lack of dignity, and is used in a derogatory manner. I use the terms "Islamic State" and "Daesh" interchangeably.

The changes in name represented more than expansion in territory held by Islamic State. They also reveal ever-increasing functionality and institutionalization of governance. Al-Tamimi (2015) shows how the group set up institutions and ministries as early as 2007 even though it lacked enforcement mechanisms, and that these became meaningful and operational by 2013. During this phase, Daesh relied upon coercion and extortion to "collect taxes" from local businesses (Hansen-Lewis and Shapiro 2015) while at the same time setting up bases for recruitment through offers of employment, dispute resolution, and propaganda. Those who failed to conform or submit to its rule have been ruthlessly executed, alternative centers of authority—whether traditional tribal structures or state ones—thus being eradicated. This dual-pronged strategy meant that by 2014 it impacted all areas of everyday life. From billboards promoting "correct" Islamic dress for women, to marriage licenses, market regulation, fishing permits, agricultural crop plans, school curricula, and immunization programs, Islamic State bureaucratized everyday life and institutionalized its authority. The proliferation of rules and institutions is justified through a religious ideal—that Islam is a "way of life" and governs all aspects of one's existence. The provision of security to live according to that way of life (*sharia*) is the basis of its claim to the caliphate. The caliphate comprises the mechanisms through which the *umma* can live "the good life" (i.e., one compliant with God's will); it exists in a territorial space known as *dar al-Islam* (the world of Islam and peace) and is contrasted with *dar al-Harb* (world of war). Consequently, the caliphate depends upon transnational ideas of citizenship (*umma*) and of governance (*sharia*) while necessarily being rooted in place (*dar al-Islam*) where the institutions of governance (as the caliphate) are operational. This is its existential paradox—both dependent on, and denying, "territory."

Postdeclaration Daesh still controls approximately 65,000 square kilometers (Gutowski 2016), with a population of approximately 6 million and formal membership of between 20,000 and 100,000 people (Institute for the Study of War n.d.; Gartenstein-Ross 2015). Its members' violence is infamous for its ruthlessness and its spectacular nature; it is estimated that between 19,000 and 30,000 people have died at the hands of Islamic State, and around 3.2 million people have been internally displaced or are living as refugees (Norwegian Refugee Council 2016; New York Times n.d). In early 2016 Islamic State appears to have been unable to sustain its territorial control, losing approximately 14% of its territory (Johnson 2016) and its Arabic-language magazine reports that it "can to return to the desert" in order to regroup if it is forced to do so. Setbacks are framed as confirmation of the impending apocalypse, which will see the group's final victory after a wave of defeats, and it insists that the caliphate transcends territory.

Given Islamic State's violent competition with local rivals and state institutions, condition of territorial flux, dependency upon a transnational citizenship, and rejection of sovereign boundaries while simultaneously controlling the daily lives of millions, imposing new laws and extracting resources, how does Islamic State cohere and maintain structural integrity? I argue that the answer lies in three extreme mechanisms of controlling gender roles. First is the construction of a "Muslimwoman" dependent upon a religious nationalism. Defined by purdah, piety, and nonviolent jihad, she transcends local culture and race, paradoxically utilizing transnational ideals to create a nationalist framework of the proto-state. Second is the creation of the "warrior-monk" built upon a militarized nationalism. He overcomes preexisting tribal allegiances for the "brotherhood." These two figures operate in gender-segregated but codependent imagined spaces (the latter in the "battlefield," the former in the "home"), but they are brought together through Daesh's public demonstrations of organized and highly symbolic, gendered violence in a third space: the street. This third mechanism redefines access, acceptable conduct, and governance of Daesh across the public and private spheres. In doing so it enforces order and cohesion by creating new centers of power in the proto-state that affect all lives regardless of membership of the caliphate. The first two mechanisms, therefore, create gender-essentialized citizens of the new proto-state formed of transnational and transhistorical ideals and made real through daily practices that locate Daesh as a particular nationalist and statist construct. The third mechanism legitimizes and reinforces Daesh's actions and ideals in the home and on the battlefield, thereby unifying—in principle if not in practice—its areas of power and authority. These complex gender maneuvers, which hold together in tension both the rejection and the desire for nationalism and statehood, are necessary because Daesh remains trapped as a proto-state.

MECHANISM 1: CONSTRUCTING THE MUSLIMWOMAN

For a proto-state such as Islamic State, where there are competing institutions of governance in the local environment, the ability to intertwine a new global religious narrative into everyday living is key to building power. The image of the national "woman" creates a singularly understood place of belonging, a community of kinship, a haven for family, and a home (Layoun

1992), and is very effective at achieving cohesion regardless of local divisions. This is because it builds a linkage between the mother/woman and the nation, and the man/father and the state, reinforcing citizenship and identity (Chatterjee 1993; Walby 2006). Cooke (2008) reflects on a form of the "national woman"—the "Muslimwoman" archetype, who is characterized by modesty, motherhood, and chastity. Islamic State prioritizes a similar construction of the "Muslimwoman"—an essentially privatized ideal coalescing around purdah, piety, and nonviolent jihad (Sonbol 2005). Combined, these elements control women in Islamic State, drawing on a transnational ideal that trumps local manifestations of womanhood; yet they are also being used to create a religio-nationalist framework of the proto-state that operates to define the symbolic and physical boundaries of Daesh. For women who cannot or will not uphold this singular "Muslimwoman" ideal, the consequences are life threatening.

Purdah is "life behind the veil," an extremely cloistered female lifestyle. The idea of purdah is to promote privacy, and through this women's chastity and the honor of the male head of household. Purdah is important because it symbolizes the home to be protected, and is a microcosm of the state that needs to be shielded from the outside. Moreover, upholding purdah shows that homes are created in Islamic State, and that Daesh is more than a "war zone." Maintaining purdah shows that members of Daesh live a "full life," one that includes a "home life," not just a fighting life. As well as placing women in a position of dependency on male heads of household, purdah demonstrates the wealth and power of those men and by extension the system in which they live. Women are thus required to carry their purdah with them when they leave the home, by wearing a niqab and gloves, to protect them from the "outside" world. Women are encouraged not to travel outside the home without need, they must be in their homes by nightfall, and a male guardian must accompany them if they are to travel any distance. While some women have official positions in Islamic State, they are usually confined to working in the home, with roles determined by their husband's status (Youssef and Haris 2015). Women with exceptional status are permitted additional freedoms; notably some foreign women belong to an all-female police force whose role is mainly to enforce purdah and "modest" behaviors (Winter 2015). Purdah therefore determines women's relationships in the home and in the public sphere. It homogenizes womanhood, overwriting national or local customs and differences.

Accompanying the physical manifestations of purdah is a series of feminine values that embody this lifestyle—modesty and self-sacrifice (Mahmood 2005). These combine in an overarching concept of piety—understood by Daesh as submission to sharia.[2] Umm Layth (a supporter of Daesh on Twitter and reportedly living in Daesh territories) argues that women of Daesh are "trying to build an Islamic state that lives and abides by the law of Allah." Daesh's emphasis on purdah is in accordance with its understanding of sharia and Islam as a complete way of life. It is essential to its status as the caliphate. Piety, as submission, is for women of Islamic State expressed through fulfilling God's purpose—namely becoming wives and mothers. Marriage is not linked to romance or love, but a contract that unifies the private and public lives toward a common goal (Brown 2014). Analysis of the social media accounts of seventeen female recruits to Daesh reveals that "it is ideological devotion to the creation of an Islamic state, not sexual or romantic desire, which drives these [marital] relationships" (Loken and Zeleny 2016, 17). Combining this with the idea of submission and service to the state, women of Islamic State perceive themselves as the "ultimate wives of *jihad*" (Saul 2014). Islamic State facilitates this understanding by strictly regulating marriages so that unions best serve Daesh. It stipulates who can be a guardian for the woman in the shaping and signing of a *nikah* (marriage contract) that must be concluded in the presence of an Islamic State official. There is now a minimum dowry of US$5,000. Daesh says it is to make marriage a serious commitment and to protect foreign women (*muhajiraat*)[3] because they had asked for so little in terms of dowry in comparison to local women (Navest, de Koning, and Moor 2016; Al Muhajirat blog, July 2015). By imposing regulations on marriages, Islamic State is attempting to add layers of legitimacy by instilling a veneer of religious and state approval to the new families and kin/gender relations created by the regime. The regulations prove to followers that Allah governs their new lives even as they transgress local customs. This detailed regulation is not unprecedented; as Mackenzie writes, "The disorder that tends to come with conflict reveals the intense effort necessary to regulate sex, and construct gender identities, or protect what I call 'conjugal order'" (2010, 205). The conjugal order within a religious nationalism project utilizes "God's privileged code" for the new political project (Friedland 2002). Heterosexual-religious marriage, created and instigated out of loyalty, piety, and submission to the caliphate rather than from love or family ties, is thus one of the cornerstones of the proto-state.

Islamic State, like the Lord's Resistance Army, has a political vision, which is not only to create a new caliphate, but to create a new cast of Muslims to fill it (Baines 2014). Governing the conjugal order generates a "new cast" of Muslims, defines their relationship with each other, and creates the proto-state. The universality of this gendered code of reproduction unifies an ethnically diverse population. Daesh claims that it is racially blind, and it truly represents a postracial political order. This claim is present in several videos and media, for example, in Islamic State's online magazine *Dabiq* "[Here] is where the Arab and non-Arab, the white man and the black man, the easterner and westerner are all brothers,": (Issue 1, p. 7), and in a video fronted by a black American "jihadist" after Baton Rouge, who emphasizes that his skin color doesn't matter in Daesh. As part of this new cast of Muslims, interracial marriages are important in order to prove racism doesn't exist. For example, Umm Abyan of Islamic State tweeted about an acquaintance of hers: "2 of his wives are Somali and he's a revert [white] Alhumduillah no discrimination" [*sic*]. The promotion of these interracial marriages is important for the governance of the group, as in 2015 there were over twenty-five thousand foreign fighters from over one hundred different countries (UNASSMT 2015, 8).

As a result of the emphasis on piety and purdah, Islamic State has largely rejected the idea of violent jihad for women within the territorial confines of the state. Its propagandists suggest that it is possible to simultaneously uphold purdah and piety while carrying out other forms of jihad. Jihad is redefined as service. The wife of Aymen Al-Zawahiri wrote in 2009, "We [Muslim women] put ourselves in the service of the jihadis, we carry out what they ask, whether supporting them financially, servicing their [practical] needs" (Lahoud 2010). Among the six hundred or so European women who have traveled to join Daesh, we only have a few accounts of their motivations; however, Hunt (2014) argues that many are driven by a sense of service to others. One woman interviewed upon her return to Europe said, "I always wanted to live under *sharia*. . . . Besides my Muslim brothers and sisters over there need help" (Hunt 2014). Shannon Maureen Conley, an eighteen-year-old from Denver who was arrested in April 2014 on her way to Syria, claimed she wanted to be a soldier's wife and a nurse. However, outside of the territories that Daesh controls, the role of jihad for women is more complex. Living in an environment where purdah and piety cannot be guaranteed, women are permitted to carry out violent jihad. In the same open letter cited above, Umayma al Zawahiri doesn't rule out jihad; instead she argues that "the path of fighting is not easy for women—for it requires a companion with whom it is lawful for a woman to be." It is largely posited as an act of last resort, and while women are trained in defensive combat and battlefield triage within Daesh territory, participation in violent jihad would violate purdah and therefore undermine the narrative of the group (Ali 2016; Eggert 2015). Reconciling the contradiction of women's violence being both permissible and prohibited is only possible because of Islamic State's proto-state nature.

This discussion about the "Muslimwoman" shows how the creation of this archetype by Daesh is necessary so as to manage the inherent tensions that characterize its condition as a proto-state. It shows that Daesh must craft and make "real" this "God code" and create the dominance of religion in public and private identities. This becomes evident in the proliferation of rules governing women's lives and bodies. Its interventions show that this is not an organic process; it is constantly dealing with instability, and its viscosity is temporary. Moreover, while interventions in the marriage market may create the "new cast" of Muslims, for example, they also reveal how local power structures still challenge them. The need for a minimum dowry was not only to protect *muhajiraat*, but because the *muhajiraat* were undercutting potential marriages for local women; it was also reported that local women were reluctant to marry "foreign fighters" (Speckard and Yayla 2015). Daesh has had to create a transnational religious identity by creating the "Muslimwoman" to override local and radical politics. Additionally, in acknowledging the potential violence of women while limiting it to the peripheries of the state, Daesh reveals that the caliphate both seeks and transcends territory.

MECHANISM 2: THE WARRIOR-MONK

Although Daesh attempts to demonstrate that it is "more than" a fighting force to affirm its claims to the caliphate, the structure of the organization, the hero worship of fighters almost to point of deification, the daily privileges afforded to military personnel, and other signs of militarism all show the limitations of this assertion. In a condition of extreme competition for allegiance and authority, Islamic State must enforce its dominance continually, over both the Iraqi and Syrian military, and over local forms of patriarchy. One mechanism that competes against both is its exposition of the ideal Muslim man. In Daesh, the ideal Muslim male is the "warrior-monk," and he epitomizes a militarized religious nationalism. The term "warrior-monk" is more common in Buddhist nationalisms (Adolphson 2007); here it combines ideas of heroism and publicly performed piety. The warrior-monk is a variation on the combination of "brain and brawn" idealized in Western militaries (Duncanson 2013) and exhibiting a "virulent masculinity" (Chatterjee 2016, 2). Performance of heroic brawn is insufficient, however; fighters for Daesh must act with correct intentions and the correct belief (Wood 2015). The piety of the warrior-monk is felt and experienced by upholding religious obligations rather than an outcome of intellectual endeavor. *Dabiq* stated: "They [the *mujaheddin*] do not complicate their knowledge by philosophizing their religion and thus abstaining from obligations through complex analysis. Rather their knowledge flows from their hearts" (issue 5, p. 27). While the motives of individual fighters are contested (Wood 2015), and we can easily question whether they seek martyrdom or material reward, the myth of the warrior-monk remains potent for Daesh, as the figure unites (together with the Muslimwoman) its claims for control, authority, and legitimacy.

The warrior-monk reveals how the glorification of war promotes the belief that men are "natural protectors," that they deserve special praise for their actions, that hierarchies are the natural order of society, that physical force is valued as a dispute resolution mechanism, and that having enemies is a normal condition (Enloe 2016; Highgate and Henry 2011). The warrior-monk figure unites the two spaces of Daesh—the battlefield and the home. This is similar to Elshtain's discussions on the "beautiful soul" and the "just warrior" (1987). The warrior-monk protects purdah, and he is rewarded for his action in the battlefield "as man"—by being offered women slaves as payments, and given priority by Daesh in the marriage market over other men. Slaves are considered legitimate reward for fighting jihad because conquered populations, their wealth, and property become "bounty" for the warriors. Official UN sources found that Islamic State held nearly 3,500 slaves (UNHRC/UNAMI 2016). Umm Abbas confirms the success of this strategy: "The *Jazrawis* [fighters from the Gulf] here are the ones who have the most *sabiyas* [slaves]. They love their women. . . . He purchased one for 1000$ [*sic*] looool . . . then another for 10000$" (Twitter, September 23, 2015). An article in *Dabiq* justified slavery of non-Muslims as punishment for "abandoning God's favor." Moreover, taking concubines is necessary because of "men's instincts," which have been suppressed in Western society because women there no longer hold purdah. It further argues that sexual sins are "the consequences of abandoning jihad and chasing after the *dunyā* [temporal worldly pleasures]" (*Dabiq*, issue 4, p. 17). As with marriage, Daesh has produced a set of guidelines regarding the proper treatment of slaves, including prohibiting a father and son from raping the same slave. That it has created such documents confirms to many the abhorrent and cruel treatment of slaves by the group. The commodification of women is not limited to slavery; women are used as financial mules, for transactional sex, and kidnapping for ransom, and are strategically used to negotiate borders and checkpoints and in prisoner exchanges (Nasar 2013; Alhayek 2015; Hojati 2016). The twin economies of war and heteronormativity are overtly and unashamedly linked by Daesh to uphold the centers of power around which its authority coalesces. Highlighting the role of slaves alongside the warrior-monk and the Muslimwoman shows the apparent viscosity of Daesh—a certain fluidity of ontology of "human" beyond a male-female binary, and the strong connections between the spheres of life—and so confirms their proto-state condition.

The warrior-monk doesn't only combine the battlefield and purdah within the territories of Islamic State in the present tense, but also creates a new mythological future. Daesh is working toward an "end of days" battle against the forces of unbelievers that will bring about the recreation of "God's earth" through violence on a cosmic scale. Daesh's account of history is one of perpetual conflict, in which the forces of evil have continuously sought to undermine and destroy the world of Islam. It anticipates violence on a global, transhistorical, and cosmic scale, which leads it to justify retaliation against perceived humiliations, injustices, and aggressions through highly organized and spectacular violence filled with symbolic messages. According to its key treatise, *The Management of Savagery* (Naji 2006), the violence of civil war is to be coaxed or disciplined into a future legal order by Daesh. It argues such savagery is natural after centuries of humiliation and is innate to the warrior-monk. A video it produced featuring "Jihadi John" (Mohammed Emwazi) and others carrying out a mass execution, declares: "Know that we have armies in Iraq and an army in Sham [Syria] of hungry lions whose drink is blood and [whose] play is carnage." Unlike other militaries, who obfuscate their extreme violence, Daesh celebrates and extends it because it confirms the totalizing and apocalyptic aesthetic of its violence.

While individual acts of violence are barbaric, the savagery is not random; it is justified and framed in a narrative of religious war, and it serves a strategic purpose of disrupting existing local tribal loyalties, lineages, and power/authority. The cult of the warrior-monk transforms local patriarchal relations, because leadership is no longer based on genealogy, nobility or even *hazz* (good fortune) but upon piety, loyalty to the new organization, and military prowess. Daesh insists that fighting men of local tribes and cities declare allegiance through the *bayaa* (the laying of hands and declaration of fealty) that binds individuals not only to Islamic State but to the leader upon whom they lay their hands. Such allegiances provide Daesh with additional fighters, financial aid, and weapons (Gambher 2014), while simultaneously usurping the authority of traditional leaders (derived through age, kinship, and patronage) by empowering young men because of their ability to fight and their new loyalty. Combined with slavery and the transnational Muslimwoman archetype, Daesh is eliminating local ways of life by rewriting relations of patriarchy and modes of masculinity and femininity. The warrior-monk is valued for his overt signs of piety and physicality—there is a clear objectification of the male body. In the Twitter avatars of male Daesh members, in its media output, and in magazines, it promotes ideals of vitality, fitness, and strength. In its propaganda, protein shakes, free weights, and AK47s and other rifles feature prominently in images of men in the home or in the street as well as the battlefield, and tracksuits or camouflage uniforms are essential to the *"jihadi* look." Maffesoli argues that aesthetics has the power of creating effective social affinities and sympathies experienced by individuals in relation to others (1991, 12–13). The sense of brotherhood or homosociability is central to Daesh, a core component of cohesion recognized in the study of military effectiveness (King 2013). The featured stories of martyrs in editions of *Dabiq* are always stories of great friends and participation in a great adventure under God's protection, in their mission sometimes achieving death. The accompanying pictures show the men looking happy, confident, proud—and in death, smiling with a halo about them. This "uniform" of jihad takes control of the meaning and social practice of death away from local institutions and practices, and toward a more homogeneous experience of grief and mourning. This is combined with the enforcement rules of mourning for widows and family regardless of local custom. Reshaping the institutions of death, as well as life, is highly significant in a conflict and war zone.

This combination of controlling the institutions of life and death in a religio-militarized proto-nationalism is part of a total-war mentality. Ottoway (2015) claims that Daesh is state-building to fund the war, and argues that without territorial rule the top-down military structure would crumble. However, this conceptualization fails to account for the symbiotic nature of Daesh's ideology of the caliphate and the Apocalypse. Imposing a hierarchy of priorities between controlling violence and life, forces us, unsatisfactorily, to view Daesh as either a state or not. Instead, the idea of the proto-state as existing in a nucleic condition of flux enables us to reconcile tensions without resorting to binaries. Daesh's focus on war provides the basis for protecting and organizing the good life of submission, but also brings the chaos of conflict into the ordered imaginary of submissive-civilian living. The warrior-monk cannot exist only in the battlefield. The distinction between the "killing fields" and "home" cannot be sustained despite purdah—rather, there is a continuum. Brickell (2008) discusses where cultures of conflict are infused into the core constituents of a society, and shows how the violence of conflict at the state level of war continues to influence micro-level behavior postconflict. For Daesh, as a proto-state, this isn't only a legacy of conflict, but a parallel effect, and a parallel geography. The warlike violence is brought home from the war front through the public and staged execution of tribes who resist Daesh, and the systematic sectarian-based violence in nominal civilian spaces—such as destroying shrines, Shiite mosques, and ancient monuments. Thus in proto-states the distinction between civilian and military and ideas of territory fluctuate, but their gendered ideal types as mechanisms of control remain stable.

MECHANISM 3: STREET VIOLENCE

The two figures of the Muslimwoman and warrior-monk operate in gender-segregated but codependent imagined spaces (the latter in the "battle-field," the former in the "home"), but they are brought together through Daesh's public demonstrations of organized, gendered violence in a third space: the street. This third mechanism redefines access, acceptable conduct, and governance of the so-called caliphate across the public and private spheres. Utilizing a gender-informed analytical framework shows that the proto-state is more than a nascent or "prestate" condition, but rather is constantly rewriting spatial understandings. The violence of the street blurs the boundaries between the warrior-monk and the Muslimwoman and between the civilian and military actions of Daesh. This violence shows how proto-states become inscribed and embodied through coercion. In the archetypes of Daesh the submission of the warrior-monk and the Muslimwoman is consensual and agentic, but behind every promise of paradise is a threat of punishment. Its acts of coercion operate at two levels: first, in the creation of boundaries and borders that shape and contain the *umma*, and, second, in creating the boundaries and borders that define the caliphate.

According to Islamic State, existing international treaties do not determine the borders of the caliphate. A popular video demonstrates this when in a dramatic climax a fighter speaks of breaking the "barrier of Sykes Picot"[4] as he purportedly crosses it, claiming it no longer prevents Muslims from living together as the *umma*. Esposito (2015) argues that Daesh's commitment to eliminating state borders seeks to evoke the glories of Islamic history in the face of centuries of Western invasions, occupation, and colonialism. Within its expansionist global political vision though, Daesh still requires control of the local, and recognition of the importance of territory (Hamdan 2016). In July 2014, Daesh announced the issuance of "caliphate passports" to approximately eleven thousand citizens in a conscious effort to create a new permanent Islamic State identity. Doing so, Daesh paradoxically presents itself as sustaining harmonious "safe spaces" (for "rightly believing" Muslims), a zone of peace (*dar-al-Islam*) that is contrasted with a zone of war (*dar-al-Harb*). Despite aerial bombardment from opponents, *Muhajiraat* claim that living under Islamic State is safer than in *dar-al-Kufr* ("land of the unbeliever"). Bint Mujahid, a *muhajirat,* presented an environment of protection and safety: "Now I was home from Taraweeh in complete safety, comfort and honor. Surrounded by *mujahidin* [male fighters] knowing none can harm me. What a difference" (Twitter, July 17, 2015). The warrior-monk maintains his status through a less than subtle "protection racket" (Sjoberg and Peet 2011). This sets up a binary logic between anarchy-evil outside its borders and governance and peace within it. This logic of sovereignty has been criticized by Cynthia Weber (1994), who shows how the performance of statecraft based on the assumption of a disordered anarchical international system leads to a gendered order within the domestic borders of the state. For Daesh's worldview and raison d'être to be sustained, it cannot tolerate desertion. Violence is central to maintaining jurisdiction; that is, the ability to define its borders even as they override older state borders. Daesh violently polices its borders, through identity cards, passports, import and export duties, and the introduction of a visa-type system for movement within Daesh. This contrasts with its earlier days, when members of Islamic State reported fluid movement and the ability to travel back and forth to Europe and elsewhere. To reinforce the shift, it became a crime to assist anyone trying to leave the caliphate without permission, and a violation of sharia to seek to leave. To deter others, an Austrian teenager was reportedly beaten to death with a hammer, after she repeatedly tried to leave Raqqa in November 2015 (Sommers 2015). In another case, a son publically executed his mother after she tried to persuade him to leave (Hall 2016).

Violence governs the borders within Islamic State too. In 2003–2009 Iraq's state infrastructure was the target of Islamic State's violence. Most casualties were Shi'a because they dominated state institutions. Post-2012 the ratio shifted and Daesh focused more on targets from everyday life (Economics and Peace 2015). In 2016, six thousand people were killed as a result of Daesh nonmilitary violence (Economics and Peace 2016). The scale is not to be dismissed and is well documented in United Nation reports (2015, 2016); Daesh is responsible for thousands of men being buried in mass graves, enslaving thousands of women, and the degrading treatment of prisoners (Spence 2014). The violence by Daesh against those they define as "Other" also defines the actions and activities of the collective *umma* for the proto-state; transgressions of behavior or belief cast an individual outside of the ordered submission of sharia and the caliphate. The display of mutilated bodies, public slave auctions, and summary executions by crucifixion or beheading for alleged traitors, witches, homosexuals, and rapists are not incidental or ad hoc (Zech and Kelly 2015). The torture of individuals and the manner of their death is highly symbolized and is designed to refer to historic examples, thereby reinforcing Daesh's foundation myth, and meant to dehumanize those who are suffering. It treats enemies and prisoners as animals—ritually slaughtering them as if they were meat, or keeping them in cages (Cheterian 2015). The so-called rightness of its violence is premised upon a narrow and unorthodox reading of sharia and from a romanticized vision of an Islamic "golden age." Daesh derive its legal legitimacy not from the fact that it is culturally conservative or traditional, but paradoxically because it is "new" and believes itself to be "re-establishing" a much older, sacred tradition that overturns local custom (*ibadaa*, or unwarranted innovation). The many instances of beheading, stoning, and amputation are explained to the public as examples of justice from the time of the Prophet and those who immediately followed him.[5] This torture is made meaningful as a deterrent and punishment because there is a continuum of violence—before, during, and after conflict, and from personal and household to the international (Enloe 2016). Violence is inflicted upon those, and creates those, who are deemed "ungovernable" because they cannot be brought into the *umma*. We should therefore see the violence carried out against thieves or traitors as operating alongside that against women who fail to wear the correct *niqab* and gloves. At least fifteen women have been disfigured with acid for this "crime," and another woman reportedly had an animal trap used on her breast (and died of her injuries) as a result of breast-feeding in public (Smith 2015). Tellingly, it was the Al-Khansaa police brigade of women who carried out these public and symbolic punishments for violations of purdah—for not upholding the Muslimwoman ideal-type, and for violating the "natural" order of the street. The rules of dress and conduct in the public sphere, in the street, become important because they demonstrate the new juridical structures, and quash vestiges of the old tainted political and cultural power. Through this violence, only a particular class of pious male is cast as political in the public sphere.

CONCLUSION

This chapter has introduced the concept of the "proto-state" to develop our understanding of so-called Islamic State, and demonstrates that a gendered perspective helps us explain underlying paradoxes of its existence. The chapter shows that Daesh exhibits classic characteristics of a proto-state, trapped in a perpetual state of instability, flux, and fluidity, and yet coalesces and finds form as it challenges and forcibly remakes authority. Daesh manages to cohere around three core control mechanisms: the

Muslimwoman archetype, the warrior-monk archetype, and "violence of the street." These mechanisms reveal that the viscosity of Islamic State is possible because of the imposition of an overarching gender hierarchy that places a particular class of man, the warrior-monk, at the pinnacle, and the nonbelieving female slave at the bottom. The purpose of this gender hierarchy is not only to create "God's order on Earth" but also to transcend race-based ideas of nationalism and territorially limited ideas of statehood. The hierarchy is manufactured through a war economy, a militarized culture and society, and the policing and coercion of territory and of the identities permitted within it. These are made meaningful to the people living under Daesh's control by redefining womanhood via a transnational ideal that also governs private relations; through the preferential treatment of jihadi soldiers; and through the symbolic, sexualized, and systematic violence used to coerce. This helps us understand why Daesh simultaneously denies and depends on local territorial formations of itself. The analysis reveals that the process of statehood is never complete; Daesh exists in a state of flux and consequently seeks extreme control. Daesh is caught in a constant and never-ending assertion of control—in the home, the battlefield, and the street—against both local and global competitors. This self-assertion reveals that Islamic State is not simply a nascent or weak state, or a terrorist or guerrilla movement, but a proto-state. Moreover, this insight into Daesh as a proto-state helps challenge the exceptionalist narrative concerning Daesh, and through a gendered analysis, its paradoxical mechanisms, discourse, and practices are demystified.

NOTES

1. I hope readers will forgive the pun on "Schrödinger's cat." Schrödinger carried out a thought experiment to help us understand quantum physics and the flaws of the Copenhagen interpretation of quantum mechanics and Heisenberg's uncertainty principle regarding knowledge and observation. The cat, trapped in a box, is to be thought of as both dead and alive because we cannot be sure of its death until it is observed. For more information: http://www.informationphilosopher.com/solutions/experiments/schrodingerscat/.

2. *Sharia* is often misunderstood as a codified legal system but should be understood as jurisprudence. Sharia is not a singular body of relations, but a history of judgments on public, private, and political life that current authorities may draw upon in their formulations.

3. *Muhajirat* (pl. *muhajiraat*) means female migrants. Islamic State uses it to describe women who have traveled to join Daesh, in contrast with women already residing in territory it controls. The term implies a holy pilgrimage, hajj. Another term is *mujahidat*, meaning female fighter; the Arabic root for the word is *jihad*. The male equivalent is *mujahidin*.

4. This is a reference to the Sykes-Picot agreement signed in 1916 between Great Britain and France. Popular understanding is that it created state boundaries of the Middle East, many of which are seen unrelated to ethnic or sectarian affiliations (Pursely 2015).

5. It is worth noting that these interpretations are disputed. Stoning does not exist as a punishment in the Qur'an or Sunna. The verse used by Daesh to justify beheadings ("smite their necks") needs to be read in conjunction with the next verse, which demands, "When ye have thoroughly subdued them, bind captives firmly. Thereafter is the time for either generosity or ransom" (chapter 47, verse 4). Beheading, clearly, is not intended. And removing a thief's hand is justified only if the state has guaranteed food for all, which is not so in Daesh.

AFTERWARDS

CHRISTINE SYLVESTER

Aftermaths are everywhere. That is not especially good news for ordinary people suffering sour states and sour afterwards—of elections, of aerial bombardments, of lost EU community, of recession, of terrorist attacks, of right-wing rantings, of life in refugee camps, of lives with illness and hunger. State-sponsored afterwalls are engineered to keep aliens who suffer out, notwithstanding increased uncertainty about exactly who is eligible and privileged enough to get walled in. Nostalgia for a greatly simplified and sugar-coated past is an afterward; it harkens back to a time when queer people were closeted, and classified ads in newspapers listed jobs for men separate from jobs for women. Afterwards today can relieve the state of civility and install spaces of convulsive rudeness, where assaults on facts become trendy, okay, alternative, pretty cool. Facebook and Twitter seduce us with kingpin platforms full of afterwords that give as good as they get, bestowing on connection- addicted users the thrill of faux popularity and the afterwards of death threats. Meanwhile, a lot of people do expire in afterworlds of state-involved war zones.

People also toss and turn with anxiety knowing that a few others massage their own sourness into real-life insufferability. Shooters fancy public places. They like gunning down kids in schoolrooms, or shooting everyday people in their churches, movie theaters, restaurants, concerts, and dance clubs. So far the shooters have been men fueled by Nietzchean levels of *ressentiment*, which the wise in society tend to pass off as mental problems. That says something about gender and about women who have mental health problems and do not perform their issues through shootings. "Last week they shot a woman, right about here. She was a Martha. She was fumbling in her robe, for her pass, and they thought she was hunting for a bomb. They thought she was a man in disguise" (Atwood, *The Handmaid's Tale*, 1985, 17.)

"They." Who are they if not guardians, supremacists, dowry doubters, god-made-me-do-it haters, and militarized misogynists? Feminist IR knows that when states go sour, one afterward foretold is that people called women will be in danger. Jacqui True and Christine Agius point toward such dangers in this collection.

These and other afterwards direct our attention as readers to a question the editors have raised: "Would the state survive without gender, and can we ungender the state?"(page 13)? Let us take this question a little further. Do we want to ungender the state? Do we want the state, run by better angels, to survive? Is the state not self-referential no matter what kind it is? Bluntly put, would the absence of gender modify loathsome afterwards of contemporary statecraft and international relations? Or would such hopes be Daeshed in the world's many anguished streets? Check Katherine Brown here (p. 24). Whose afterward would be the model?

The fact that this renewed volume on gendered states comes out now, at this moment in history, is consequential. The state in 2017 is fraught, disappearing in some places and coming on strong in others. It is in transition or under pressure in some of my favorite spots: Zimbabwe, the UK, Sweden, Korea, France, the Netherlands, Japan, the United States. The existential situation is truly dire in Sudan, Yemen, Somalia, Syria, Afghanistan, Iraq, and DR Congo; but the states of Belgium, Germany, Greece, Italy, Spain, Ukraine, Turkey, Iran, Pakistan, Brazil, Mexico, and Argentina are also experiencing what might be called "afterwards politics." These range from austerities imposed to cure chronic debt, to the decline of Labor parties before the combined onslaught of neoliberalism, nationalism, and intolerance associated with scary right-wing strongmen like Geert Wilders and Donald Trump, and strongwoman Marine le Pen. We see women heads of state singled out for popular impeachments, and social democratic Sweden instituting all-citizens conscription in case the primo strongman in Russia tries funny business in the region. We see too much trouble.

WHERE TO TURN?

Worry and watch TV news? There is the horror of knowing some women are going through nine months of pregnancy only to have babies with impossibly large Zika heads or offspring who will succumb to Ebola, malaria, starvation, girl killings, or hate crimes; diseases often battled hard in the tony West are allowed to run riot elsewhere. We can see their scourges. The men of Boko Haram get it into their entitled heads to kidnap hundreds of schoolgirls and force them to become sex slaves. Meanwhile some promising girl scholars in the UK take it into their heads to fly off to Turkey and slip into Syria to join a glorious fight against their own futures. In the United States, children watch undocumented mothers get kicked out and see their dreams disappear. "Women can't hold property anymore, she said. It's a new law. Turned on the TV today? . . . Don't worry, I'm sure it's temporary" (Atwood 1985, 231, 232). "Something is happening: there's a commotion, a flurry among the shoals of cars. Some are pulling over to the side, as if to get out of the way. I look up quickly: it's a black van, with the white-winged eye on the side. It doesn't have the siren on, but the other cars avoid it anyway. It cruises slowly along the street, as if looking for something: shark on the prowl" (Atwood 1985, 219). Watch white policemen of state shoot black men of not the state—often, it seems, because they can. The police do not go wary in front of all the phone cameras recording their deeds. They have an answer: the victims made us do it, don't you see? Thus is the citizenry admonished to support police as they break up protests from inside tank turrets, wielding excess military equipment the Pentagon sells off to finance overseas wars. Police lives are the lives that matter.

Keep going? Refugees and asylum seekers languish on Pacific islands or in UNHCR camps for nearly ever—sent by a paranoid Australian state or encountered as they run as individuals from the Lord's Resistance Army in Uganda. "Not all of you will make it through. Some of you will fall on dry ground or thorns. Some of you are shallow-rooted" (Atwood 1985, 25). Lucky ones gain citizenship somewhere and do their bit for the new country, only to find themselves denigrated, as was the Khan family, originally from Pakistan and now American citizens, whose son died fighting the American war in Iraq; they were chastised for scolding a gauche presidential candidate who showed cluelessness about the Constitution he could, and soon would, be sworn to uphold. Or you might get to your dream country at last and find it so alien and outside your imaginings that you cannot embrace it: "This place doesn't look like my America, doesn't even look real. It's like we are in a terrible story, like we're in the crazy parts of the Bible, there where God is busy punishing people for their sins" (Bulawayo, *We Need New Names*, 2013, 152–153). Then there are all those proper citizens, most of them men, who reside in Arlington National Cemetery near Washington, DC. They heeded the call to serve, to be heroes for the warrior state. Look where it got them (be careful to avoid saying anything about the many times more bodies on the other side of all the wars. They don't count).

Sit it all out? Perhaps the Hegelian dialectic, though coughing up phlegm, is still alive and gasping in some version. If so, would that not suggest the prospect of syntheses percolating up, nudging or catapulting stagnant, stubborn, stupid-acting, secretive, mean-spirited, and dinosaur-ish states in some progressive directions? What of women who march and workers who picket, those who sign petitions, phone their representatives, and adjudicate in ways that do not let cruel laws go into effect? Still. I don't know about you, kind reader, but I get cranky, crabby, out of sorts—old feminist feathers ruffle—when, I see retro mores revived and lovingly embraced as the smart afterwards of feminism, like stiletto heels or very much younger women walking a bit behind their very, very much older men partners. It floors me that the ideal heterosexual woman in much of the Western world is, or at least can say she has been, a photographed model, certainly not a thinker, reader, or humanitarian doer (Amal Clooney not-withstanding) who ventures out of her comfort zone. American working-class people—and those are my own roots—slay me when they seem to believe they can become favored apprentices to billionaires; or imagine that billionaires will blow resources their way, do right by us, value us, give us lovely jobs, and pay us a lot. For once, the working class seemed ahead of the political game, reading the tea leaves well enough to elect their man president of the United States. And then we all get a retro aftermath. Of course, he does not deliver, cannot even think straight, and the working class is mocked once again, because monsters care not a whit about you and me. Four people called women take up residence in the state cabinet of the new American president. Only four. Feminists should not cry over this. It is probably reasonable that women who think, as well as all other stout-hearted souls, steer clear of that state afterward.

Better to work as peacekeepers perhaps, helping to control, as best as possible, moments and belligerences of a war and its afterwards? Not nec-essarily. That is a situation where pieces of peace sidle up to states of war; at opposite ends both are gendered masculine, as Lesley Pruitt writes here. Katharine Lee-Koo shows how difficult it is to de-gender a state, even in an afterward where a devastating tsunami lands on top of an armed struggle. The men win on the Aceh issue, no matter what shape the aftermath takes. That is the rule. It happened in Zimbabwe at the end of its war for inde-pendence years ago and repeats over time. Women comrades fought along-side men for the new country and found they were meant to go home at the end, have babies, sweep their yards. Status quo ante restored was perceived as an urgent but also fair afterward of war against the British-bolstered Rhodesian state. The state of Zimbabwe was now in the hands of ex-mili-tary commanders and expatriot men with no mud on their shoes when they arrived back home. The state was all theirs to negotiate and to fill mostly with others like themselves. Of course, that state paid some obeisance to socialist "women's rights," for a little while. Then "women's rights" were hosed off the women. With intent and purpose, the new gender relations of the new Zimbabwe became the old gender normal revivified.

Get away from it all for a while? Tarted-up theme parks present themselves online and in brochures as enchanted vacation spots by the sea. Never mind the conveniently walled- off beggars and the barrios visible from top floors of towering hotels, built to encase inhabitants in splendid isolation—away from nature, from people, from culture, from caring. These are the serenity escapes for people who have more means than empathy.

WHAT TO DO?

In an era of human rights, where has security gone? Gone to militarized afterwards of fearful states, risk-taker states, bombastic states, cleverly manipulative states, hacker states, and emotional states like India, which Swati Parashar writes about here. The United States is certainly one of those emotional states, a country where reason, let alone critical reasoning, is popularly replaced by feel-good patriotism and an always enlarging sense of American exceptionalism. National anthems abound, flags are vigorously waved, and those always already heroes march off into the ether of permanent war—state symbols, hierarchical insistences, commuter tickets, and lunch pails in hand. Affective militarized citizenship is one more afterward of democracy-proud states determined to ward off the ghosts and the blowback they have created, while listening to the music of boots on the ground and killer eyes humming in the sky.

"There were some who appeared speechless, without words, and for a long while they walked around in silence, like the returning dead. But then with time, they remembered to open their mouths. Their voices came back like tiptoeing thieves in the dark . . . " (Bulawayo 2013, 77). And so we speak, gather, phone, film, denounce, fret, teach, read, write, ruminate. We are awake now. Fully awake, that is, as add-on contributors to this volume. In my mind, however, the task ahead is to refocus attention from the state to the ordinary people in societies all over the world who are suffering most from the afterwards of sour and misguided states. *I recommend strongly that we study the state as people's experiences of the state, not so much the state itself.* The state shell is there, filling and emptying, filling and emptying. It will remain, persevere. The state is the problematic, though, of everyday men, women, children, animals, coral reefs, forests, air, water, soil, food, health, and on and on. Just as I have advocated that IR study war as experience, it is time to spend our precious resources, time, and written work on people registering and responding to their experiences of the state. That is where the bulk of women are, not in the world's state structures. Take off those stilettos and move quickly to places of people. Heed their calls and the power they show now, and have shown in the past, to topple regimes, walk through walls, end apartheid, resist conscription, and defy retrograde and sentimental notions of gender. "It's your country, Darling? Really, it's your country, are you sure? she says, and I can feel myself starting to get mad" (Bulawayo 2013, 288).

REFERENCES

Ackerly, Brooke. 2017. *Just Responsibility: A Human Rights Theory of Global Justice*. New York: Oxford University Press.

Acuto, Michele, and Simon Curtis, eds. 2014. *Reassembling International Theory: Assemblage Thinking and International Relations*. New York: Palgrave Macmillan.

Adolphson, Mikael S. 2007. *The Teeth and Claws of the Buddha: Monastic Warriors and Sōhei in Japanese History*. Honolulu: University of Hawaii Press.

Affiat, Rizki. 2011. *Women's Participation in Decision Making Processes in Post-Conflict Aceh*. European Union: Crisis Management Initiative.

Afrianty, Dina. 2011. "Local Women's Movements in Aceh and the Struggle for Equality and Justice: The Women's Network for Policy." *RIMA: Review of Indonesian and Malaysian Affairs*. 45(1/2): 37–68.

Afrianty, Dina. 2015. *Women and Sharia Law in Northern Indonesia: Local Women's NGOs and the Reform of Islamic Law in Aceh*. London: Routledge.

Agathangelou, Anna M., and L. H. M. Ling. 2004. "Power, Borders, Security, Wealth: Lessons of Violence and Desire from September 11." *International Studies Quarterly* 48(3): 517–538.

Agathangelou, Anna M., and Heather M. Turcotte. 2016. "Reworking Postcolonial Feminisms in the Sites of International Relations." In Jill Steans and Daniela Tepe-Belfrage, eds., *Handbook on Gender in World Politics*. Cheltenham: Edward Elgar, pp. 41–49.

Agenda. 2014. "Georgia Protests against Domestic Violence." http://agenda.ge/news/25166/eng. Accessed March 5, 2016.

Aggestam, Karin, and Annika Bergman Rosamond. 2016. "Swedish Feminist Foreign Policy in the Making: Ethics, Politics, and Gender." *Ethics and International Affairs* 30(3): 323–334.

Agius, Christine. 2006. *The Social Construction of Swedish Neutrality: Challenges to Swedish Identity and Sovereignty*. Manchester: Manchester University Press.

Agius, Christine. 2011. "Transformed beyond Recognition? The Politics of Post-Neutrality." *Cooperation and Conflict* 46(3): 370–395.

Aguilar, Filomeno V. 2014. *Migration Revolution: Philippine Nationhood and Class Relations in a Globalized Age*. Singapore: Singapore University Press.

Åhäll, Linda, and Thomas Gregory, eds. 2015. *Emotions, Politics and War*. London: Routledge.

Ahmed, Sara. 2004. *The Cultural Politics of Emotion*. Edinburgh: Edinburgh University Press.

Al Ali, Nadje. 2016. "Sexual Violence in Iraq: Challenges for Transnational Feminist Politics." *European Journal of Women's Studies* 1–18. doi:10.1177/1350506816633723.

Albanese, Patrizia. 2006. *Mothers of the Nation*. Toronto: University of Toronto Press.

Alhayek, Katty. 2015. "Untold Stories of Syrian Women Surviving War" *Syria Studies* 7(1): 1–30 https://ojs.st-andrews.ac.uk/index.php/syria/issue/view/112.

Ali, M. R. 2015. "ISIS and Propaganda: How ISIS Exploit Women." Outer Institute Fellowship Paper, Oxford. https://reutersinstitute.politics.ox.ac.uk/sites/default/files/Isis%20and%20Propaganda-%20How%20Isis%20Exploits%20Women.pdf.

Aljazeera America. 2014. "Putin: Russia Must 'Cleanse' Itself of Gays, but No Need to Fear in Sochi." January 19. http://america.aljazeera.com/articles/2014/1/19/putin-russia-mustcleanseitselfofgays.html. Accessed December 31, 2016.

Al-Tamimi, A. 2015. "The Evolution in Islamic State Administration: The Documentary Evidence." *Perspectives on Terrorism* 9(4). http://www.terrorismanalysts.com/pt/index.php/pot/article/view/447/html

Amnesty International. 2004. *New Military Operations, Old Patterns of Human Rights Abuses in Aceh (NAD)*. New York: Amnesty International.

Anand, Utkarsh. 2016. "National Anthem Must Be Played before Movies in Theaters, Rules Supreme Court." *Indian Express*, December 1. http://indianexpress.com/article/india/india-news-india/national-anthem-national-flag-supreme-court-theater-4402827/. Accessed April 10, 2017.

Anthias, Floya, and Nira Yuval-Davis. 1989. "Introduction." In Nira Yuval-Davis and Floya Anthias, eds., *Woman—Nation—State*. Palgrave Macmillan, pp. 1–15.

Appleby, Joyce, Lynn Hunt, and Margaret Jacob. 1996. *Telling the Truth about History*. New York: Norton.

Araoye, A. 2012. "Hegemonic Agendas, Intermesticity and Conflicts in the Postcolonial State." *African Journal on Conflict Resolution* 12(1): 33–60.

Arat, Zehra F. Kabasakal. 2015. "Feminisms, Women's Rights and the United Nations: Would Achieving Gender Equality Empower Women?" *American Political Science Review* 109(4): 674–689.

Åse, Cecilia, 2016. "Ship of Shame: Gender and Nation in Narratives of the 1981 Submarine Crisis in Sweden." *Journal of Cold War Studies* 18(1): 112–132.

Ashwin, Sarah. 2000. "Introduction: Gender, State and Society in Soviet and Post-Soviet Russia." In Sarah Ashwin, ed., *Gender, State and Society in Soviet and Post-Soviet Russia*. London: Routledge, pp. 1–29.

Ashwin, Sarah, and Lytkina, Tatyana. 2004. "Men in Crisis in Russia: The Role of Domestic Marginalization." *Gender and Society* 18(2): 189–206.

Aspinall, Edward. 2008. "Peace without Justice? The Helsinki Peace Process in Aceh." Centre for Humanitarian Dialogue, April.

Aspinall, Edward. 2009. *Islam and Nation: Separatist Rebellion in Aceh, Indonesia*. Stanford, CA: Stanford University Press.

Atherton-Zeman, Ben. 2009. "Minimizing the Damage: Male Accountability in Stopping Men's Violence against Women." http://www.xyonline.net/content/minimizing-damage-%E2%80%93-male-accountability-stopping-men%E2%80%99s-violence-against-women. Accessed December 15, 2015.

Atwood, Margaret. 1985. *The Handmaid's Tale*. New York: Fawcett Crest.

Bäckstrand, Karin, and Annica Kronsell, eds. 2015. *Rethinking the Green State: Environmental Governance towards Climate and Sustainability Transitions*. New York: Routledge.

Baines, Erin. 2014. "Forced Marriage as a Political Project: Sexual Rules and Relations in the Lord's Resistance Army." *Journal of Peace Research*. DOI:10.1177/0022343313519666.

Baker, Garth. 2013. "Effectively Involving Men in Preventing Violence against Women." Issues Paper No. 5, New Zealand Family Violence Clearinghouse, Auckland.

Banerjee, Dipankar. 2013. "India." In Alex J. Bellamy and Paul D. Williams, eds., *Providing Peacekeepers: The Politics, Challenges, and Future of United Nations Peacekeeping Contributions*. Oxford: Oxford University Press.

Banerjee, S. 2006. "Beyond Naxalbari." *Economic and Political Weekly* 41.29.

Banerjee, S. 2015. "Indian Maoism: As Victim and Agency of Violence." In Kalpana Kannabiran, ed., *Violence Studies*. New Delhi: Oxford University Press.

Bannedthoughts.net. 2015a. "Pamphlet on Martyr Com. Dharmu." East Bastar Divisional Committee, Communist Party of India (Maoist), pamphlet in Hindi. http://www.bannedthought.net/India/CPI-Maoist-Docs/Statements-2015/150600-EastBastarPamph-MartyrComDharmu-Hin.pdf. Accessed April 10, 2017.

Bannedthoughts.net. 2015b. "Call to the CRPF." Abhay, Spokesperson, Central Committee, Communist Party of India (Maoist), pamphlet in Hindi. http://www.bannedthought.net/India/CPI-Maoist-Docs/Statements-2015/150500-CC-CallToCRPF-ByAbhay-Hindi-BadTitleFont.pdf. Accessed April 10, 2017.

Barry, Kathleen. 2010. *Unmaking War, Remaking Men*. North Melbourne: Spinifex Press.

Bartlett, Rosamund. 2007. "The Meaning of Motherland." In Simon Roberts, *Motherland*. London: Chris Boot, pp. 1–29.

Basham, Victoria. 2013. *War, Identity and the Liberal State: Everyday Experiences of the Geopolitical in the Armed Forces*. New York: Routledge.

Basu, S. 2016a. "Gender as National Interest at the UN Security Council." *International Affairs* 92(2): 255–273.

Basu, S. 2016b. "The Global South Writes 1325 (Too)." *International Political Science Review* 37(3): 362–374.

Basu, Tapan. 2016. "A Tale of Two Elections: How Trump 2016 Echoed Modi 2014." *The Wire*, November 18. https://thewire.in/80919/a-tale-of-two-elections-how-trump-2016-echoed-modi-2014/. Accessed April 10, 2017.

BBC News. 2012. "Pussy Riot Members Jailed for Two Years for Hooliganism." August 17. http://www.bbc.com/news/world-europe-19297373. Accessed April 10, 2017.

BBC Russian Service. 2009. "'Rodina-mat' mozhet okazat'sia na grani padeniia." May 8. http://www.bbc.com/russian/russia/2009/05/090507_stalingrad.shtml. Accessed December 30, 2016.

Beasley, C. 2015. "Caution! Hazards Ahead: Considering the Potential Gap between Feminist Thinking and Men/Masculinities Theory and Practice." *Journal of Sociology* 51 (3): 566–581.

Beeson, Mark. 2011. "Can Australia Save the World? The Limits and Possibilities of Middle Power Diplomacy." *Australian Journal of International Affairs* 65(5): 563–577.

Bergman Rosamond, Annika. 2013. "Protection beyond Borders: Gender Cosmopolitanism and Co-constitutive Obligation." *Global Society* 27(3): 319–336.

Bildt, Carl. 2013. Statement of Government Policy in the Parliamentary Debate on Foreign Affairs. February 13. http://www.regeringen.se/contentassets/

c1f7e438b32f4d6e995a09bd34508695/statement-of-government-policy-in-the-parliamentary-debate-on-foreign-affairs-2013.

Bilgic, Ali. 2016. *Turkey, Power and the West: Gendered International Relations and Foreign Policy*. London: I.B. Tauris.

Birnbaum, Michael. 2016. "How to Understand Putin's Jaw-Droppingly High Approval Ratings." *Washington Post*, March 6. https://www.washingtonpost.com/world/europe/how-to-understand-putins-jaw-droppingly-high-approval-ratings/2016/03/05/17f5d8f2-d5ba-11e5-a65b-587e721fb231_story.html. Accessed December 31, 2016.

Bjereld, Ulf. 2014. "Svensk Nato-Opinion i Förändring?" [Change in Swedish opinion on NATO?]. In Henrik Oscarsson and Annika Bergström, eds., *Ittfåra och marginal*. Gothenburg: SOM Institute.

Bleiker, Roland. 2000. "We Don't Need Another Hero." *International Feminist Journal of Politics* 2(1): 30–57.

Bleiker, Roland, and Emma Hutchison. 2008. "Fear No More: Emotions and World Politics." *Review of International Studies* 34: 115–135.

Booth, Ken, Steve Smith, and Marysia Zalewski, eds. 1996. *International Theory: Positivism and Beyond*. Cambridge: Polity Press.

Brickell, K. 2008. "Fire in the House: Gendered Experiences of Drunkenness and Violence in Siem Reap, Cambodia." *Geoforum* 9: 1667–1675.

Brown, Katherine E. 2014. "Analysis: Why Are Young Western Women Joining Islamic State?" BBC Online, October 6. http://www.bbc.co.uk/news/uk-29507410. Accessed August 14, 2017.

Brown, Katherine E. 2015. "The Cult of the Islamic State." *The Conversation*. http://theconversation.com/bethnal-green-girls-need-to-know-there-is-a-way-out-of-islamic-state-cult-38004.

Brown, Wendy. 1992. "Finding the Man in the State." *Feminist Studies* 18(1): 7–34.

Brown, Wendy. 1995. *States of Injury: Power and Freedom in Late Modernity*. Princeton, NJ: Princeton University Press.

Brown, Wendy. 2010. *Walled States, Waning Sovereignty*. New York: Zone Books.

Bruff, Ian. 2014. "The Rise of Authoritarian Neoliberalism." *Rethinking Marxism* 26(1): 113–129.

Bryson, V. 1999. "Patriarchy: A Concept Too Useful to Lose?" *Contemporary Politics* 5 (4): 311–324.

Bulawayo, NoViolet. 2013. *We Need New Names*. New York: Back Bay Books.

Burke, Anthony. 2007. "Australia Paranoid: Security Politics and Identity Security." In Anthony Burke and Matt McDonald, eds., *Critical Security in the Asia-Pacific*. Manchester: Manchester University Press.

Burke, Anthony. 2008. *Fear of Security: Australia's Invasion Anxiety*. Cambridge: Cambridge University Press.

Butler, Judith. 1990. *Gender Trouble*. Kindle ed. London: Routledge.

Butler, Judith. 2004. *Precarious Life: The Powers of Mourning and Violence*. Verso: London.

Butler, Judith. 2009. *Frames of War: When Is Life Grievable*. New York: Verso.

Caneva, Lina. 2015. "White Ribbon Ambassador Charged with Domestic Violence." http://www.probonoaustralia.com.au/news/2015/10/white-ribbon-ambassador-charged-domestic-violence#. Accessed December 20, 2015.

Carter, Jimmy. 2014. "Patriarchy and Violence against Women and Girls." *The Lancet* doi:10.1016/S0140-6736(14)62217-0.

Casey, E., and T. Smith. 2010. "'How Can I Not?': Men's Pathways to Involvement in Anti-violence against Women Work." *Violence against Women* 16 (8): 953–973.

Chambers, Peter. 2015. "The Embrace of Border Security: Maritime Jurisdiction, National Sovereignty, and the Geopolitics of Operation Sovereign Borders." *Geopolitics* 20(2): 404–437.

Charrad, Mounira M. 2001. *States and Women's Rights: The Making of Postcolonial Tunisia, Algeria, and Morocco*. Berkeley: University of California Press.

Chatterjee, D. 2016. "Gendering ISIS and Mapping the Role of Women." *Contemporary Review of the Middle East*. 3(2): 201–218

Chatterjee, Partha. 1993. *The Nation and Its Fragments: Colonial and Postcolonial Histories*. Princeton, NJ: Princeton University Press.

Cheeseman, Graeme. 2004. "Australia: A Fractured Cosmopolitan." In Lorraine Elliott and Graeme Cheeseman, eds., *Forces for Good: Cosmopolitan Militaries in the Twenty-First Century*. Manchester: Manchester University Press.

Cheng, Yi'En, Brenda S. A. Yeoh, and Juan Zhang. 2015. "Still 'Breadwinners' and 'Providers': Singaporean Husbands, Money and Masculinity in Transnational Marriages." *Gender, Place and Culture* 22(6): 867–883.

Cherniavsky, Michael. 1958. "'Holy Russia': A Study in the History of an Idea." *American Historical Review* 63(3): 617–637.

Chernova, Zhanna. 2012. "New Pronatalism? Family Policy in Post-Soviet Russia." *REGION: Regional Studies of Russia, Eastern Europe, and Central Asia* 1(1): 75–92.

Cheterian, V. 2015. "ISIS and the Killing Fields." *Survival* 57(2): 105–118.

Chigateri, Shraddha, Mubashira Zaidi, and Anweshaa Ghosh. 2016. "Locating the Processes of Policy Change in the Context of Anti-rape and Domestic Worker Mobilizations in India." UNRISD Research Report, United Nations Research Institute for Social Development, Geneva. http://www.unrisd.org/80256B3C005BCCF9/%28httpPublications%29/03AB499766D6FDB2C1257F9B004F6BDF?OpenDocument. Accessed April 21, 2017.

Clapham, Christopher S. 1996. *Africa and the International System*. Cambridge: Cambridge University Press.

Clarke, Ross, Galuh Wandita, and Samsidar. 2008. *Considering Victims: The Aceh Peace Process from a Transitional Justice Perspective*. New York: International Center for Transitional Justice.

Clinton, Bill. 2005. "A New Dawn for the Tsunami Survivors." *The Independent*, June 25. http://www.independent.co.uk/voices/commentators/bill-clinton-a-new-dawn-for-the-tsunami-survivors-5544789.html.

Clunan, Anne L., and Harold A. Trinkunas, eds. 2010. *Ungoverned Spaces: Alternatives to State Authority in an Era of Softened Sovereignty*. Stanford, CA: Stanford University Press.

Cohn, Carol 1993. "Wars, Wimps, and Women: Talking Gender and Thinking War." In Miriam Cooke and Angela Woollacott, eds., *Gendering War Talk*. Princeton, New Jersey: Princeton University Press, pp. 227–246.

Conaway, C. P., and J. Shoemaker. 2008. *Women in United Nations Peace Operations: Increasing the Leadership Opportunities*. Washington, DC: Women in International Security, Georgetown University.

Confortini, Catia. 2012. *Intelligent Compassion: Feminist Critical Methodology in the Women's International League for Peace and Freedom*. New York: Oxford University Press.

Connell, Raewyn. 1987. *Gender and Power: Society, the Person and Sexual Politics.* Cambridge: Polity Press.

Connell, Raewyn. 1990. "The State, Gender, and Sexual Politics: Theory and Appraisal." *Theory and Society* 19(5): 507–544.

Connell, Raewyn. 1995. *Masculinities.* Berkeley: University of California Press.

Connell, Raewyn. 2004. "Encounters with Structure." *International Journal of Qualitative Studies in Education* 17(1): 10–27.

Connell, Raewyn. 2005. *Masculinities.* 2nd ed. Cambridge: Polity Press.

Constable, Nicole. 2014. *Born Out Of place: Migrant Mothers and the Politics of International Labor.* Berkeley: University of California Press.

Cooke, Miriam. 2008. "Religion, Gender, and the Muslimwoman: Deploying the Muslimwoman." *Journal of Feminist Studies of Religion* 24(1): 91–99.

Couldry, Nick. 2010. *Why Voice Matters: Culture and Politics after Neoliberalism.* London: Sage.

Credit Suisse Research Institute. 2012. *Gender Diversity and the Impact on Corporate Performance, 2005–2011.* Zurich: Credit Suisse.

Crisis Management Initiative. 2006. *The Aceh Peace Process: Involvement of Women.* Helsinki: CMI.

Crisis Management Initiative. 2012. *Aceh Peace Process Follow-Up Project, Final Report.* Helsinki: CMI.

Cullen, Sam. 2012. "Labor MPs Speak Out over Aid Diversion." *ABC News*, December 19. http://www.abc.net.au/news/2012-12-19/backbenchers-unhappy-over-aid-diversion/4436022.

Cunliffe, S., Riyadi, E., Arwalembun, R., and Boli Tobi, H. 2009. *Negotiating Peace in Indonesia: Prospects for Building Peace and Upholding Justice in Maluku and Aceh.* European Union: Initiative for Peacebuilding.

Dagens Nyheter. 2015a. "Stöd för Nato-medlemskap nu större än motståndet" [Support for NATO membership is now greater than the resistance]. May 6. http://www.dn.se/debatt/stod-for-nato-medlemskap-nu-storre-an-motstandet.

Dagens Nyheter. 2015b. "Sveriges trovärdighet som handelspartner står på spel" [Sweden's credibility as a trading partner is at stake]. March 6. http://www.dn.se/debatt/sveriges-trovardighet-som-handelspartner-star-pa-spel-1/.

Daily Mirror. 2013. "New Rules to Protect SL Maids." *Daily Mirror*, September 23. http://www.dailymirror.lk/news/35880-new-rules-to-protect-sl-maids.html. Accessed September 14, 2016.

Daily Mirror. 2016. "Worker Remittances Likely to Slow Down in 2016." January 4. https://www.pressreader.com/sri-lanka/daily-mirror-sri-lanka/20160104/282020441272500. Accessed April 3, 2017.

Daily News. 2013. "Call to Provide Higher Wages for Housemaids." September 10. http://www.dailynews.lk/local/call-provide-higher-wages-housemaids. Accessed September 21, 2013.

Daily News. 2016. "Capping Women's Economic Freedom." January 6. http://www.dailynews.lk/?q=2016/01/06/features/capping-womens-economic-freedom. Accessed January 23, 2017.

Dangerfield, George. 1966. *The Strange Death of Liberal England.* London: MacGibbon & Kee.

Das, Shaswati. 2017. "Govt to Revise Anti-Maoist Strategy in Wake of Sukmanaxal Attack." *Hindustan Times*, April 26. http://www.livemint.com/Politics/TKNWeh

PCKnFUcfiEgNev4I/Rajnath-Singh-pays-homage-to-25-CRPF-
men-killed-in-Naxal-att.html. Accessed April 27, 2017.

Davies, Sara E. 2013. "Pursuing Women's Peace and Security, and Justice." *Australian Journal of International Affairs* 67(4): 540–548.

Davies, Sara E., and Jacqui True. 2015. "Reframing Conflict-Related Sexual and Gender-Based Violence: Bringing Gender Analysis Back In." *Security Dialogue* 46(6): 495–512.

Davies, Sara, and Jacqui True. 2017. "Norm Entrepreneurship in Foreign Policy: William Hague and the Prevention of Sexual Violence in Conflict." *Foreign Policy Analysis.* https://doi.org/10.1093/fpa/orw065.

De Haas, Hein. 2012. "The Migration and Development Pendulum: A Critical View on Research and Policy." *International Migration* 50(3): 8–25.

De Jong, Sara. 2017. *Complicit Sisters: Gender and Women's Issues across North and South Divides.* New York: Oxford University Press.

De la Cadena, Marisol. 2005. "The Production of Other Knowledges and Its Tensions: From Andeanist Anthropology to Interculturalidad?" *Journal of World Anthropology Network* 1: 13–33.

Delgado-Wise, R. 2014. "A critical overview of migration and development: the Latin American challenge." *Annual Review of Sociology.* 40, 643–663.

De Mel, Neloufer. 2001. *Women and the Nation's Narrative: Gender and Nationalism in Twentieth Century Sri Lanka.* Lanham, MD: Rowman & Littlefield.

DeKeseredy, Walter S., and Martin D. Schwartz. 2005. "Masculinities and Interpersonal Violence." In Jeff Hearn, Michael S. Kimmel, and Raewyn Connell, eds., *Handbook of Studies on Men and Masculinities.* Thousand Oaks, CA: Sage, pp. 353–366.

Delanda, Michael. 2006. *A New Philosophy of Society: Assemblage Theory and Social Complexity.* New York: Continuum.

Deleuze, Giles, and Félix Guattari. 1998. *A Thousand Plateaus: Capitalism and Schizophrenia.* Trans. Brian Massumi. New York: Bloomsbury.

Detraz, Nicole. 2016. *Gender and the Environment.* Malden, MA: Polity Press.

Diamond, S. 1996. "Dahomey: The Development of a Proto-State." *Dialectical Anthropology* 21(2): 121–216.

Dickinson, D. 2016. "First All-Female UN Police Unit Leaves Liberia." United Nations Radio.

Doeser, Fredrik. 2014. "Sweden's Participation in Operation Unified Protector: Obligations and Interests." *International Peacekeeping* 21(5): 642–657.

Doucet, A. 2004. "'It's Almost Like I Have a Job, but I Don't Get Paid': Fathers at Home Reconfiguring Work, Care, and Masculinity." *Fathering* 2(3): 277–303.

Dower, John W. 1986. *War Without: Mercy Race and Power in the Pacific War.* New York: Random House.

Drexler, Elizabeth. 2006. "History and Liability in Aceh, Indonesia: Single Bad Guys and Convergent Narratives." *American Ethnologist* 33(3): 313–326.

Duggan, Lisa. 2004. *The Twilight of Equality: Neoliberalism, Cultural Politics, and the Attack on Democracy.* Boston: Beacon Press.

Duncanson, Claire. 2013. *Forces for Good? Military Masculinities and Peacebuilding in Afghanistan and Iraq.* Basingstoke. Palgrave Macmillan.

Duramy, Benedetta Faedi. 2014. *Gender and Violence in Haiti: Women's Path from Victims to Agents.* New Brunswick, NJ: Rutgers University Press.

Eggert, J. P. 2016. "Women Fighters in the 'Islamic State' and Al-Qaida in Iraq: A Comparative Analysis." *Journal of International Peace and Organization* 90(3–4): 363–380.

Eichler, Maya. 2014. "Militarized Masculinities in International Relations." *Brown Journal of World Affairs* 21(1): 81–93.

Eisenstein, Hester. 1996. *Inside Agitators: Australian Femocrats and the State.* Philadelphia: Temple University Press.

Eisenstein, Zillah R. 1979. "Developing a Theory of Capitalist Patriarchy and Socialist Feminism." In Zillah R. Eisenstein, ed., *Capitalist Patriarchy and the Case for Socialist Feminism.* New York: Monthly Review Press, pp. 5–40.

Elder, Miriam. 2013. "Feminism Could Destroy Russia, Russian Orthodox Patriarch Claims." *The Guardian*, April 9. http://www.theguardian.com/world/2013/apr/09/feminism-destroy-russia-patriarch-kirill. Accessed December 29, 2016.

Elias, Juanita. 2013. "Foreign Policy and the Domestic Worker: The Malaysia-Indonesia Domestic Worker Dispute." *International Feminist Journal of Politics* 15(3): 391–410.

Elias, Juanita, and Samanthi Gunawardana, eds. 2014. *The Global Political Economic of the Household in Asia.* London: Palgrave.

Ellsberg, Mary, et al. 2014. "Prevention of Violence against Women and Girls: What Does the Evidence Say?" *The Lancet* 385: 1555–1566.

Elshtain, Jean-Bethke. 1992. "Sovereignty, Identity, Sacrifice." In V. Spike Peterson, ed., *Gendered States. Feminist (Re)visions of International Relations Theory.* Boulder, CO: Lynne Rienner.

Encinas-Franco, Jean. 2013. "The Language of Labor Export in Political Discourse: 'Modern-Day Heroism' and Constructions of Overseas Filipino Workers (OFWs)." *Philippine Political Science Journal* 34(1): 97–112.

Endo, Isaku, and Gabi G. Afram. 2011. *The Qatar-Nepal Remittance Corridor: Enhancing the Impact and Integrity of Remittance Flows by Reducing Inefficiencies in the Migration Process.* Washington, DC: World Bank.

Enloe, Cynthia H. 2016. *Globalization and Militarism: Feminists Make the Link.* 2nd ed. Lanham, MD: Rowman & Littlefield.

Erofeeva, Lyubov V. 2013. "Traditional Christian Values and Women's Reproductive Rights in Modern Russia: Is a Consensus Ever Possible?" *American Journal of Public Health* 103(11): 1931–1935.

Esposito, J. L. 2015. "Islam and Political Violence." *Religions* 6(3): 1067–1081.

Evans, Gareth. 1990. "Foreign Policy and Good International Citizenship." Address by the Minister for Foreign Affairs, Senator Gareth Evans, Canberra, March 6. http://www.gevans.org/speeches/old/1990/060390_fm_fpandgoodinternationalcitizen.pdf.

Evans, Nancy J., and Jamie Washington. 1991. "Becoming an Ally." In Vernon A. Wall and Nancy J. Evans, eds., *Beyond Tolerance: Gays, Lesbians, and Bisexuals on Campus.* Washington, DC: American College Personnel Association.

Fanon, Frantz. 1967a. *Black Skin White Masks.* Trans. Richard Philcox. New York: Grove Press.

Fanon, Frantz. 1967b. *The Wretched of the Earth.* Trans. Constance Farrington. Harmondsworth: Penguin.

Felten-Biermann, Claudia. 2006. "Gender and Natural Disaster: Sexualized Violence and the Tsunami." *Dialogue* 49 (3): 82–86.

Filipovic, Jill. 2013. "The UN Commission on the State of Women Unmasks Equality's Enemies." *The Guardian*, March 19. https://www.theguardian.com/

commentisfree/2013/mar/18/un-commission-status-women-enemies-equality. Accessed March 27, 2017.

Flood, Michael. 2014. "Men's Anti-violence Activism and the Construction of Gender-Equitable Masculinities." In À. Carabí and J. Armengol, eds., *Alternative Masculinities for a Changing World*. New York: Palgrave, pp. 35–50.

Flood, Michael. 2015. "Work with Men to End Violence against Women: A Critical Stocktake." *Culture, Health and Sexuality* 17(2): 159–176. doi:10.1080/13691058.2015.1070435.

Forsberg, Oskar. 2013. "ÖB: 'Sverige kan försvara sig en vecka'" [Supreme commander: Sweden can be defended for one week]. *Aftonbladet*, March 1. http://www.aftonbladet.se/nyheter/article16013259.ab.

Fortier, Anne-Marie. 2008. *Multicultural Horizons: Diversity and the Limits of the Civil Nation*. New York: Routledge.

Fortier, Anne-Marie. 2010. 'Pride politics and multiculturalist citizenship.' *Ethnic and Racial Studies*, 28: 3, 559–78.

Foxall, Andrew. 2013. "Photographing Vladimir Putin: Masculinity, Nationalism and Visuality in Russian Political Culture." *Geopolitics* 18(1): 132–156.

Frantz, Elizabeth. 2013. "Jordan's Unfree Workforce: State-Sponsored Bonded Labour in the Arab Region." *Journal of Development Studies* 49(8): 1–16.

Fraser, Nancy. 1997. *Justice Interruptus: Critical Reflections on the Post-Socialist Condition*. New York: Routledge.

Fraser, Nancy. 2005. "Reframing Justice in a Globalized World." *New Left Review* 76: 79–88.

Friedland, R. 2002. "Money, Sex and God: The Erotic language of Religious Nationalism." *Sociological Theory* 20(3): 381–425.

Fukuyama, Francis. 1998. "Women and the Evolution of World Politics." *Foreign Affairs*. https://www.foreignaffairs.com/articles/1998-09-01/women-and-evolution-world-politics

Galstyan, Areg. 2016. "Third Rome Rising: The New Ideologues Calling for a New Russian Empire." *National Interest*, June 27. http://nationalinterest.org/feature/third-rome-rising-the-ideologues-calling-new-russian-empire-16748. Accessed December 31, 2016.

Gambher, Haleen K. 2014. Dabiq: *The Strategic Messaging of the Islamic State*. Washington, DC: Institute for the Study of War.

Gamburd, Michelle Ruth. 2000. *The Kitchen Spoon's Handle: Transnationalism and Sri Lanka's Migrant Housemaids*. Ithaca, NY: Cornell University Press.

Gamburd, Michelle Ruth. 2008. "Milk Teeth and Jet Planes: Kin Relations in Families of Sri Lanka's Transnational Domestic Servants." *City and Society* 20(1): 5–31.

Gandhi, Leela. 1998. *Postcolonial Theory: A Critical Introduction*. New Delhi: Oxford University Press.

Gartenstein-Ross, Daveed. 2015. "How Many Fighters Does the Islamic State Really Have?" *War on the Rocks*. Feburary 9. http://warontherocks.com/2015/02/how-many-fighters-does-the-islamic-state-really-have/.

Garton, Stephen. 1998. "War and Masculinity in Twentieth Century Australia." *Journal of Australian Studies* 22(56): 86–95.

Gaub, F. 2016. "The Cult of ISIS." *Survival* 58(1): 113–130.

Ghosh, Dipankar. 2016. "Outsiders vs Patriotic Voices: The New Lines in Bastar." *Indian Express*, March 6. http://indianexpress.com/article/india/india-news-india/the-new-lines-in-bastar-naxalites-new-line-bastar-chhatisgarh-police. Accessed April 5, 2017.

Giustozzi, A. 2003. "Respectable Warlords? The Politics of State-Building in Post-Taleban Afghanistan." Crisis States Research Centre working papers series No. 1, 33. London School of Economics and Political Science.

Goldstein, S., and Davis, D. 2010. "Heterosexual Allies: A Descriptive Profile." *Equity and Excellence in Education* 43(4): 478–494.

Gopinath, M. 2015. "Her Voice." Paper presented at School of Social Sciences Seminar Series, Monash University.

Gowan, R. and Singh, Sushant K. 2013. "India and UN Peacekeeping: The Weight of History and a Lack of Strategy." Sidhu, Waheguru Pal Singh; Mehta, Pratap Bhanu; Jones, Bruce, eds., *Shaping the Emerging World: India and the Multilateral Order*. Washington, DC: Brookings Institution.

GQ Australia. 2015. "Our Exclusive Interview with Malcolm Turnbull." September 14. http://www.gq.com.au/success/career/malcolm+turnbull+to+be+australias+next+prime+ministerr,37215.

Gramsci, Antonio. 1971. *Selections from the Prison Notebooks*. Edited by Quintin Hoare and Geoffrey Nowell-Smith. London: International Publishers.

Grant, Rebecca. 1992. "The Quagmire of Gender and International Security." V. Spike Peterson, ed., *Gendered States: Feminist (Re)visions of International Relations Theory*. Boulder, CO: Lynne Rienner.

Grossman, Kristina. 2012. "Women as Change Agents in the Transformation Process in Aceh, Indonesia." In Andrea Fleschenberg and Claudia Derichs, eds., *Women and Politics in Asia*. Singapore: Lit Verlag.

Grossman, Kristina. 2016. "Women's Rights Activists and the Drafting Process of the Islamic Criminal Law Code (*Qanun Jinayat*)." In Michael Feener and Annemarie Samuels, eds., *Islam and the Limits of the State: Reconfigurations of Practice, Community and Authority in Contemporary Aceh*. Leiden: Brill.

Guevarra, Anna Romina. 2006. "Managing 'Vulnerabilities' and 'Empowering' Migrant Filipina Workers: The Philippines's Overseas Employment Program." *Social Identities: Journal for the Study of Race, Nation and Culture* 12(5): 523–541.

Guha, R. 2007. "Adivasis, Naxalites and Indian Democracy." *Economic and Political Weekly* 42 (32): 3305–3312.

Gunawardana, Samanthi. 2014. *Movement Responses to Migration in Sri Lanka*. Solidarity Centre. http://www.solidaritycenter.org/wp-content/uploads/2015/09/Labor-Movement-Responses-to-Migration-in-Sri-Lanka.report.1.2014.pdf. Accessed September 24, 2015.

Gutowski, Alexandra. 2016. *ISIS Sanctuary*. Map, December. http://www.understandingwar.org/backgrounder/isis-sanctuary-map-december-8-2016.

Hague, William. 2010. "Speech: Britain's Foreign Policy in a Networked World." Foreign and Commonwealth Office, July 1. https://www.gov.uk/government/speeches/britain-s-foreign-policy-in-a-networked-world--2.

Hall, John. 2016. "Isis Militant Ali Saqr al-Qasem Executes Own Mother Accusing Her of Apostasy." *The Independent*, January 8. http://www.independent.co.uk/news/world/middle-east/isis-militant-ali-saqr-al-qasem-publicly-executes-his-own-mother-in-raqqa-after-accusing-her-of-a6801811.html.

Hamdan, A. N. 2016. "'Breaker of Barriers?' Notes on the Geopolitics of the Islamic State in Iraq and Sham." *Geopolitics* 21(3): 605–627.

Hansen, Lene. 2000. "The Little Mermaid's Silent Security Dilemma and the Absence of Gender in the Copenhagen School." *Millennium* 29(2): 285–306.

Hansen-Lewis, Jamie, and Jacob N. Shapiro. 2015. "Understanding the Daesh Economy." http://www.terrorismanalysts.com/pt/index.php/pot/article/viewFile/450/881.

Harrington, Mona. 1992. "What Exactly Is Wrong with the Liberal State as an Agent of Change?" In V. Spike Peterson, ed., *Gendered States: Feminist (Re)visions of International Relations Theory*, 65–82. Boulder, CO: Lynne Rienner.

Harris Rimmer, Susan. 2015. "A Critique of Australia's G20 Presidency and the Brisbane Summit 2014." *Global Summitry* 1(1): 41–63.

Harris, Simon. 2004. "Gender, Participation and Post-conflict Planning in Northern Sri Lanka." *Gender and Development* 12(3): 60–69.

Hasan, Zoya. 2000. *Politics and the State in India*. New Delhi: Sage.

Hasan, Zoya. 2010. "Gender, Religion and Democratic Politics in India." *Third World Quarterly* 31(6): 939–954.

Hautzinger, Sarah J. 2007. *Violence in the City of Women: Police and Batterers in Bahia, Brazil*. Berkeley: University of California Press.

Hearn, Jeff. 1998. *The Violence of Men*. London: Sage.

Hearn, Jeff. 2014. "Men, Masculinities and the Material(-)Discursive." *NORMA: The Nordic Journal* 9(1): 5–17.

Hearn, Jeff, and David H. J. Morgan. 1990. "The Critique of Men." In Jeff Hearn and David H. J. Morgan, eds., *Men, Masculinities and Social Theory*. London: Unwin Hyman, pp. 203–205.

HeegMaruska, Jennifer. 2010. "When Are States Hypermasculine?" In Laura Sjoberg, ed., *Gender and International Security: Feminist Perspectives*. New York: Routledge.

HeForShe. 2014. "IMPACT 10x10x10: In Brief." http://www.heforshe.org/~/media/HeForShe/Files/impactchampion/HeForShe_IMPACT10X10X10_Brief.pdf. Accessed June 14, 2016.

HeForShe. 2016. "Take Action: Violence." http://www.heforshe.org/en/take-action/violence. Accessed July 12, 2016.

Held, David, Anthony McGrew, David Goldblatt, and Jonathan Perraton. 1999. *Global Transformations: Politics, Economics and Culture*. Stanford, CA: Stanford University Press.

Heldt, Birgir. 2012. "Peacekeeping Contributor Profile: Sweden." Providing for Peacekeeping. September. http://www.providingforpeacekeeping.org/2014/04/03/contributor-profile-sweden/. Accessed August 14, 2007.

Hercus, C. 1999. "Identity, Emotion and Feminist Collective Action." *Gender and Society* 13(1): 34–55.

Herek, G. M., and J. P. Capitanio. 1996. "'Some of My Best Friends': Intergroup Contact, Concealable Stigma, and Heterosexuals' Attitudes toward Gay Men and Lesbians." *Personality and Social Psychology Bulletin* 22(4): 412–424.

Higate, Paul, and Marsha Henry. 2011. "Militarising Spaces: A Geographical Exploration of Cyprus." In Scott Kirsch and Colin Flint, eds., *Reconstructing Conflict: Integrating War and Post-war Geographies*. Surrey: Ashgate.

Hojati, Z. 2016. "Violence against Women under ISIS Occupation: A Critical Feminist Analysis of Religious and Political Factors That Commodify Women's Sexuality in the War Zone." *International Relations and Diplomacy* 4(4): 302–310.

Hooper, Charlotte. 2001. *Manly States: Masculinities, International Relations and Gender Politics*. New York: Columbia University Press.

Howard, John. 2001. Address at the Federal Liberal Party campaign launch, Sydney, October 28. http://electionspeeches.moadoph.gov.au/speeches/2001-john-howard.

Hozic, Aida, and Jacqui True, eds. 2016. *Scandalous Economics: The Politics of Gender and Financial Crises*. New York: Oxford University Press.

Hozic, Aida, and Jacqui True. 2017. "Brexit as a Scandal: Gender and Global Trumpism." *Review of International Political Economy* 24(2): 270–287.

Htun, Mala. 2003. *Sex and the State: Abortion, Divorce, and the Family under Latin American Dictatorships and Democracies*. Cambridge: Cambridge University Press.

Htun, Mala, and L. Weldon. 2012. "The Civic Origins of Progressive Policy Change: Combatting Violence against Women in Global Perspective." *American Political Science Review* 106(3): 548–569.

Human Rights Watch. 2001. *Indonesia: The War in Aceh*. New York: Human Rights Watch.

Human Rights Watch. 2013. "Russia: Harsh Toll of 'Foreign Agents' Law." June 25. https://www.hrw.org/news/2013/06/25/russia-harsh-toll-foreign-agents-law. Accessed December 30, 2016.

Human Rights Watch. 2016. "Russia: Government vs. Rights Groups." December 21. https://www.hrw.org/russia-government-against-rights-groups-battle-chronicle. Accessed December 30, 2016.

Hunnicutt, Gwen. 2009. "Varieties of Patriarchy and Violence against Women." *Violence against Women* 15(5): 553–573.

Hunt, C. 2014. "Young Vulnerable Women Being Groomed for Jihad: Jihadists of the Islamic State Are Using Social Media to Attract Female Brands and Fighters." *Sunday Independent*, August 24.

Hunt, Krista. 2002. "The Strategic Co-optation of Women's Rights: Discourse in the 'War on Terrorism.'" *International Feminist Journal of Politics* 4: 116–121.

Inskeep, Steve. 2015. *Jacksonland: President Andrew Jackson, Cherokee Chief John Ross, and the Great American Land Grab*. New York: Penguin Random House.

Institute for Economics and Peace. 2015. *Global Terrorism Index 2015*. University of Maryland. http://economicsandpeace.org/wp-content/uploads/2015/11/Global-Terrorism-Index-2015.pdf.

Institute for Economics and Peace. 2016. *Global Terrorism Index 2016*. University of Maryland. http://economicsandpeace.org/wp-content/uploads/2016/11/Global-Terrorism-Index-2016.2.pdf.

Institute for the Study of War. n.d. "ISIS Sanctuary Map" http://www.understandingwar.org/project/isis-sanctuary-map

International Organisation of Migration (IOM) 2007. "A Psychosocial Needs Assessment of Communities in 14 Conflict-Affected Districts in Aceh, 2007."

Issoupova, Olga G. 2000. "From Duty to Pleasure? Motherhood in Soviet and Post-Soviet Russia." In Sarah Ashwin, ed., *Gender, State, and Society in Soviet and Post-Soviet Russia*. London: Routledge, pp. 30–54.

Isupova, Olga G. 2002. "The Social Meaning of Motherhood in Russia Today ('Only You Need Your Child')." *Russian Social Science Review* 43(5): 24–43.

Ivanova, Maria. 2015. "Paris Climate Summit: Why More Women Need Seats at the Table." *The Conversation*.

Jabri, V. 2004. "Feminist Ethics and Hegemonic Global Politics." *Alternatives: Global, Local, Political* 6(1): 265–284.

Jackson, Robert H. 1993. *Quasi-States: Sovereignty, International Relations and the Third World*. Cambridge: Cambridge University Press.

Jacobson, Robert H. 2013. "Women 'after' Wars." In Carol Cohn, ed., *Women and Wars*. Cambridge: Polity Press.

Jaquette, Jane S. 2003. "Feminism and the Challenges of the 'Post–Cold War' World." *International Feminist Journal of Politics* 5(3): 331–354.

Jaquette, Jane S., ed. 2009. *Feminist Agendas and Democracy in Latin America*. Durham, NC: Duke University Press.

Jauhola, Marjaana. 2013. *Post-tsunami Reconstruction in Indonesia*. London: Routledge.

Jayasuriya, Kanishka. 2005. "Beyond Institutional Fetishism: From the Developmental to the Regulatory State." *New Political Economy* 10(3): 381–387.

Jeffery, Renée. 2014. *Reason and Emotion in International Ethics*. Cambridge: Cambridge University Press.

Jeffreys, Sheila. 2005. *Beauty and Misogyny: Harmful Cultural Practices in the West*. New York: Routledge.

Joenniemi, Pertti. 1988. "Models of Neutrality: The Traditional and Modern." *Cooperation and Conflict* 23(1): 53–67.

Johnson, Carol. 2010. "The Politics of Affective Citizenship: From Blair to Obama." *Citizenship Studies* 14(5): 495–509.

Johnson, Carol. 2015. "Playing the Gender Card: The Uses and Abuses of Gender in Australian Politics." *Politics and Gender* 11(2): 291–319.

Johnson, Henry. 2016. "The Isslamic State is losing its territory and fast" *Foreign Policy*, March 16. http://foreignpolicy.com/2016/03/16/mapped-the-islamic-state-is-losing-its-territory-and-fast/

Jones, Sidney. 2008. "Keeping the peace: Security in Aceh." *Accord* 20: 72–75.

Kamaruzzaman, Suraiya. 2008. "Agents for Change: The Roles of Women in Aceh's Peace Process." *Accord* 20: 70–71.

Kanatola, J. 2007. "The Gendered Reproduction of the State in International Relations." *British Journal of Politics and International Relations* 9(2): 270–283.

Kandiyoti, Deniz. 1989. "Bargaining with Patriarchy." *Gender and Society* 2(3): 274–290.

Katz, Jackson. 2006. *The Macho Paradox: Why Some Men Hurt Women and How All Men Can Help*. Naperville, IL: Sourcebooks.

Kaviraj, Sudipta. 2000. "The Modern State in India." In Zoya Hasan, ed., *Politics and the State in India*. New Delhi: Sage.

Kay, Rebecca. 2006. *Men in Contemporary Russia: The Fallen Heroes of Post-Soviet Change?* Aldershot: Ashgate.

King, Anthony. 2013. *The Combat Soldier: Infantry Tactics and Cohesion in the Twentieth and Twenty-First Centuries*. Oxford: Oxford University Press.

Krasner, Stephen D., ed. 1983. *International Regimes*. Ithaca, NY: Cornell University Press.

Kronsell, Annica. 2012. *Gender, Sex and the Postnational Defense: Militarism and Peacekeeping*. Oxford: Oxford University Press.

Kronsell, Annica, and Erika Svedberg. 2001. "The Duty to Protect: Gender in the Swedish Practice of Conscription." *Cooperation and Conflict* 36(2): 153–176.

Kutz, Christopher. 2000. *Complicity: Ethics and Law for a Collective Age*. Cambridge: Cambridge University Press.

Lahoud, Nelly. 2010. "Umayma al-Zawahiri on Women's Role in Jihad." *Jihadica*, February 26. http://www.jihadica.com/umayma-al-zawahiri-on-women%E2%80%99s-role-in-jihad/.

Lake, Marilyn. 2009. "Fight Free of Anzac, Lest We Forget Other Stories." *The Age*, April 23. http://www.theage.com.au/federal-politics/

fight-free-of-anzac-lest-we-forget-other-stories-20090422-afb5.
html#ixzz48s8DYYHT.

Lan, Pei-Chia. 2006. *Global Cinderellas: Migrant Domestics and Newly Rich Employers in Taiwan*. Durham, NC: Duke University Press.

Lan, Pei-Chia. 2016. "Born Out Of Place: Migrant Mothers and the Politics of International Labor." *Pacific Affairs*. 89(1): 140–142.

Lapointe, A. A. 2015. "Standing 'Straight' Up to Homophobia: Straight Allies' Involvement in GSAs." *Journal of LGBT Youth* 12(2): 144–169.

Laqueur, Thomas. 1990. *Making Sex: Body and Gender from the Greeks to Freud*. Cambridge, MA: Harvard University Press.

Layoun, Mary. 1992. "Telling Spaces: Palestinian Women and The Engendering of National Narratives." In Andrew Parker, Mary Russo, Doris Summer, and Patricia Yaeger, eds., *Nationalisms & Sexualities*. New York: Routledge, pp. 407–423.

Le Billon, Philippe, and Arno Waizenegger. 2007. "Peace in the Wake of Disaster? Secessionist Conflicts and the 2004 Indian Ocean Tsunami." *Transactions of the Institute of British Geographers* 32(3): 411–427.

Lee-Koo, Katrina. 2012. "Gender at the Crossroad of Conflict: Tsunami and Peace in Post-2005 Aceh." *Feminist Review* 101: 59–77.

Lia, B. 2015. "Understanding Jihadi Proto-States." *Perspectives on Terrorism* 9(4): 31–41.

Liang, Li-Fang. 2011. "The Making of an 'Ideal' Live-In Migrant Care Worker: Recruiting, Training, Matching and Disciplining." *Ethnic and Racial Studies* 34(11): 1815–1834.

Liebowitz, D. J., and S. Zwingel. 2014. "Gender Equality Oversimplified: Using CEDAW to Counter the Measurement Obsession." *International Studies Review* 6: 362–389.

Life.ru. 2013. "Na gej-frika Alenu Piskun napali za oskverenie Mamaeva kurgana." November 1. https://life.ru/t/новости/122096. Accessed January 1, 2017.

Lipset, Seymour Martin. 1996. *American Exceptionalism: A Double Edged Sword*. New York: Norton.

Lister, Charles. 2016. "Jihadi Rivalry: Islamic State Challenges al-Qaida." Brookings Doha Center Analysis Paper No. 16. https://www.brookings.edu/wp-content/uploads/2016/07/en-jihadi-rivalry-2.pdf.

Lloyd, Genevieve. 1993. *The Man of Reason: "Male" and "Female" in Western Philosophy*. 2nd ed. London: Routledge.

Loken, M., and A. Zelenz. 2016. "Explaining Extremism: Western Women in Daesh." Working paper, International Studies Association Conference.

Lovett, M. 1988. "Gender Relations, Class Formation, and the Colonial State in Africa." In Jane L. Parpart and Kathleen A. Staudt, eds., *Women and the State in Africa*. Boulder, CO: Lynne Rienner, pp. 23–46.

Lynch, Caitrin. 2007. *Juki Girls, Good Girls: Gender and Cultural Politics in Sri Lanka's Global Garment Industry*. Ithaca, NY: Cornell University Press.

Mackenzie, M. 2010. "Securitizing Sex?" *International Feminist Journal of Politics* 12(2): 202–221.

MacKinnon, Catharine A. 1989. *Towards a Feminist Theory of the State*. Cambridge: Harvard University Press.

Macleod, C. 2007. "The Risk of Phallocentrism in Masculinities Studies: How a Revision of the Concept of Patriarchy May Help." *Psychology in Society* 35(1): 4–14.

Maffesoli, M. 1991. "The Ethics of Aesthetics." *Theory Culture and Society* 8: 7–20.

Mahmood, Sabz. 2005. *Politics of Piety: The Islamic Revival and the Feminist Subject.* Princeton, NJ: Princeton University Press.

Maley, William. 2015. "The War in Afghanistan. Australia's Strategic Narratives." In Beatrice De Graaf, George Dimitriu, and Jens Ringsmose, eds., *Strategic Narratives, Public Opinion, and War: Winning Domestic Support for the Afghan War*, 282–299. London: Routledge.

Mansbridge, Jane. 2003. "Anti-statism and Difference Feminism in International Social Movements." *International Feminist Journal of Politics* 5(3): 355–360.

Marhaban, S. 2011. "Women and Peace in Aceh: A Struggle of Identity and Patronage Politics." https://ligainongachehdotorg.wordpress.com/2011/11/11/women-and-peace-in-aceh-a-struggle-of-identity-in-patronage-politics/.

Mapping Militants. 2017. "Islamic State." Stanford University. April 14. http://web.stanford.edu/group/mappingmilitants/cgi-bin/groups/view/1.

Marchand, Marianne, and Anne Sisson-Runyan, eds. 2000. *Gender and Global Restructuring: Sites and Sightings.* New York: Routledge.

Marcus, George E., W, Russell Neuman, and Michael MacKuen. 2002. *Affective Intelligence and Political Judgment.* Chicago: University of Chicago Press.

Matz, Johan. 2013. "Parliamentary Decision Making and Foreign Policy: Sweden's Participation in International Armed Missions and the Crucial Role of the Riksdag." *Parliaments, Estates and Representation* 33(2): 186–201.

Mazurana, Dyan, Prisca Benelli, Huma Gupta, and Peter Walker. 2011. "Sex and Age Matter: Improving Humanitarian Response in Emergencies." http://www.pacificdisaster.net/pdnadmin/data/original/FIC_2011_sex_age_matter.pdf.

McKay, Steven. 2007. "Filipino Sea Men: Constructing Masculinities in an Ethnic Labour Niche." *Journal of Ethnic and Migration Studies* 33(4): 617–633.

McKinsey and Company. 2007. *Women Matter, Gender Diversity: A Corporate Performance Driver.* New York.

McLeod, Travers. 2014. "Winning the Border War by Keeping Secrets." *The Age*, January 14. http://www.theage.com.au/comment/winning-the-border-war-by-keeping-secrets-20140113-30qmd.html.

McNevin, Anne. 2011. *Contesting Citizenship: Irregular Migrants and New Frontiers of the Political.* New York: Columbia University Press.

Meger, Sara. 2016. *Rape Loot Pillage: The Political Economy of Sexual Violence in Armed Conflict.* New York: Oxford University Press.

Mehta, Pratap Bhanu. 2016. "Unconstitutional Patriotism: Order on National Anthem Shows What Is Wrong with the Court." *Indian Express*, December 3. http://indianexpress.com/article/opinion/columns/national-anthem-cinema-halls-supreme-court-order-unconstitutional-patriotism-4407560/. Accessed April 5, 2017.

Mehta, Ved. 1977. *Mahatma Gandhi and His Apostles.* London: Andre Deutsch.

Menon, N. 2015. "Fighting Patriarchy and Capitalism." *Journal of Contemporary African Studies* 33(1): 3–11.

Meo, Nick. 2005. "Tsunami was God's Revenge for Your Wicked Ways, Women Told", *The Times.* 22 December. http://www.truth-out.org/archive/item/59481-tsunami-was-gods-revenge-for-your-wicked-ways-women-told. Accessed August 12, 2016.

Mezzadra, Sandro, and Brett Neilson. 2013. *Border as Method; or, the Multiplication of Labor.* Durham, NC: Duke University Press.

Michael, Bachelard. 2015. "Aceh's Sharia Law: Raped and Beaten; then formally whipped." *Sydney Morning Herald*, January 9. http://www.smh.com.au/world/acehs-sharia-law-raped-and-beaten-then-formally-whipped-20150109-12kucb.html?deviceType=text. Accessed August 12, 2016.

Mies, Maria. 1986. *Patriarchy and Accumulation on a World Scale*. London: Zed Books.

Mill, John Stuart. 1971. "On Liberty." In A. D. Lindsay, ed., *Utilitarianism, Liberty, Representative Government*. London: J. M. Dent and Sons.

Miller, Michelle Ann. 2009. *Rebellion and Reform in Indonesia: Jakarta's Security and Autonomy Policies in Aceh*. London: Routledge.

Millett, Kate. 1969. *Sexual Politics*. Urbana: University of Illinois Press.

Ministry of Foreign Affairs, Sweden. 2015. Statement of Foreign Policy. February 11. http://www.government.se/speeches/2015/02/statement-of-foreign-policy-2015/.

Mohanty, C. T. 1984. "Under Western Eyes: Feminist Scholarship and Colonial Discourse." *Boundary 2* 12(3): 333–358.

Moisi, Dominique. 2009. *The Geopolitics of Emotion: How Cultures of Fear, Humiliation and Hope Are Reshaping the World*. London: The Bodley Head.

Montgomery, Peter. 2016. International Backlash: The Religious Right at the UN. *The Public Eye*, Fall, 10–16. http://www.politicalresearch.org/wp-content/uploads/2016/10/PE_Fall16_Montgomery.pdf. Accessed March 27, 2017.

Mookherjee, M. 2005. "Affective Citizenship: Feminism, Postcolonialism and the Politics of Recognition." *Critical Review of International Social and Political Philosophy* 8(1): 31–50.

Morrison, Scott. 2014. "A New Force Protecting Australia's Borders." Address to the Lowy Institute for International Policy, Sydney, May 9. http://www.minister.immi.gov.au/media/sm/2014/sm214247.htm.

Mountz, Alison. 2011. "The Enforcement Archipelago: Detention, Haunting, and Asylum on Islands." *Political Geography* 30(3): 118–128.

Muhammad, Kh. Husein, et al. 2007. *Dawrah Fiqh Concerning Women: Manual for a Course on Islam and Gender*. 2nd ed. West Java: Fahmina Institute.

Murphy, Craig. 1984. *The Emergence of the NIEO Ideology*. Boulder CO: Westview Press.

Murphy, M. J. 2010. "An Open Letter to the Organizers, Presenters and Attendees of the First National Conference for Campus Based Men's Gender Equality and Anti-Violence Groups." *Journal of Men's Studies* 18(1): 103–108.

Nagel, Joane. 1998. "Masculinity and Nationalism: Gender and Sexuality in the Making of Nations." *Ethnic and Racial Studies* 21(2): 242–269.

Naji, Abu Bakr. 2006. *The Management of Savagery*. Trans. William McCants. Cambridge, MA: John M. Olin Institute for Strategic Studies, Harvard University.

Nandy, Ashis. 1983. *The Intimate Enemy: Loss and Recovery of Self under Colonialism*. Delhi: Oxford University Press.

Nandy, Ashis. 2003. *The Romance of the State: And the Fate of Dissent in the Tropics*, Delhi: Oxford University Press.

Nandy, Ashis, and Phillip Darby. 2015. "International Relations as Variations on Everyday Human Relations." *Postcolonial Studies* 18(2): 103–114.

Naples, Nancy A., and Manisha Desai, eds. 2002. *Women's Activism and Globalization: Linking Local Struggles and Transnational Politics*. New York: Routledge.

Narain, Vrinda. 2001. *Gender and Community: Muslim Women's Rights in India*. Toronto: University of Toronto Press.

Narayan, Uma. 1997. *Dislocating Culture: Identities, Traditions and Third World Feminism*. New York: Routledge.

Narayan, Uma, and Sandra Harding, eds. 2000. *Decentering the Center: Philosophy for a Multicultural, Postcolonial World*. Bloomington: Indiana Univeristy Press.

Nasar, Sema. 2013. "Violence against Women, Bleeding Wound in the Syrian Conflict." Euro-Mediterranean Rights Network, November. http://www.wluml.org/sites/wluml.org/files/Euromedrights-VAW-Syria-Nov-2013.pdf.

Navest, Ayesha, Martijn de Koning, and Annalies Moors. 2016. "Chatting about Marriage with Female Migrants to Syria: Agency beyond the Victim versus Activist Paradigm." *Anthropology Today* 32(2): 22–25.

Nayak, Meghana. 2006. "Orientalism and 'Saving' US State Identity after 9/11." *International Feminist Journal of Politics* 8(1): 42–61.

Nduka-Agwu, A. 2009. "'Doing Gender' after the War: Dealing with Gender Mainstreaming and Sexual Exploitation and Abuse in UN Peace Support Operations in Liberia and Sierra Leone." *Civil Wars* 11(2): 179–199.

Nehru, Jawharlal L. 1961. *India's Foreign Policy: Selected Speeches, September 1946–April 1961*. New Delhi: Publications Division, Ministry of Information and Broadcasting, Government of India.

New York Times. 2013. "Russia: Orthodox Leader Condemns Feminism." April 9. http://www.nytimes.com/2013/04/10/world/europe/russia-orthodox-leader-condemns-feminism.html. Accessed April 9, 2017.

New York Times. n.d. "Interactive Map ISIS Attacks around the World." http://www.nytimes.com/interactive/2016/03/25/world/map-isis-attacks-around-the-world.html?_r=0.

News.com.au. 2013. "Russian Patriarch Denounces Feminism." April 10. http://www.news.com.au/world/breaking-news/russian-patriarch-denounces-feminism/news-story/6bb63ff02150da0a3302771373d247ac. Accessed April 9, 2017.

Nordberg, Jenny. 2015. "Who's Afraid of a Feminist Foreign Policy?" *New Yorker*, April 15. http://www.newyorker.com/news/news-desk/swedens-feminist-foreign-minister.

Norwegian Refugee Council. 2016. "GRID: Global Report on Internal Displacement." http://www.internal-displacement.org/assets/publications/2016/2016-global-report-internal-displacement-IDMC.pdf.

Nussbaum, Martha. 2001. *Upheavals of Thought: The Intelligence of Emotions*. Cambridge: Cambridge University Press.

Nussbaum, Martha. 2015. *Political Emotions: Why Love Matters for Justice*. Cambridge, MA: Harvard University Press.

O'Reilly, Maria. 2012. "Muscular Interventionism: Gender, Power and Liberal Peacebuilding in Post-conflict Bosnia-Herzegovina." *International Feminist Journal of Politics* 14(4): 529–548.

O'Reilly, Marie, A. Ó Súilleabháin, and T. Paffenholz. 2015. *Reimagining Peacemaking: Women's Roles in Peace Processes*. Washington, DC: International Peace Institute.

Ogley, Roderick. 1970. *The Theory and Practice of Neutrality in the Twentieth Century*. London: Routledge and Kegan Paul.

Ohmai, Kenichi. 1991. *The Borderless World: Power and Strategy in the Interlinked Economy*. New York: HarperCollins.

Orlova, Alexandra V. 2014. "Plugging the Baby Gap? The Struggle to Reverse Demographic Decline in Russia." *Eurasia Studies Society of Great Britain and Europe Journal* 3(2): 1–15.

Ostner, Ilona, and Jane Lewis. 1995. "Gender and the Evolution of European Social Policies." In Stephen Leibfried and Paul Piierson, eds., *European Social Policy: Between Fragmentation and Integration*. Washington, DC: Brookings Institution Press.

Ottoway, Marina. 2015. "ISIS: Many Faces, Different Battles." Middle East Program, Woodrow Wilson Center, Occasional Paper Series, Winter.

Oxfam. 2005. "The Tsunami's Impact on Women." Oxfam Briefing Note.

Oyěwùmí, Oyèrónké. 2003. "The White Woman's Burden: African Women in Western Discourse." In Oyèrónké Oyěwùmí, ed., *African Women and Feminism: Reflecting on the Politics of Sisterhood*. Trenton, NJ: Africa World Press.

Paffenholz, Thania, Nick Ross, Steven Dixon, Anna-Lena Schluchter, and Jacqui True. 2016. *Making Women Count—Not Just Counting Women: Assessing Women's Inclusion and Influence on Peace Negotiations*. New York: Inclusive Peace and Transition Initiative and UN Women.

Pande, Amrita. 2014. "'I Prefer to Go Back the Day before Tomorrow, but I Cannot': Paternalistic Migration Policies and the 'Global Exile.'" *Critical Social Policy* 34(3): 374–393.

Pandey, Prashant. 2017. "Sukma Attack: He Would Have Gone on a Pilgrimage." *Indian Express*, April 26. http://indianexpress.com/article/india/sukma-attack-he-would-have-gone-on-a-pilgrimage-4628524. Accessed April 27, 2017.

Parashar, Swati. 2011a. "Embodied 'Otherness' and Negotiations of Difference: A Critical Self Reflection on the Politics of Emotions in Researching Militant Women." In Christine Sylvester, ed., "Forum: Emotion and the Feminist IR Researcher." *International Studies Review* 13(4): 687–708

Parashar, Swati. 2011b. "Gender, Jihad and *Jingoism:* Women as Perpetrators, Planners and Patrons of Militancy in Kashmir." *Studies in Conflict and Terrorism* 34(4): 295–317.

Parashar, Swati. 2014. *Women and Militant Wars: The Politics of Injury*. New York: Routledge.

Parashar, Swati. 2015. "Anger, War and Feminist Storytelling." In Linda Åhäll and Thomas Gregory, eds., *Emotions, Politics and War*. London: Routledge.

Paris, R. 2003. "Peacekeeping and the Constraints of Global Culture." *European Journal of International Relations* 9(3): 441–473.

Parpart, Jane L., and Staudt, Kathleen A. 1988. "Women and the State in Africa." In Jane L. Parpart and Kathleen A. Staudt, eds., *Women and the State in Africa*. Boulder, CO: Lynne Rienner, pp. 1–19.

Parreñas, Rhacel. 2005. "Long Distance Intimacy: Class, Gender and Intergenerational Relations between Mothers and Children in Filipino Transnational Families." *Global Networks* 5(4): 317–336.

Pateman, Carole. 1988a. "The Patriarchal Welfare State: Women and Democracy." In Amy Gutman, ed., *Democracy and the Welfare State*. Princeton, NJ: Princeton University Press, pp. 231–260.

Pateman, Carole. 1988b. *The Sexual Contract*. Stanford, CA: Stanford University Press.

Pease, B. 2015. "Disengaging Men from Patriarchy: Rethinking the Man Question in Masculinities Studies." In Michael Flood and Richard Howson, eds., *Engaging Men in Building Gender Equality*. London: Cambridge Scholars Press, pp. 55–70.

Pecherskaya, Nataliya V. 2013. "Perspektivy rossiiskoi semejnoi politiki: prinuzhdenie k traditsii." *Zhurnal sotsiologii i sotsialnoi antropologii* 69(4): 94–105.

Pegg, Scott. 1998. *International Society and the De Facto State*. Basingstoke: Ashgate Publishing.

Perelli-Harris, Brienna, and Olga Isupova. 2013. "Crisis and Control: Russia's Dramatic Fertility Decline and Efforts to Increase It." In Ann Buchanan and Anna Rotkirch, eds., *Fertility Rates and Population Decline*. London: Palgrave Macmillan, pp. 141–156.

Perera, Suvendrini. 2013. "Oceanic Corpo-Graphies, Refugee Bodies and the Making and Unmaking of Waters." *Feminist Review* 103: 58–79.

Persson, Alma. 2013. "Gendered Military Divisions: Doing Peacekeeping as Part of the Postnational Defence." *Kvinder, Køn & Forskning* 22(2): 30–45.

Peterson V. Spike, ed. 1992a. *Gendered States: Feminist (Re)visions of International Relations Theory*. Boulder, CO: Lynne Rienner.

Peterson, V. Spike. 1992b. "Introduction." In V. Spike Peterson, ed., *Gendered States: Feminist (Re)visions of International Relations Theory*. Boulder, CO: Lynne Rienner, pp. 1–30.

Peterson, V Spike. 1992c. "Security and the Sovereign State: What Is at Stake in Taking Feminism Seriously?" In V. Spike Peterson, ed., *Gendered States: Feminist (Re)visions of International Relations Theory*. Boulder, CO: Lynne Rienner, pp. 31–64.

Peterson, V. Spike. 2004. "Feminist Theories within, Invisible to, and beyond IR." *Brown Journal of World Affairs* 10(2): 35–46.

Peterson, V. Spike. 2010. "Gendered Identities, Ideologies, and Practices in the Context of War and Militarism." In Laura Sjoberg and Sandra Via, eds., *Gender, War, and Militarism: Feminist Perspectives*. Santa Barbara, CA: Praeger.

Peterson, V. Spike. 2014. "Family Matters: How Queering the Intimate Queers the International." *International Studies Review* 16: 604–608.

Peterson, V. Spike, and Anne S. Runyan. 2010. *Global Gender Issues in the New Millennium*. Boulder, CO: Westview Press.

Pettman, Jan Jindy. 1996. *Worlding Women: A Feminist International Politics*. Sydney: Allen & Unwin.

Phillips, John. 2006. "Agencement/Assemblage." *Theory, Culture and Society* 23(2–3): 108–109.

Picq, Manuela L. 2013. "Indigenous Worlding: Kichwa Women Pluralizing Sovereignty." In Arlene B. Tickner and David Blaney, eds., *Claiming the International*. New York: Routledge.

Piper, Nicola, Stuart Rosewarne, and Matt Withers. 2016. "Addressing Multiple Forms of Migrant Precarity: Beyond 'Management' of Migration to an Integrated Rights-Based Approach. UNRISD Working Paper 2016-11, September. http://www.unrisd.org/80256B3C005BCCF9/(httpAuxPages)/72E2E53E545B067BC12580250043BA1D/$file/Piper%20et%20al.pdf. Accessed August 14, 2017.

Plait, P. 2014. #YesAllWomen. http://www.slate.com/blogs/bad_astronomy/2014/05/27/not_all_men_how_discussing_women_s_issues_gets_derailed.htm. Accessed December 20, 2015.

Pruitt, Lesley J. 2013. "All-Female Police Contingents: Feminism and the Discourse of Armed Protection." *International Peacekeeping* 20(1): 67–79.

Pruitt, Lesley J. 2016. *The Women in Blue Helmets: Gender, Policing and the UN's First All-Female Peacekeeping Unit*. Berkeley: University of California Press.

Pursley, S. 2015. "'Lines Drawn on an Empty Map': Iraq's Borders and the Legend of the Artificial State." *Jadaliyya* (Arab Studies Institute).

Queerussia. 2013. "Deputy Mizulina to Russian Gay Teenager: I Defend Majority Values and Demographics, Not Responsible for Crimes." December 19. https://web.archive.org/web/20160806075802/http://queerussia.info/2013/12/19/3220/#sthash.ghAMAqUi.dpbs. Accessed January 1, 2017.

Quilliam Foundation. 2015. *Women of Islamic State, an English Translation from Arabic*. London.

Rai, Shirin M. 1996. "Women and the State in the Third World: Some Issues for Debate." In Shirin M Rai and Geraldine Lievesley, eds., *Women and the State: International Perspectives*. London: Routledge.

Rao, Varavara. 2010. *Captive Imagination: Letters from Prison*. New Delhi: Penguin Viking.

Ratha, Dilip, Sonia Plaza, and Erwin Dervisevic. 2016. *Migration and Remittances Factbook 2016*. World Bank Publications.

Reus-Smit, Christian. 2013. *Individual Rights and the Making of the International System*. Cambridge: Cambridge University Press.

Reveal News. 2016. "Russia's New Scapegoats." September 24. https://www.revealnews.org/episodes/russias-new-scapegoats/. Accessed December 29, 2016.

RIA Novosti. 2014. "Putin ob otnosheniiakh RF i Zapada: medvedya vsegda khotiat posadit- na tsep'." December 18. https://ria.ru/politics/20141218/1038943319.html. Accessed December 31, 2016.

Riabov, Oleg V. 2006. "'Rodina-mat': istoriaobraza." *Zhenshchina v rossijskomobshchestve* 3: 33–46.

Riabov, Oleg V., and Tatiana B. Riabova. 2014. "The Remasculization of Russia?" *Problems of Post-Communism* 61(2): 23–35.

Riabova, Tatyana B. 2015. "'Rodina-mat' v praktikakh politicheskoj mobilizatsii sovremennoj Rossii." *Zhenshchina v rossijskom obshchestve* 3–4(76/77): 124–137.

Riabova, Tatiana B., and Anastasiia A. Romanova. 2015. "'Rodina-mat' kak kul'turno-semioticheskij factor sovremennogo rossijskogo antiamerikanizma." *Labirint: Zhurnal sotsial'no-gumanitarnykh issledovanij* 4: 168–183.

Riabova, Tatiana B., and Oleg Riabov. 2010. "Nastoiashshij muzhchina Rossijskoj politiki? (K voprosu o gendernom diskurse kak resurce vlasti)." *Polis* 5: 48–65.

Rinaldo, R. 2011. "Muslim Women, Moral Visions: Globalization and Gender Contraversies in Indonesia." *Qualitative Sociology* 34(4): 539–560.

Robinson, Mary. 2016. "Gender Equality and Climate Change: The Vital Link for Success beyond Paris." *The Elders*, March 7. http://theelders.org/article/gender-equality-and-climate-change-vital-link-success-beyond-paris.

Robinson, V. 2003. "Radical Revisionings? The Theorizing of Masculinity and (Radical) Feminist Theory." *Women's Studies International Forum* 26(3): 129–137.

Rodriguez, Robyn Magalit. 2010. *Migrants for Export: How the Philippine State Brokers Labor to the World*. Minneapolis: University of Minnesota Press.

Rotberg, Robert I. 2011. *Failed States, Collapsed States, and Weak States: Causes and Indicators*. Washington, DC: Woodrow Wilson Center for Peace.

Rothrock, Kevin. 2014. "Russian Lawmakers Will Debate Legislation against Back Tattoos for Women." *Global Voices*, October 10. http://globalvoicesonline.org/2014/10/10/russia-duma-tattoos-women-epidural/. Accessed December 31, 2016.

Roul, K. 2016. "The Kandhamal Encounter: Reality and Response." *Mainstream Weekly*, November 12. http://www.mainstreamweekly.net/article6812.html. Accessed April 10, 2017.

Roy, Arundhati. 2011. *Broken Republic: Three Essays.* New Delhi: Hamish Hamilton.

Roy, S. 2009. "The Ethical Ambivalence of Resistant Violence: Notes from Postcolonial South Asia." *Feminist Review* (91): 135–153. Retrieved from http://www.jstor.org/stable/40663984.

Rubin, Gayle S. 1984. "Thinking Sex: Notes for a Radical Theory of the Politics of Sexuality." In Carole Vance, ed., *Pleasure and Danger.* New York: Routledge, pp. 143–178.

Rupert, James. 2015. "Sweden's Foreign Minister Explains Feminist Foreign Policy." *Olive Branch*, February 9. http://www.usip.org/olivebranch/2015/02/09/sweden-s-foreign-minister-explains-feminist-foreign-policy.

Rutland, Peter. 2014. "The Pussy Riot Affair: Gender and National Identity in Putin's Russia." *Nationalities Papers* 42(4): 575–582.

Ryabov, Oleg V., and Tatiana B. Ryabova. 2016. "Simbol Rodiny-materi kak resurs formirovaniia rossijskoj grazhdanskoj identichnosti." *Chelovek. Soobshchestvo. Upravlenie* 2(17): 99–114.

Salter, M. 2015. "'Real Men Don't Hit Women': Constructing Masculinity in the Prevention of Violence against Women." *Australian and New Zealand Journal of Criminology* 49(4): 463–479.

Samath, Faizal. 2013. "Migrant Worker Challenges Govt. on Restrictive Rule." *Sunday Times*, September 1. http://www.sundaytimes.lk/130901/business-times/migrant-worker-challenges-govt-over-restrictive-rule-59771.html. Accessed October 2, 2013.

Sassen, Saskia. 2006. *Territory, Authority, Rights: From Medieval to Global Assemblages.* Princeton, NJ: Princeton University Press.

Saul, Heather. 2014. "Isis now targeting women with guides on how to be the 'ultimate wives of jihad'" *The Independent*. 31st October. http://www.independent.co.uk/news/world/middle-east/isis-now-targeting-women-with-guides-on-how-to-be-the-ultimate-wives-of-jihad-9830562.html

Sawer, Marian. 2003a. "Constructing Democracy." *International Feminist Journal of Politics* 5(3): 361–365.

Sawer, Marian. 2003b. *The Ethical State: Social Liberalism in Australia.* Melbourne: Penguin.

Schulze, Kirsten E. 2003. "The Struggle for an Independent Aceh: The Ideology, Capacity and Strategy of GAM." *Studies in Conflict and Terrorism* 26(4): 241–271.

Scrutton, Alistair, and Johan Sennero. 2014. "Sweden's Palestine Statement Signals Start of Weightier Global Role." Reuters, October 7. http://www.reuters.com/article/2014/10/07/us-sweden-diplomacy-idUSKCN0HW1N520141007.

Seymour, K. 2012. "The Violence of Gender: Australian Policy Response to Violence." PhD dissertation, Deakin University.

Shah, Alpa. 2010. *In the Shadows of the State.* New Delhi: Oxford University Press.

Sharafutdinova, Gulnaz. 2014. "The Pussy Riot Affair and Putin's Demarche from Sovereign Democracy to Sovereign Morality." *Nationalities Papers* 42(4): 615–621.

Sharan, R. 2005. "Alienation and Restoration of Tribal Land in Jharkhand: Current Issues and Possible Strategies." *Economic and Political Weekly* 40(41): 4443–4446.

Sharma A., and A. Gupta. 2006. "Introduction: Rethinking Theories of the State in an Age of Globalization." In Aradhana Sharma and Akhil Gupta, eds., *The Anthropology of the State: A Reader.* Oxford: Blackwell.

Sharma, Richa, and S. Bazilli. 2014. "A Reflection on Gang Rape: What's Law Got to Do with It?" *International Journal of Crime, Justice and Social Democracy* 3.3: 4–21. https://www.crimejusticejournal.com/article/view/155/154.

Shepherd, Laura J. 2006. "Veiled References: Constructions of Gender in the Bush Administration Discourse on the Attacks on Afghanistan Post-9/11." *International Feminist Journal of Politics* 8(1): 19–41.

Shepherd, Laura J. 2011. "Sex, Security and Superhero(in)es: From 1325 to 1820 and Beyond." *International Feminist Journal of Politics* 13(4): 504–521.

Shepherd, Laura J., and Jacqui True. 2014. "The Women, Peace and Security Agenda and Australian Leadership in the World: From Rhetoric to Commitment?" *Australian Journal of International Affairs* 68(3): 257–284.

Siapno, Jacqueline Aquino. 2001. "Gender, Nationalism, and the Ambiguity of Female Agency in Aceh, Indonesia and East Timor." In Marguerite R. Waller and Jennifer Rycenga, eds., *Frontline Feminisms: Women, War, and Resistance*. New York: Routledge.

Silvey, Rachel. 2004. "Transnational Migration and the Gender Politics of Scale: Indonesian Domestic Workers in Saudi Arabia." *Singapore Journal of Tropical Geography* 25(2): 141–155.

Simić, O. 2010. "Does the Presence of Women Really Matter? Towards Combating Male Sexual Violence in Peacekeeping Operations." *International Peacekeeping* 17(2): 188–199.

Simpson, L. C. 2000. "Communication and the Politics of Difference." *Constellations* 7(3): 430–442.

Singh, S. 2010. "Women's Autonomy in Rural India: Need for Culture and Context." *International Social Work* 53(2): 169–186.

Sinha, Mrinalini. 1995. *Colonial Masculinity: The "Manly Englishman" and the "Effeminate Bengali" in the Late Nineteenth Century*. Manchester: Manchester University Press.

Sivkova, Alena. 2014. "Est' Putin—est' Rossia, net Putina—net Rossii." *Izvestiya*, October 22. http://izvestia.ru/news/578379. Accessed January 1, 2017.

Sjoberg, Laura ed. 2009. *Gender and International Security: Feminist Perspectives*. New York: Routledge.

Sjoberg, Laura. 2012. "Gender, Structure and War: What Waltz Couldn't See." *International Theory* 4(1): 1–38.

Sjoberg, Laura. 2013. *Gendering Global Conflict: Toward a Feminist Theory of War*. New York: Columbia University Press.

Sjoberg, Laura, and Jessica Peet. 2011. "A(nother) Dark Side of the Protection Racket: Targeting Women in Wars." *International Feminist Journal of Politics* 13(2): 163–182.

Smith, Nicola. 2015. "ISIS Kills Mother Who Fed Baby in Public." *Sunday Times*, December 27. http://www.thesundaytimes.co.uk/sto/news/world_news/Middle_East/article1649568.ece.

Sommers, Jack. 2015. "Isis 'Poster Girl' Samra Kesinovic Murdered for Trying to Flee Raqqa: Austrian Press Report." *Huffington Post*, November 25. http://www.huffingtonpost.co.uk/2015/11/25/samra-kesinovic-isis-murdered-reports_n_8645622.html.

Sonbol, Amira El-Azhary, ed. 2005. *Beyond the Exotic: Women's Histories in Islamic Societies*. Syracuse, NY: Syracuse University Press.

Speckhard, Anne, and Ahmet S. Yayla. 2015. "Eyewitness Accounts from Recent Defectors from Islamic State: Why They Joined, What They Saw, Why They

Left." *Perspectives on Terrorism* 9(6). http://www.terrorismanalysts.com/pt/index.php/pot/article/view/475/html.

Sperling, Valerie. 2015. *Sex, Politics, and Putin*. Oxford: Oxford University Press.

Sperling, Valerie. 2016. "Putin's Macho Personality Cult." *Communist and Post-Communist Studies* 49(1): 13–23.

Spivak, Gayatri Chakravorty. 1995. *The Spivak Reader: Selected Works of Gayatri Chakravorty Spivak*. London: Routledge.

Spivak, Gayatri Chakravorty. 2013. "Europa and the Bull Market." Nicos Poulantzas Institute on Vimeo. Uploaded February 8. https://vimeo.com/59215616. Accessed August 9, 2014.

Stachowitsch, Saskia. 2013. "Military Privatization and the Remasculinization of the State: Making the Link between the Outsourcing of Military Security and Gendered State Transformations." *International Relations* 27(1): 74–94.

Staff Reporter. 2008. "Overwhelming Response to CRPF Marathon 2008 in City." *The Hindu*, August 31.

Stetson McBride, Dorothy, and Amy G. Mazur. 1995. *Comparative State Feminisms*. Thousand Oaks, CA: Sage.

Stewart-Harawira, Makere. 2005. *The New Imperial Order: Indigenous Responses to Globalization*. New York: Zed Books.

Stiehm, Judith Hicks. 1982. "The Protected, the Protector, the Defender." *Women's Studies International Forum* 5(3/4): 367–376.

Sundar, Nandini. 2012. "'Winning Hearts and Minds': Emotional Wars and the Construction of Difference." *Third World Quarterly*.

Sundar, Nandini. 2016. *The Burning Forest: India's War in Bastar*. New Delhi: Juggernaut.

Suslov, M. D. 2014. "'Holy Rus': The Geopolitical Imagination in the Contemporary Russian Orthodox Church." *Russian Politics and Law* 52(3): 67–86.

Suspitsina, Tatiana. 1999. "The Rape of Holy Mother Russia and the Hatred of Femininity: The Representation of Women and the Use of Feminine Imagery in the Russian Nationalist Press." *Anthropology of East Europe Review* 17(2): 114–123.

Sydney Morning Herald. 2012. "Saving Lives Trumps Politics, Says Gillard." August 19. http://www.smh.com.au/federal-politics/political-news/saving-lives-trumps-politics-says-gillard-20120819-24g0i.html.

Sydney Morning Herald. 2014. "'I'm No Feminist': Julie Bishop." October 29. http://www.smh.com.au/federal-politics/political-news/im-no-feminist-julie-bishop-20141029-11dn7m.html.

Sylvester, Christine. 1992. "Feminists and Realists View Autonomy and Obligation in International Relations." In V. Spike Peterson, ed., *Gendered States: Feminist (Re)visions of International Relations Theory*. Boulder, CO: Lynne Rienner.

Sylvester, Christine. 2011. *Experiencing War*. London: Routledge.

Sylvester, Christine. 2011. "Forum: Emotion and the Feminist IR Researcher." *International Studies Review* 13(4): 687–708.

Szekely, O. 2016. "Proto-state Realignment and the Arab Spring." *Middle East Policy* 23(1): 75–91.

Tansel, Cemal Burak, ed. 2017. *States of Discipline: Authoritarian Neoliberalism and the Contested Reproduction of Capitalist Order*. Lanham, MD: Rowman & Littlefield.

Tanyag, Maria. 2017. "Global Gag Rule and the Political Economy of Sexual and Reproductive Freedoms." *Quarterly Access* 22(56): 86–95. http://www.internationalaffairs.org.au/

global-gag-rule-and-the-political-economy-of-sexual-and-reproductive-freedoms/.

Taylor, Lenore. 2016. "Turnbull Suggests Australia Is Not Responsible for Asylum Seekers Held Offshore." *The Guardian*, June 27. https://www.theguardian.com/australia-news/2016/jun/28/turnbull-suggests-australia-is-not-responsible-for-asylum-seekers-held-offshore.

Telegraph. 2013. "Russian Orthodox Patriarch Denounces 'Dangerous Feminism.'" April 10. http://www.telegraph.co.uk/women/womens-life/9984591/Russian-Orthodox-Patriarch-denounces-dangerous-feminism.html. Accessed April 9, 2017.

Tetreault, Mary Ann. 1992. "Women and Revolution: A Framework for Analysis." In V. Spike Peterson, ed., *Gendered States: Feminist (Re)visions of International Relations Theory*. Boulder, CO: Lynne Rienner.

Tickner, J. Ann. 1987. *Self-Reliance versus Power Politics: American and Indian Experiences in Building Nation States*. New York: Columbia University Press.

Tickner, J. Ann. 1988. "Hans Morgenthau's Principles of Political Realism: A Feminist Reformulation. *Millennium* 17(3): 429–440.

Tickner, J. Ann. 1992. *Gender in International Relations: Feminist Perspectives on Achieving Global Security*. New York: Columbia University Press.

Tickner, J. Ann. 1996. "Identity in International Relations Theory: Feminist Perspectives." In Yosef Lapid and Friedrich Kratochwil, eds., *The Return of Culture and Identity in IR Theory*. Boulder, CO: Lynne Rienner.

Tickner, J. Ann. 2001. *Gendering World Politics: Issues and Approaches in the Post-Cold War Era*. New York: Coloumbia University Press.

Tickner, J. Ann. 2014. *A Feminist Voyage through International Relations*. Oxford: Oxford University Press.

Tickner, J. Ann. 2015. "Revisiting IR in a Time of Crisis: Learning from Indigenous Knowledge." *International Feminist Journal of Politics* 17(4): 536–553.

Tilly, Charles. 1985. "War Making and State Making as Organized Crime." In Peter Evans, Dietrich Rueschemeyer, and Theda Skocpol, eds., *Bringing the State Back In*. Cambridge: Cambridge University Press.

Times of India. 26 April 2017. http://timesofindia.indiatimes.com/elections/delhi-mcd/news/no-celebrations-bjp-to-dedicate-mcd-win-to-slain-crpf-jawans/articleshow/58375613.cms.

Towns, Ann E. 2010. *Women and States: Norms and Hierarchies in International Society*. Cambridge: Cambridge University Press.

True, Jacqui. 2003. *Gender, Globalization, and Post-Socialism: The Czech Republic after Communism*. New York: Columbia University Press.

True, Jacqui. 2012. *The Political Economy of Violence against Women*. New York: Oxford University Press.

True, Jacqui. 2015a. "A Tale of Two Feminisms in International Relations? Feminist Political Economy and the Women, Peace and Security Agenda." *Politics and Gender* 11(2): 419–424.

True, Jacqui. 2015b. "Why We Need a Feminist Foreign Policy to Stop War." *Open Democracy*. April 20. https://www.opendemocracy.net/5050/jacqui-true/why-we-need-feminist-foreign-policy-to-stop-war.

True, Jacqui. 2016. "Gender and Foreign Policy." In Shahar Hamieri and Mark Beeson, eds., *Australia in World Affairs: Navigating the New International Disorder (2011– 2015)*. Melbourne: Oxford University Press.

Uchendu, Egodi. 2008. "Introduction: Are African Males Men? Sketching African Masculinities." In Egodi Uchendu, ed., *Masculinities in Contemporary Africa*. Oxford: Codesria.

UN Women. 2011. *Progress of the World's Women: In Pursuit of Justice*. New York: UN.

UN Women. 2014. HeForShe UN Women Solidarity Movement for Gender Equality Action Kit. New York: UN Women.

UN Women. 2015. Press release: "UN Women Launches HeForShe IMPACT 10x10x10 Initiative." http://www.unwomen.org/en/news/stories/2015/01/emma-watson-launches-10-by-10-by-10. Accessed July 18, 2016.

United Nations Analytical Support and Sanctions Monitoring Team. 2015. *The Threat Posed by Foreign Terrorist Fighters*. www.un.org/en/sc/ctc/docs/2015/N1508457_EN.pdf.

United Nations Human Rights Commission and United Nations Assistance Mission Iraq (UNHRC/UNAMI). 2016. *Report on the Protection of Civilians in the Armed Conflict in Iraq May–October 2015*. http://www.uniraq.org/images/humanrights/UNAMI-OHCHR_%20POC%20Report_FINAL_01%20May-31%20October%202015_FINAL_11Jan2016.pdf.

United Nations Mission in Liberia (UNMIL). 2010. *Gender Mainstreaming in Peacekeeping Operations Liberia, 2003–2009: Best Practices Report*.

United Nations Population Fund (UNFPA). 2005. *Gender-Based Violence in Aceh, Indonesia: A Case Study*.

UNORC. 2009. *Tsunami Recovery Indicator Package (TRIP): The Third Report for Aceh and Nias*. Jakarta: UNORC.

Vershinina, Kseniya. 2013. "Internet-zvezda Alena Piskun mozhet pojti pod sud za oskorblenie Mamaeva kurgana." 1tvnet.ru. October 2. http://www.1tvnet.ru/content/show/internet-zvezda-alena-piskun-mojet-poiti-pod-sud-za-oskorblenie-mamaeva-kurgana_22327.html. Accessed March 20, 2017.

Voronina, Olga. 2009. "Has Feminist Philosophy a Future in Russia?" *Signs* 34(2): 252–257.

Wadley, Jonathan D. 2010. "Gendering the State: Performativity and Protection in International Security." In Laura Sjoberg, ed., *Gender and International Security: Feminist Perspectives*. New York: Routledge.

Walby, Sylvia. 1990. *Theorising Patriarchy*. Oxford: Basil Blackwell.

Walby, Sylvia. 2006. "Gender Approaches to Nations and Nationalism." In Gerard Deland and Krishan Kumar, eds., *Sage Handbook of Nations and Nationalism*. London: Sage.

Walker, Shaun. 2014. "Vladimir Putin: Gay People at Winter Olympics Must 'Leave Children Alone.'" *The Guardian*, January 18. https://www.theguardian.com/world/2014/jan/17/vladimir-putin-gay-winter-olympics-children. Accessed December 31, 2016.

Walker, Shaun. 2017. "Putin Approves Legal Change That Decriminalises Some Domestic Violence." *The Guardian*, February 8. https://www.theguardian.com/world/2017/feb/07/putin-approves-change-to-law-decriminalising-domestic-violence. Accessed March 27, 2017.

Wallström, Margot. 2016. State of the Government Policy in Parliamentary Debate on Foreign Affairs. February 24. http://www.government.se/speeches/2016/02/statement-of-government-policy-in-the-parliamentary-debate-on-foreign-affairs-2016/.

Walsh, Shannon D. 2008. "Engendering Justice: Constructing Institutions to Address Violence against Women." *Studies in Social Justice* 2: 48–62.

Walsh, Shannon D. 2016 "Advances and Limitations of Policing and Human Security for Women: Nicaragua in Comparative Perspective." In Victoria Sanford, Katerina Stefatos, and Cecilia M. Salvi, eds., *Gender Violence in Peace and War: States of Complicity*. New Brunswick, NJ: Rutgers University Press.

Waltz, Kenneth. 1959. *Man, the State and War*. New York: Columbia University Press.

Waltz, Kenneth. 1979. *Theory of International Politics*. Boston: Addison-Wesley.

Weber, Cynthia. 1994. *Simulating Sovereignty*. New York: Cambridge University Press.

Welland, J. 2015. "Liberal Warriors and the Violent Colonial Logics of 'Partnering' and 'Advising.'" *International Feminist Journal of Politics* 17(2): 289–307.

Wells, Kristopher. 2006. *Gay-Straight Student Alliances in Alberta Schools: A Guide for Teachers*. Alberta, Canada: Alberta Teachers' Association.

Wibben, Annick. 2011. *Feminist Security Studies: A Narrative Approach*. New York: Routledge.

Wickramasekara, Piyasiri. 2015. *Bilateral Agreements and Memoranda of Understanding on Migration of Low Skilled Workers: A Review*. Report Prepared for the Labour Migration Branch, International Labour Office. Geneva: ILO.

Wilkinson, Cai. 2014. "Putting 'Traditional Values' into Practice: The Rise and Contestation of Anti-homopropaganda Laws in Russia." *Journal of Human Rights* 13(3): 363–379.

Winter, Charlie, trans. 2015. *Women of the Islamic State: A Manifesto on Women by the Al-Khanssaa Brigade*. London: Quilliam Foundation.

Women against Sexual Violence and State Repression (WSS). 2013. Representation to the Justice Verma Commission, January 5. http://wssnet.org/2013/01/05/represenation-to-the-justiceverma-commission/. Accessed January 6, 2016.

Wood, Elizabeth A. 2016. "Hypermasculinity as a Scenario of Power." *International Feminist Journal of Politics* 18(3): 329–350.

Wood, Graeme. 2015. "What ISIS Really Wants." *The Atlantic*, March. http://www.theatlantic.com/features/archive/2015/02/what-isis-really-wants/384980/. Accessed August 15, 2017.

World Bank. 2016. *Migration and Remittances Factbook 2016*. 3rd Edition. International Bank for Reconstruction and Development / The World Bank: Washington DC, https://openknowledge.worldbank.org/bitstream/handle/10986/23743/9781464803192.pdf. Accessed January 15 2017.

World Economic Forum. 2013. *The Global Gender Gap Report*. Geneva, Switzerland: World Economic Forum. http://www3.weforum.org/docs/WEF_GenderGap_Report_2013.pdf

World Economic Forum. 2014. *The Global Gender Gap Report*. Geneva, Switzerland: World Economic Forum. http://reports.weforum.org/global-gender-gap-report-2014/

World Economic Forum. 2015. *The Global Gender Gap Report*. Geneva: World Economic Forum. http://www3.weforum.org/docs/GGGR2015/cover.pdf http://www3.weforum.org/docs/GGGR2015/cover.pdf.

Xiang, Biao, Brenda Yeoh, and Johan Lindquist. 2012. "Opening the Black Box of Migration: Brokers, the Organization of Transnational Mobility and the Changing Political Economy in Asia." *Pacific Affairs* 85(1): 7–19.

Yeoh, Brenda. 2016. "Migration and Gender Politics in Southeast Asia." *Migration, Mobility, and Displacement* 2(1): 79–98.

Young, Iris Marion. 2003. "The Logic of Masculinist Protection: Reflections on the Current Security State." *Signs* 29(1): 1–25.

Youssef, Nancy A., and Haris, Shane. (2015, May 7). The women who secretly keep ISIS running. *The Daily Beast*. http://www.thedailybeast.com/articles/2015/07/05/the-women-who-secretly-keep-isis-running.html

Yuval-Davis, Nira. 1997. *Gender and Nation*. London: Sage.

Yuval-Davis, Nira, and Floya Anthias, eds. 1987. *Woman—Nation—State*. Basingstoke: Macmillan.

Zech, Steven T., and Zane M. Kelly. 2015. "Off with Their Heads: The Islamic State and Civilian Beheadings." *Journal of Terrorism Research* 6(2). http://doi.org/10.15664/jtr.1157.

Zembylas, M. (2014). "Affective Citizenship in Multicultural Societies: Implications for Critical Citizenship Education." *Citizenship Teaching & Learning* 9(1): 5–18.

INDEX

Abbas, Umm, 183
Abbott, Tony, 77–79
Abu Dhabi Dialogue, 93
Abyan, Umm, 181
Aceh: Aceh Monitoring Mission and, 145–47; Acehnese Democratic Women's Organisation and, 142; All Acehnese Women Congress and, 142; "Build Back Better" campaign in, 13, 148–49; Cessation of Hostilities Agreement (2002) in, 145; Charter for the Rights of Women in Aceh and, 152; Commission for Truth and Reconciliation in, 146; disaster relief in, 140, 143–46, 148; female fighters in conflict in, 142; Gerakan Aceh Merdeka (GAM; Free Aceh Movement) in, 141–42, 145–46, 149; homosexuality criminalized in, 151; human rights in, 140–42, 146; Indian Ocean tsunami (2004) and, 13, 139, 142–43, 145, 149; Law on Governing Aceh (2006) and, 139, 146, 153; legislative elections (2009 and 2014) in, 146; military conflict (1976–2004) in, 140–43; nongovernmental organizations in, 144, 148–49, 152–53; oil and natural gas reserves in, 140; patriarchy in, 13, 139–40, 143–44, 146–51, 153–54, 194; peace process in, 140, 143–49; qanun (provincial regulations) in, 149–51; rape and sexual slavery during military conflict in, 141–42; Reconstruction and Rehabilitation Agency for Aceh and Nias in, 152; regional legislature in, 153; semi-autonomous status of, 13, 139, 149; sharia law in, 140, 142, 149–51; vigilante justice in, 150; women in political institutions and public life in, 151–53; Women's Committee for the Revival of Aceh and, 152; women's role as primary caregivers in, 143–44

Adivasis: communal ownership of property among, 164; Communist Party of India and, 164; human rights violations against, 167; Maoist insurgency in India and, 13, 165, 167–68; "Mother India" appeals to, 170; political marginalization of, 162, 173n3; regional concentrations of, 164

affective citizenship: gendered emotion and, 13, 171–72; in India, 162; multiple intersecting communities recognized in, 161; postcolonial statehood and, 159–63, 171–72; ruling elite discourse and, 161–62

affective nationalism, 160

Affiat, Rizki, 151, 153

Afghanistan: Australian military deployments in, 77; British military experiences in, 57–58; masculinity in, 58; patriarchy and gendered violence in, 42; Sweden's role in peace missions in, 73–74; The Taliban in, 45; U.S. invasion (2001) of, 54, 158; women's rights compromised during peace negotiations in, 45

Afrianty, Dina, 150

Ahmed, Sara, 159, 163

Ahtisaari, Martti, 145–46
alt-right movements (United States), 45
American exceptionalism, 20, 31n2, 195
anarchy, 19, 22, 25, 71
Anthias, Floya, 110
anticolonialism. *See also* postcolonial
    states: affective nationalism and,
    160, 162; gendered nationalism
    and, 90; in India, 8, 169; masculinity
    and, 169; the state as ideal in, 1, 8
Appleby, Joyce, 27–28
Arab Spring, 176
Argentina, 15n1, 192
Ashwin, Sarah, 111
assemblage, 4, 11, 85–88
Association of Southeast Asian
    Nations, 145
Atwood, Margaret, 191, 193
austerity policies, 2, 192
Australia: Afghanistan deployments
    by, 77; Australia and New Zealand
    Army Corps (ANZAC), 77; Battle
    of Gallipoli (1916) and, 77; border
    control policy in, 78–84; corporate
    masculinities in, 55; feminism
    in, 32n13; gender equality goals
    promoted by, 38; humanitarian
    missions led by, 77; immigration and
    asylum policy in, 11, 70–71,
    78–82; indigenous femininities in, 55;
    Indonesia and, 141; international
    aid funding and, 79; "middle power"
    status of, 70, 76; misogyny in, 77–78;
    nationalism and national identity
    in, 81; offshore detention policies
    of, 71, 78–82; Operation Sovereign
    Borders in, 70, 79–80; Pacific Solution
    and, 78–79; Responsibility to Protect
    doctrine and, 77; security policies in,
    70–71, 77–82; ultraright nationalism
    in, 160; United Nations Women, Peace
    and Security (WPS) agenda and, 78;
    White Australia policy (early twentieth
    century), 77; White Ribbon Campaign
    and, 59–61
Austria, 73
autonomy, 14, 22–23, 28, 35

Badawi, Raef, 84n5
al-Baghdadi, Abu Bakr, 176

Bahrain, 93
Banderas, Antonio, 63
Bartlett, Rosamund, 109
Basu, Soumita, 127
Bedi, Kiran, 124
Belgium, 192
Bharatiya Janata Party (BJP), 160,
    166, 171
Bildt, Carl, 72, 76
bin Laden, Osama, 173n1
Bishop, Julie, 78
Bleiker, Roland, 158
Boko Haram, 45, 192
Bolivia, 30
borders: Australia's policies
    regarding, 78–84; Islamic State
    and, 187; nationalism and, 80; as
    porous social constructs, 75; refugee
    crises and, 29, 70–71; security
    and, 11, 80–81; Sweden's policies
    regarding, 71
Brazil, 192
Brown, Wendy, 80
Buddha, 170
Buddhism, 182
Bulawayo, NoViolet, 193, 195–96
Burke, Anthony, 77
Bush, George W., 173n1
Butler, Judith, 24, 168

Cambodia, 15nn1–2
Campbell, Angus, 79
capitalism: globalization and,
    41, 126; Islamic State's response
    to, 45; the liberal state and, 53;
    patriarchy and, viii; state's role in
    buffering negative impacts of, 126;
    U.S. faith in, 28
Carl XVI Gustaf (king of Sweden), 76
Central Reserve Police Force (CRPF,
    India), 124, 166, 168, 171
Chambers, Peter, 80
Charrad, Mounira, 175
Charter for the Rights of Women in
    Aceh, 152
Chechen War (1994–96), 105
Chhotanagpur Tenancy Act (India), 164
Chile, 15n1
China, 36, 38
chivalry, 35, 59, 71

Fanon, Frantz, 8, 58
Felten-Biermann, Claudia, 144
female formed police units (FFPUs) in peacekeeping: challenges in staffing, 123–24; cultural norms regarding gender challenged by, 130–32, 136–37; Global South as source of personnel in, 12, 122–23, 125–26, 129, 134–37; India as source of personnel in, 12, 122, 124–28, 131, 133–34, 137; Liberia as theater of deployment for, 12, 124–25, 134; "second shifts" of, 125
femininity. *See also* gender: colonialism and, 57; indigenous populations and, 55; Maoist insurgency in India and, 168–70; masculinity and, 106–8; patriarchy and, 35, 46; Russia and, 107–12, 114, 120; the state and, 33, 108–12, 159, 163
feminism: anti-violence campaigns and, 51; bottom-up methodologies in, 6; international relations discipline and, vii–ix, 3–7, 9, 20–22, 24, 33, 35, 158, 160; lesbianism associated with, 116; the liberal state and, 51–53, 56, 58–59, 65–66; men's role in, 59–60, 62–65, 67; political economy and, 4; Russia's criticism of, xi, 107, 115–17, 119; the state and, 2, 5–7, 21–22, 25–27, 30, 69; Sweden's foreign policy and, 7, 44, 48n4, 70, 75–76, 128, 135
Finland, 73
Flood, Michael, 61
Flower Aceh organization, 142
France, 192
Frantz, Elizabeth, 97
Fraser, Nancy, 46
Free Aceh Movement. *See* Gerakan Aceh Merdeka
French Revolution, 27

G20 (Group of Twenty counties), 38
Gallipoli, Battle (1916) of, 77
Gamburd, Michelle Ruth, 90–91
Gandhi, Leela, 8
Gandhi, Mahatma: on agrarian self-reliance and state-building, 20–21, 28; bisexuality aspiration of, 170; gender equality promoted

by, 21, 170; nationalism and, 8, 169–70
Ganges River, 169–70
gender: citizenship and, 7, 41–42, 91, 111; gendered militarism and, 25; gender mainstreaming and, 27, 48, 134, 152; global data regarding equality in, 135–36; globalization and, 37–39, 42, 46, 69; labor migration and, 85–86, 90–100; nationalism and, xi, 3, 14, 24–25, 90–91, 95; neoliberalism and, 4, 136; postcolonialism and, 5–6, 8–9, 11, 13; quotas and, 27; security and, x, 3–4, 23, 70–72, 74–78, 81–82; sovereignty and, x, 14, 23, 25, 29, 35–36, 74, 83, 176; war and, 7, 24
Gendered States (edited volume published in 1992), viii, 3, 21–25, 176
Gendered States Revisited Conference (2014), 4–5
Gender in International Relations conference (2000), 23
Gerakan Aceh Merdeka (GAM; Free Aceh Movement), 141–42, 145–46, 149
Germany, 192
Gillard, Julia, 77–79
Global Financial Crisis (2008–9), 2, 4
Global Gender Gap Report (World Economic Forum), 135
globalization: capitalism and, 41, 126; gendered violence and, 34, 41; gender equality gains and gender inclusion as consequence of, 37–39, 42, 46, 69; patriarchy undermined in, x, 10, 33–34, 37, 41–43, 47; the state and, 1, 41, 69, 80–81
Global North: feminism in, 53; Global South's problems criticized in, 61, 66, 123, 136; masculinity and, 57; peacekeeping forces from, 134–36; state system in, 159–60
Global South. *See also* postcolonial states: development and, 20; ethnic diversity in, 29; gendered aspects of labor migration and, 93; gender equity issues in, 123, 129, 134–37; Global North's criticism of problems in, 61, 66, 123, 136; India as leader in, 127; the liberal state and, 53; masculinity

and, 57; peacekeeping units from
states in, 12, 122–23, 125–26,
129, 134–37
Göranson, Sverker, 75
Grant, Rebecca, 23
Great Britain. *See* United Kingdom
Greece, 192
Guattari, Félix, 87

Hague, William, 44, 84n4
Hague Congress for Peace (1915), 43
Haiti earthquake (2010), 139
Hamilton, Alexander, 20, 27
The Handmaid's Tale (Atwood), 191, 193
Hansen, Lene, 80
Harrington, Mona: caring social
democratic state advocated by, 28–29;
on isolationist agrarianism, 26–27;
liberal state defended by, 10, 25–26,
52–54, 56–58, 66, 67n1, 69–70, 128;
on Nordic states' women-friendly
policies, 26
Hasan, Zoya, 126
Hautzinger, Sarah J., 134
HeForShe campaign, 10, 52, 63–64,
66, 68n8
hegemonic masculinity: male athletes
and, 60; resistance to, 62, 65; Russian
culture and, 106–7, 114; the state
and, 3, 25
heteronormativity: Islamic State
and, 180, 183; LGBT allies' role in
questioning, 62; masculinity and, 56;
motherland tropes and, 11–12; Russia
and, xi, 11–12, 113–14, 118; the
state and, 7
Hobbes, Thomas, 24
Holy See, 120
homosexuality. *See also*
heteronormativity; LGBT
populations: Aceh's criminalization
of, 151; Russia's suppression of, xi, 7,
12, 107–8, 115, 117–20
Hooper, Charlotte, 55–58, 67–68n6
housemaids. *See under* labor migration
Howard, John, 77–79
human rights: in Aceh, 140–42, 146;
gendered dimensions of, 3,
39, 41–42, 47; in India, 167;
postcolonial states and, 1, 15n1;

Saudi Arabia and, 76; states' role in
promoting, 3, 39
Hunt, Lynn, 27, 181
Hutchison, Emma, 158

Iceland, 65
immigration. *See* labor migration
IMPACT 10x10x10 Initiative, 64, 68n8
India: Adivasis in, 13, 162, 164–65,
167–68, 170, 173; affective citizenship
in, 162; anticolonial movement in,
8, 169; anti-rape protests (2012)
in, 40; Bharatiya Janata Party (BJP) in,
160, 166, 171; Central Reserve Police
Force (CRPF) in, 124, 166, 171; Dalits
("untouchables") in, 13, 162, 165,
167, 173n3; Dantewada ambush (2010)
in, 166, 168, 171; female formed police
units (FFPUs) for peacekeeping from,
12, 122, 124–28, 131, 133–34, 137;
gender and nationalism in, xi, 13;
gender-based violence in, 39–40;
gender equality measures in, 135–36;
as Global South leader, 127; Hindu
Right in, 126; human rights violations
in, 167; Justice Verma Commission
in, 40; Maoist (Naxalite) insurgency in,
8, 13, 159, 163–68, 170–73; "Mother
India" and, 169–72, 173n9; national
anthem Supreme Court case (2017)
in, 160; nationalism and national
identity in, 160, 170–71; neoliberalism
in, 164; Operation Green Hunt
in, 164–65, 170; partition (1947)
of, 162; political leaders' emotional
discourse in, 161–62; protectionism
as development strategy in, 20; state-
building strategies in, 9, 20–21, 28, 30;
Sukma attack (2017) in, 166, 171;
Supreme Court in, 160, 165; United
Progressive Alliance government
in, 165
Indian Ocean tsunami (2004), 13, 139,
142–43, 145, 149
indigenous populations: citizenship
and, 30; colonial powers' removal
of, 28; femininity and, 55; justice
systems and governance outside the
state among, 29–30; sovereignty and,
9, 29–30; state power and, 7, 56

masculinity (*cont.*)
and, 160; femininity and, 106–8; globalization's challenge to, 41; hegemonic masculinity and, 3, 25, 60, 62, 65, 106–7, 114; heteronormativity and, 56; homophobia and, 61; hypermasculinity and, 25, 58, 106–8, 120, 169; the liberal state and, 10, 51–59, 61–62, 64–67; Maoist insurgency in India and, 168–70; militarized masculinity and, 47, 67n5, 81, 171, 173; neoliberalism and, 4; patriarchy and, 35, 46; peacekeeping and, 74, 129, 134, 136; postcolonial states and, 159–60; protection and, 61, 70–72, 83, 95, 98, 114, 119; rationalism associated with, 4, 33, 35, 55, 57–58, 158, 163; Russia and, 105–9, 112–20; security policies and, 77–78, 83–84; Soviet Union and, 111; the state and, 3, 10, 25, 33, 35, 38, 52, 54, 71–72, 81–83, 163

Mayo, Katherine, 173n9
McIntosh, Peggy, viii
McNevin, Anne, 80
Menon, Nivedita, 126
Mexico, 192
Mies, Maria, 53
Mill, John Stuart, 57
Millennium Development Goals, 39
Millett, Kate, 53
misogyny, 60, 77–78, 107, 116
Mizulina, Elena, 118
Modi, Narendra, 160–62
Moisi, Dominique, 157
Mookherjee, Monica, 161
Morgenthau, Hans, 22–23
Morrison, Scott, 79–80
Mother India (book by Mayo), 173n9
Mother India (film by Khan), 170–72, 173n9
"The Motherland Calls" poster (World War II Soviet Union), 110
Mother Russia Calls statue (Volgograd), 110, 118
Mujahid, Bint, 187
Muslims. *See* Islam
"Muslimwoman identity." *See under* Islamic State
Myanmar, 15nn1–2

My Strength Is Not for Hurting campaign (United States, 2001–11), 60

Nandy, Ashis, 8, 162, 169–70, 172
National Action Plans for the Protection and Empowerment of Women and Children during Social Conflicts, 152
nationalism: in Australia, 81; borders and, 80; gendered dimensions of, xi, 3, 14, 24–25, 90–91, 95; India and, 160, 170–71; Indonesia and, 91; participation in foreign wars and, 77; The Philippines and, 91; postcolonialism and, 5, 8; religious nationalism and, 14, 178, 180, 182; Russia and, xi, 7, 108–10, 115, 119; Sweden and, 70, 72–73, 81; twenty-first century revivals of, 192; xenophobia and, 1
Nationalist Party (Australia), 79
Nauru, 81
Naxalites. *See* Maoists in India
Nehru, Jawaharlal, 20, 31n3, 162
neoliberalism: development and, 85–86; gender and, 4, 136; global spread of, 133; in India, 164; individualism and, 136; Islamic State's response to, 45; labor migration and, 86, 89; market-based solutions championed in, 133; peacekeeping and, 133–34, 136; state autonomy diminished in, ix, 133; state's role in buffering negative impacts of, 126; structural inequalities ignored in, 133
Neo-Nazism, 45
Nepal, 95
The Netherlands, 192
neutrality and neutral states, 73–74, 76
New International Economic Order (NIEO), 31n3
New Zealand, 27, 77
Nigeria, 45, 134
nikah (marriage contract), 180
Nordic states, 26–27. *See also* Sweden
Norland, Richard, 63
North Atlantic Treaty Organization (NATO), 73–76
nuclear disarmament negotiations, 43
Nussbaum, Martha, 157, 162

Obama, Barack, 63
Odisha (state in India), 164
Oman, 97
Operation Green Hunt, 164–65, 170
Operation Sovereign Borders (OSB, Australia), 70, 79–80
O'Reilly, Maria, 74
Ottoway, Marina, 185

Pakistan, 15n2, 192
Palestine, 75–76
Papua New Guinea, 81–82
Paris, Roland, 130
Pasukan Inong Balee (female fighting force in Free Aceh Movement), 142
Pateman, Carole, 31n5, 36, 53
patriarchy: in Aceh, 13, 139–40, 143–44, 146–51, 153–54, 194; attempts to restore, 47; capitalism and, viii; chivalry and, 35; definition of, 35; gendered violence and, 39–42, 45, 47; globalization and the unraveling of, x, 10, 33–34, 37, 41–43, 47; Industrial Revolution and, 36; Islamic State and, 44–45, 160, 184, 189; the liberal state and, 51–55, 63–67; men's benefiting from, 59–61; obscured nature of, 35–36; other systems of domination and, 37, 40, 42, 46, 56; postcolonial states and, 42; public-private divide in, 34–36, 55; responses to the unraveling of, 42–46; Russia and, 113; sharia law and, 149; the state and, 5, 9, 34–37, 42, 51–52, 59; war justified on account of, 54
peacekeeping: female formed police units and, 12, 122–26, 128–34, 136–37; global cultural norms regarding challenged in, 130–32; Global North states' roles in, 134–36; Global South states' role in, 12, 122–23, 125–26, 129, 134–37; Indian as source of personnel for, 12, 122, 124–28, 131, 133–34, 137; masculinity and, 74, 129, 134, 136; neoliberal perspectives on, 133–34, 136; patriarchy and, 129; Sweden and, 72–74, 135; United Nations and, 12, 74, 78, 122, 124–27
Perera, Suvendrini, 80
Peru, 30

Peterson, V. Spike: on ancient Athens and masculine state-making, 84n2; on gender and international relations theory, 70; on gender as empirical category *versus* analytical category, 81; *Gendered States* edited by, 3; Harrington and, 53; lens of protection and, 11, 107; on mutually constituted categories of masculine and feminine, 106–7; on national security and individual insecurity, 23; on queer theory's goals, 114–15; on reproduction of male domination and violence, 129; on shift from "women as knowable" to "women as knowers," 160; on state formations and power relations, 138
phallocentrism, 62
The Philippines, 89, 91, 94
Picq, Manuela, 29–30
Piper, Nicola, 92–93
Piskun, Alena, 118–19
pluriethnic citizenship, 30
political economy: feminism and, 4; gendered violence and, 41; labor migration and, 85, 93, 98–99; regimes and, 86
postcolonial states. *See also* anticolonialism: affective citizenship and, 159–63, 171–72; development and, 11, 19–21; emotions and, 13, 159–63; ethnic diversity and, 29; feminist perspectives on, 21; gendered conceptions and aspects of, 5–6, 8–9, 11, 13; human rights violations among, 1, 15n1; international relations discipline and, 4; labor brokerage and, 99; the liberal state and, 53; masculinity and, 159–60; in the Middle East, 175; nationalism and, 5, 8; patriarchy and, 42; public-private divide in, 33; self-reliance and, 19–20; state building and, 20–21; violent conflicts within, 8, 13, 29
poststructuralism, 4, 6
proto-states, 175–76
purdah. *See under* Islam
Pussy Riot, 117–18

Putin, Vladimir: Abbott and, 78; feminism criticized by, xi; homosexuality criticized by, xi; masculinity championed by, xi, 83, 106, 109, 192; pro-fertility policies promoted by, 113, 118; public opinion regarding, 106; Pussy Riot and, 117

Qatar, 93

queer populations. *See* homosexuality; LGBT populations

queer theory, 3, 114–15

Ramphal Commission on Migration and Development, 93

Rao, Varavara, 163, 169

rape: Aceh conflict and, 141–42, 144, 150; Australian offshore detention centers and, 80; India protests (2012) against, 40; Islamic State and, 45, 183; military occupation and analogies of, 168

Rata Viruwo Program (Sri Lanka), 92

realism, 4, 19, 22–24, 71

Reconstruction and Rehabilitation Agency for Aceh and Nias, 152

reproductive rights and health services, 26–27, 152

Responsibility to Protect doctrine, 77

Reus-Smit, Chris, 41

Rodgers, Elliot, 60

rodina (Russian for "motherland"), 109–10

Rodriguez, Robyn Margalit, 89

Rosewarne, Stuart, 92–93

Rousseau, Jean-Jacques, 23

Roy, Arundhati, 168

Rubin, Gayle, 115

Rudd, Kevin, 78–79

Russia. *See also* Soviet Union: Chechen War (1994–96) and, 105; demographic crisis and pro-fertility policies in, 112–14, 117–18; domestic violence law in, 120; feminism criticized in, xi, 107, 115–17, 119; Geiropa ("Gay Europe") and, 118; heteronormativity and, xi, 11–12, 113–14, 118; homosexuality suppressed in, xi, 7, 12, 107–8, 115, 117–20; masculinity and, 105–9, 112–20; misogyny in, 107, 116; "Mother Russia" and, xi, 7,

11–12, 107–12, 114–15, 117, 119–20; nationalism and national identity in, xi, 7, 108–10, 115, 119; nongovernmental organizations law in, 121n12; Orthodox Christianity in, 115–16, 118, 121n11; patriarchy and, 113; Second World War and, 110, 118–19, 121; suicide rates in, 112, 121n6; Sweden and, 75–76; "traditional family values" promoted in, 11, 108, 111, 113–15, 117, 119–20; Ukraine conflict and, 75; "Unholy Queer Peril" in, 107–8, 111, 114–15, 119–20

Rutland, Peter, 117

Salwa Judum (vigilante group in India), 165

Sassen, Saskia, 11, 85, 88

Saudi Arabia: Foreign Employment Agency in, 90; human rights and, 76; labor migration from Sri Lanka to, 89–90, 93, 96; Sweden and, 76, 84n5

Sawyer, Marian, 27

Scandinavia. *See* Nordic states

"Schrödinger's states," 176, 189n1

secondary education enrollment levels, 39

security: Australia and, 70–71, 77–82; borders and, 11, 80–81; feminist perspectives on, 4, 22, 28, 31; gender and, x, 3–4, 23, 70–72, 74–78, 81–82; logics of protection and, 72, 77, 82; outsourcing and privatization of, 81; sovereignty and, 71, 74; Sweden and, 10–11, 70–71, 74–76, 83

Self-Reliance versus Power Politics (Tickner), 20

Sen, Binyak, 167

September 11, 2001 terrorist attacks, 25, 158–59

The Sexual Contract (Pateman), 36

sex workers, 29, 91

sharia law in Aceh, 140, 142, 149–51

Shoemaker, Jolynn, 123

Solomon Islands, 77

Somalia, 192

South Asian Migration Commission, 93

sovereignty: borders and, 80; feminist perspectives on, 25; gendered aspects of, x, 14, 23, 25, 29, 35–36, 74, 83, 176; globalization and, 41, 69;